CULTURALLY DIVERSE
CHILDREN AND ADOLESCENTS

Culturally Diverse Children and Adolescents

ASSESSMENT, DIAGNOSIS, AND TREATMENT

✦

Ian A. Canino, MD
Jeanne Spurlock, MD

THE GUILFORD PRESS
New York   London

To our parents,
Gloria Jordan and Fernando Canino
and Glodene and Frank Spurlock

© 1994 The Guilford Press
A Division of Guilford Publications, Inc.
72 Spring Street, New York, NY 10012

Printed in the United States of America

This book is printed on acid-free paper.

Last digit is print number: 9   8   7   6   5   4   3   2   1

Library of Congress Cataloging-in-Publication Data

Canino, Ian A.
    Culturally diverse children and adolescents : assessment, diagnosis, and treatment / Ian A. Canino, Jeanne Spurlock.
        p.   cm.
    Includes bibliographical references and index.
    ISBN 0-89862-409-6
    1. Children of minorities—Mental health.   2. Child psychiatry—Social aspects.   3. Minority teenagers—Mental health.
4. Adolescent psychiatry—Social aspects.   I. Spurlock, Jeanne.
II. Title.
    [DNLM: 1. Mental Disorders—in infancy & childhood.   2. Mental Disorders—in adolescence.   3. Cultural Characteristics.   4. Ethnic Groups—psychology.   5. Psychotherapy.   WS 350.2 C223c 1994]
RJ507.M54C36   1994
618.92'89'008693—dc20
DNLM/DLC
for Library of Congress   93-50824
                                                                                          CIP

Foreword

✦

During their years in school most children develop a sense of belonging. They receive warmth and acceptance from other children in their neighborhoods and schools; they feel welcomed in their classrooms and playgrounds by both their peers and their teachers; and they have a sense of being valued by their communities. But these important forms of validation are marred for other children—those of minority cultures—as they are confronted with attitudes of racial and ethnic prejudice. Implicit and explicit communications based on their race, language, or customs demean their appearance, character, and abilities. These same children usually see their parents and family members similarly demeaned, in the attitudes and comments of others. Developing healthy self-esteem and enthusiasm for a successful future does not come as easily for these children and adolescents.

Mental health professionals, on the whole, think of themselves as kind and accepting, not only that they are nonjudgmental but that they validate the integrity and worth of all the children and families they see in their work. It is a surprise to them if someone views them suspiciously or anticipates something other than a positive response from them. It is, however, human nature that people who have felt denigrated by the dominant culture should anticipate the same response from health care personnel. Language difficulties seriously exacerbate this type of problem, both in the difficulty people have in explaining the pain and concerns of their families and in mental health professionals' being able to convey their empathy, understanding, and suggestions. Families can end up feeling the appointments have not been of any help.

Anyone who has been so seriously ill that he or she has consulted a physician while visiting a foreign country, perhaps with a language different from his or her own, can attest to the great difficulty in feeling understood when explaining the symptoms or in understanding the treatment offered. There is also the intense anxiety that accompanies placing oneself in the care of medical staff from a different culture: Do they know what they are doing? What strange medicine might they give or painful procedure might they do? Are they competent?

Though this discomfort seems to be understandable when we think of ourselves under the medical care of others in a country with a different language and customs, it is difficult for us to think in a similar way about the discomfort of people of other cultures in our care. We minimize the difficulty for them for several reasons. One is that we are confident that we know what we are doing and expect others to trust us. Another is that, in some instances, children in these families often speak English well enough for us to feel that we can communicate with them effectively. We can relate to the part of the child that has adapted to dealing with school and other aspects of our own culture, the part of the child that is acculturating. The child or adolescent may not mind, but the part of the child's life that has to do with the parents' and the family's culture is neglected. That we feel we understand and can communicate with the child may be reassuring but it may be uncomfortable for the parents since it appears to them that their influence is being ignored. This makes the parents even more anxious. It is in this way that we can often feel that we are providing quality services when in fact they are irrelevant or even disruptive to the family.

In a case I know of, Asian American immigrant parents were concerned that the grades of their only son, a 15-year-old, were falling. The therapist decided that the parents were overcontrolling, overanxious, and overdemanding with a timid adolescent boy who was reluctant to stand up to his parents about his social isolation. The therapist encouraged the boy to argue to convince his parents to allow him to join the school band, participate in after-school sports, choose his own school schedule, and listen to rock music. His mother did not speak English and his father was deferential and seemed to accept the therapist's suggestions. But the parents then terminated the appointments. They said it was because of transportation problems, but the boy indicated that his parents felt the therapist was "too American" and was encouraging disrespect toward them. The therapist had ignored the cultural issues by working with the boy with little attention to the parents' feelings and customs. The approach was not successful.

To provide relevant mental health services to a child and his or her family requires that we know enough about their culture for them to feel we understand and accept them, and that they feel they are active participants in their treatment. They need to feel "at home" with us while they allow us to help them with their problems.

It is specifically around these issues that this book is of great help. This is a masterful presentation of compassion, understanding, and wisdom in helping children and families of minority cultures. Clinical vignettes show vividly the difficulties and pitfalls in diagnosis and treatment. The authors demonstrate an awareness of the importance of cultural factors that have so frequently led to discontinuation of appointments, noncompliance with treatment plans, and what is perceived as "uncooperativeness." But this uncooperativeness is actually in response to the irrelevance and ineffectiveness of treatment provided without sufficient attention to cultural factors. Drs. Canino and Spurlock are to be commended for their efforts to help us replace stereotypes with real people and myths with facts. They confront us with the need, in diagnosing and treating these children and their families, to consider the powerful forces of culture in addition to intrapsychic, interpersonal, and family dynamics. We should all be more competent and compassionate therapists if we apply the knowledge contained in this book.

William H. Ayres, MD
President, American Academy of
Child and Adolescent Psychiatry
Department of Psychiatry,
University of California at
San Francisco

Acknowledgments

✦

The completion of this book could not have been accomplished without the support of Teresa, Mishara, and Ian Gabriel Canino and various members of the Spurlock clan who patiently moved us forward.

We both want to thank our respective teachers and all those community children and adolescents who were our source of inspiration. Special thanks go to the excellent multidisciplinary cadre of professionals who helped us in reviewing and identifying the literature, including Grace Yik-Heung Won, Sally Robles, Angelica Perez, Anthony Chi-Bun Cheng, Changdai Kim, and Susan Heffner. We also want to thank our colleagues Stuart Silverman and Debbie Carter for supplying us with excellent clinical vignettes and to Maribel Arcelay and Dorothy Donnelly for their secretarial support.

A book does not stand without a solid structure. In this regard, we want to thank for their editorial comments Carolyn Haynie, Stasia Madrigal, Kitty Moore, and especially Elyse Zukerman for her thorough and sensitive revision of the preliminary document. Finally, we want to thank our colleagues Joe Yamamoto and Heather Walter for reading our initial draft and offering us constructive suggestions.

The following publishers have generously given permission to use extended quotations from copyrighted works:

From "Should the Poor Get None?" by Jeanne Spurlock and Rebecca Cohen, January 1969, *Journal of the American Academy of Child Psychiatry*, 8(4), 16–35. Copyright 1969 by the American Academy of Child Psychiatry.

From *Anase and His Visitor, Turtle* (cassette recording) by E. Kaula, 1969. Copyright 1969 by Caedmon Records, Inc.

From *Savage Inequalities* by Jonathan Kozol, 1991. Copyright 1991 by Jonathan Kozol. By permission of Crown Publishers, Inc.

From *DSM-IV Draft Criteria* by the American Psychiatric Association, 1993. Copyright 1993 by the American Psychiatric Association.

Contents

✦

Introduction

✦

There are numerous obstacles that may be encountered during the course of developing or improving assessment techniques in mental health services for children. These obstacles relate to the situation specificity of many child behaviors, the influence of developmental level on cognition and skill acquisition, and a frequently subjective definition of problem behavior on the part of parents and teachers. Several additional obstacles compound the evaluation of culturally diverse children who are economically disadvantaged and who experience discrimination and problems with acculturation.

Such obstacles challenge traditional assessment, diagnostic, and treatment approaches and call upon the clinician not only to intervene sensitively, creatively, and responsibly on the basis of knowledge, but to extend his or her involvement to include the role of advocate. Current population statistics suggest that this challenge will grow as culturally diverse children come to represent increasingly large percentages of our communities and consequently intensify the demand for mental health services.

Clinicians who serve these children are frequently inadequately trained to address the problems they encounter effectively. Many training programs fail to integrate appropriate and helpful theoretical constructs, suffer from the paucity of research findings, or choose to ignore the particular needs of the communities they serve.

This book offers clinical guidelines for those individuals who work with economically disadvantaged children and adolescents from culturally diverse backgrounds, namely, social workers, psychologists, psychiatrists, and other community mental health workers. These

1

guidelines describe useful theoretical constructs, suggest ways to sensitize assessments of minority children, and outline treatment strategies to achieve better clinical results. Our focus is on the mental health needs of those children in four minority groups—African-American, Latino, Asian-American, and American Indian—who encounter multiple social stressors and whose families represent the nation's lower socioeconomic levels.

Our primary objective is to offer concrete suggestions on how to elicit the relevant history information and whom to select as the informant; how to use available diagnostic criteria; and how to intervene, with whom, and with which treatment strategies. Because of the variety of ethnic and racial minorities, the vast differences in family styles and attitudes among these groups, and the enormous impact of diverse social stressors, our intent in this book is to present an approach to clinical issues that is sensitive to all these dimensions and that addresses specific concerns as well.

Several assumptions underlie the book's approach to work with minority group children. Mental health workers find it difficult to differentiate those behaviors in children that are physiologically or genetically induced or that are related to developmental level from those with an environmental etiology. Another problem is determining whether dysfunctional behaviors are temporary or permanent. Depending on the circumstances, the stress a child experiences may either precipitate symptom expression or elicit adaptive responses. Finally, many behaviors of childhood require further study before they can be classified as either normative or pathological. Most importantly, our clinical experience with diverse populations has led us to the following conclusions: health-seeking behaviors vary across culture and socioeconomic level; the sociocultural context affects mental health and symptomatic behaviors; and it is difficult to differentiate between behavior that is unique to a particular culture and behavior that is specific to socioeconomic level.

A PERSPECTIVE
FOR THE CLINICIAN

✦

Children do not grow up in a vacuum. They cannot be understood apart from the historical, geographical, and socioeconomic characteristics of the area in which they develop. As evaluators, we are reminded, ever and again, that the children we see are members not only of families but also of wider groups, whose training patterns affect them a good deal. To do our work well, we need to be aware of these cultural patterns; only then will we be able to understand the child's own functioning and that of his family in an adequate way.

—LOOFF (1979, pp. 87–88)

When children are evaluated by mental health professionals, the influence of cultural patterns is often overlooked or attended to much too briefly. This introductory section explores the influence of culture and multiple social stressors on the mental health of minority children.

CHAPTER 1

The Influence of Culture and Multiple Social Stressors on the Minority Child

✦

THE CONCEPT OF ETHNICITY AND ETHNIC SOCIALIZATION

The concept of ethnicity encompasses a broad range of meanings. Terms such as *ethnic diversity, ethnic socialization, ethnic development,* and *ethnic identification* are used widely in both the sociological and the psychological literature and are often used interchangeably—and misused—in the political arena. Our intention is to clarify these terms and to discuss the relevance of the concept of ethnicity to clinical work with African-American, Asian-American, American Indian, and Latino children.

The term *ethnicity* often refers to group-shared patterns of social interaction, values, social customs, behavioral roles, perceptions, and language usage (Barth, 1969; Ogbu, 1981). The well-documented differences in affective, attitudinal, and behavioral patterns across cultures have been called "ethnic patterns" (Whiting & Whiting, 1975). Rotheram and Phinney (1986) suggest four dimensions to help differentiate the social patterns of cultural groups: (1) interdependence versus independence (i.e., the degree of group affiliation); (2) active achievement versus passive acceptance; (3) authoritarianism versus equalitarianism; and (4) expressive/overt/personal versus restrained/formal/impersonal style of communication. Whiting and Whiting (1975) identify two cultural dimensions that pertain specifically to the socialization of children: (1) nurturance and responsibility versus dominance and dependence and (2) reprimands and assaults versus sociability and intimacy.

Ethnic socialization refers to the developmental processes by which children acquire the values, perceptions, behaviors, and attitudes of an ethnic group and perceive themselves and others as members of the group (Rotheram & Phinney, 1986). Ethnic identification is influenced by the community in which the child grows up. For example, Asian children born in Hawaii or in urban areas where there are peers of the same or similar cultural background are more likely to feel comfortable about their ethnic identity than are Asian children who grow up in areas with no children of like background.

Foster home placement with a white family living in a predominantly white neighborhood has been known to generate identity problems for some minority children. Their attitudes and behavior, acceptable in their culture of origin, may take on negative connotations and serve to channel hostilities in their new communities. Westermeyer (1979), for example, noted identity problems among urban American Indians living in Minneapolis: youths in the 12-to-23 age range who had been placed in non-Indian foster homes were observed to be struggling with issues of "how Indian" they were.

Younger children may sometimes identify with another ethnic group. Such identification stems from either their conviction that they actually belong to that ethnic group, their wish to belong to it, or their admiration for the group because of its higher status in the culture (Rotheram & Phinney, 1986). Many youths borrow elements of ethnic patterns from other groups during adolescence and integrate these into their own patterns of behavior. This is particularly noticeable among the adolescents in communities located in close proximity to other ethnic groups.

Some theorists emphasize the benefits of socialization to the norms of more than one cultural group (Fitzgerald, 1971; McFee, 1968; Ramirez & Castaneda, 1974). Ramirez (1983), for example, reports a higher level of self-esteem and increased achievement for children with bicultural competence.

Knowledge of these concepts of ethnicity is critical to the diagnostic process and to the implementation of responsive and appropriate intervention strategies with minority children. The following case vignette illustrates the relevance of the concept of ethnicity to clinical work.

Clinical Vignette

Sean, a 15-year-old Irish-American boy, had a long history of psychiatric hospitalizations for schizophrenia and of foster care placement, owing to severe neglect by his family of origin. As a young child, Sean was reared by a Latino family, and throughout his childhood he was hospitalized in institutions with primarily Latino staff and peers.

Sean gave his name as Pedro; he refused to respond when he was called Sean. He spoke with a heavy Spanish accent and would not relate to non-Latino staff or peers. Sean so vigorously denied his genetic makeup that at times his denial reached delusional proportions, as when he proclaimed that his skin was brown, not white, and his eyes were brown, not blue. These protestations caused resentment in the Irish, as well as Latino, patients and hospital staff.

Hospital staff understood the dynamics of Sean's behavior but initially felt at a loss for an appropriate intervention. The strategy ultimately selected combined psychopharmacology with a psychotherapeutic approach designed to be particularly sensitive to Sean's issues of ethnic identity. A particularly nurturing Irish American therapist provided individual therapy and codirected Sean's group therapy with a Latino therapist. The strengths of both cultures were emphasized. Eventually, Sean was able to relate equally comfortably to both ethnic groups, an achievement that enhanced his socialization skills. He responded to the medication and in time became truly bicultural.

Sean's story shows in a clinical setting the significance of the concepts of ethnicity and ethnic identity formation. It underlines the importance of the need for mental health professionals to consider such variables as the attitudes of the majority culture toward a specific ethnic group and the strengths and competencies of the particular ethnic group in addition to individual factors within the family and the child (Rosenthal, 1986).

A Minority Child's Ethnic Identity

It is particularly important when working with minority children and adolescents to consider the individual's acquisition of ethnic group patterns and his or her sense of belonging to that ethnic group. A number of authors have explored the stages in the child's development of ethnic and racial concepts and attitudes. Goodman (1964) and Porter (1971) state that children develop an awareness of ethnic and cultural differences by age 3 or 4. Young children are aware of the more obvious ethnic cues, such as language utilization. Between ages 4 and 8, children develop an ethnic orientation (Goodman, 1964); clearer explanations of why they select one social group over another (Porter, 1971); a consolidation of group concepts (Katz, 1976); and curiosity about other groups (Aboud & Mitchell, 1977).

A child's ethnic identity depends on other factors as well. The level of cognitive functioning in children affects their attitudes and understanding of ethnicity (Aboud & Skerry, 1983; Spencer, 1982), and their reactions to ethnic stimuli depend on whether the cues are affective, perceptual, or cognitive (Aboud, 1984; Ramsey, 1986). For some minority children, the way other people see them (according to physical characteristics such as skin color and facial and bodily features) is important (Rotheram & Phinney, 1986); for other children the perception other groups have of them is relatively unimportant. According to Rosenberg and Simmons (1972), "Black children use blacks, rather than whites, as their comparison reference group" (p. 56). The conclusions of the aforementioned theorists apply to the ethnic identification of minority children in general; clearly, clinicians need to seek information from the specific children and adolescents in their care in order to determine their ethnic/racial identity.

A child's ethnic identity behavior may vary, being more salient in some situations than in others and depending on the status of the group as well as on the degree of ethnic heterogeneity in the daily life of the youngster. Changes in a child's ethnic awareness may occur in response to a variation in the sociocultural milieu, a change in cohort or generational groups, developmental changes, and the interactions among these influences. Some of these issues are illustrated in the following vignettes.

Clinical Vignette

Michael, a bright 13-year-old, was referred to the outpatient clinic because of symptoms of anxiety and acting-out behavior in school. He had been cutting classes, talking back to his teachers, displaying an "attitude problem," experiencing difficulties with his peers, and appearing overly worried and anxious at home. At his first evaluative session Michael made good eye contact. The examiner observed a Muslim star and a Christian cross around Michael's neck and a star of David attached to the back of his jacket.

Michael's mother, a Christian African-American, and his Jewish American father had recently separated after bitter battles about their cultural origins and racial differences. These differences had become increasingly apparent in their childrearing attitudes. In the past the parents had been able to respect each other's beliefs and integrate them in a balanced and enriching experience for their children. As their difficulties increased, the parents expressed their conflict in racial and religious slurs against each other and in unfortunate demands that the children take sides and define themselves as either black or white, Christian or Jewish. Michael, just entering adolescence, was already struggling with his identity in relationship to his peers, none of whom had a bicultural background.

Family therapy, co-led by therapists of mixed racial and religious backgrounds, was instituted. Early work focused on the parents' insecurities related to losing their children and to the increasing fear of each parent that the children would ally with the other parent. Family therapy then freed Michael to focus on his developmental struggle to achieve identity and autonomy.

Clinical Vignette

Laura, a 14-year-old from a traditional South American family, had begun attending a large inner-city high school. Her parents had recently separated because of the father's involvement with illegal activities and his overly seductive stance with Laura.

Laura began to modify her appearance and behavior to conform to her African-American classmates, who constituted the majority group in her school. She adopted her friends' dress style, which included a preference for large gold earrings; their fondness for rap music; and their speech patterns and slang to such an extent that the other girls complained that she was overdoing it. Laura's mother grew more concerned when Laura who insisted this was the thing to do among girls in her school, began to date 22- and 23-year-old unemployed men from another neighborhood.

Laura's efforts to make friends, to adapt, and to integrate cultural patterns that would enrich her own style were potentially healthy; however, the exaggeration and exclusivity of these efforts suggested underlying conflicts. The therapist supported Laura's wish to belong and to be accepted in her new school, helped her family understand the cultural norms of other groups, and addressed the family dynamics and conflictual issues underlying Laura's behavior with her peers and her need to date older men.

Language

Linguistic patterns are closely related to ethnicity and culture. Language provides not only a means of communication but also a "cognitive structuring of the world which is linked to one's world view, identity, self-concept, and self-esteem" (Hilliard, 1983, p. 27). Language can also prove a source of cultural conflict and controversy in the classroom. For example, Navajo children adopt a slow, methodical speech pattern. When the children pause, Anglo-American teachers often regard this as a signal that they have completed their sentence. Conversely, native Hawaiian children often overlap each other's sentences; this means involvement for them but is often interpreted by teachers as rude interruptions. More classroom rapport and student involvement has been reported when teachers follow the rhythmic patterns of the children's speech.

The oral tradition flourishes for African-Americans who live in a large social network, which includes the church, neighbors, and the extended family. Multiparty conversations are the norm, and children learn how to attend in the midst of the verbal whirl. Adults do not mediate the world for children, nor do they simplify their speech for them. Rather, adults often prod their children to show their "wit" in front of others. The child is challenged to outwit or outperform another in the context of a large group. "Children take adult roles, issue commands and counterstatements, and win arguments by negotiating nuances of meaning verbally and nonverbally. Adults expect children to show what they know rather than to tell what they know" (Heath, 1989, p. 369). Heath (1983) suggests that African-American oral traditions contain many useful skills, such as "keen listening and observational skills, quick recognition of nuanced roles, rapid-fire dialogue, hard-driving argumentation, succinct recapitulation of an event, striking metaphors and comparative analysis based on unexpected analogies" (p. 378). Poor urban children of single mothers often live in tenement buildings and consequently are less exposed to this rich oral tradition, but they may acquire it as they grow older and spend more time "in the streets." The danger exists, however, that the inner-city streets will fail to provide a safe channel for these skills.

Service providers often fail to understand the complexity of bilingualism. Children may be proficient in using a language for interpersonal communication but not for academic situations (Hakuta & Garcia, 1989). They may acquire differential skills in the two languages and may alternate between them, even within a single sentence ("code-switch"). This may not reflect a deficiency in either language but, rather, a discourse strategy that uses the richness of both languages (Hakuta & Garcia, 1989, p. 376).

Clinical Vignette

Carmen, an 8-year-old Latina, was referred to an outpatient clinic for evaluation because of her poor academic performance. Family problems were suspected to be a root cause. Carmen's parents came from the Dominican Republic and spoke Spanish at home.

A monolingual English-speaking clinician did the assessment and found Carmen to be inhibited, shy, and overly concrete in her responses. She had difficulty answering questions about her feelings and family background. When asked in English to elaborate on her fantasies and tell a story about family events, Carmen seemed unable to develop full paragraphs. Yet she seemed well informed about school matters and grew animated when describing her school experiences. Her vocabulary in English seemed delayed and her sentence structure somewhat immature, although she had been in an English-speaking school since the age of 6. The clinician suspected family problems as well as possible mild retardation or a learning disability in Carmen but wisely recommended an evaluation of the child by a bilingual clinician.

The bilingual consultant found Carmen to be quite expressive when describing her family and feelings in Spanish. There was no evidence of family or cognitive dysfunction. It was clear that the child needed extra help with English grammar and vocabulary. Special bilingual help was provided in school, and a homework helper was found in the community. At a 6-month follow-up Carmen was reported to be doing well.

MULTIPLE SOCIAL STRESSORS AND THEIR IMPACT

The acquisition of ethnic identity and language involves normal and necessary processes for all children. The issues involved in these processes, as well as the presence of other life stressors, have to be considered and understood fully by clinicians if they are to be competent evaluators of those inner-city minority children who are at risk. During the course of an assessment the clinician must be aware of and evaluate the impact of multiple life stressors on the child.

The question of the role of life stressors remains unclear: Do life stressors cause health and adjustment problems (Johnson, 1986)? Do health and adjustment problems cause life changes? Do these problems result from another factor (such as genetic factors in the child), or are they related to each other? Holmes and Masuda (1974) claim that life stress can increase the likelihood of illness and/or influence the timing of disease onset. More recent studies suggest that experiencing certain stressors may increase the competence of the immune system (Jemmott & Locke, 1984) while other stressors may tax and eventually overwhelm it.

Life changes in children seem to be associated with a variety of illness-related variables, such as the number of physician visits, reports of physical health problems, and number of school day absences (Johnson, 1986). Other variables, such as the frequency and timing of stressors, are equally important to consider. Data suggest that when coping abilities are taxed, health-related difficulties may result, especially if many stressful events are experienced within a short period of time (Holmes & Rahe, 1967). Clinicians working with inner-city children who are exposed to daily acts of violence have noted this to be so.

The relative stress of an event for a child is determined by the extent of his or her personal control over it. In assessing the impact of an event the clinician must determine whether it is positive, neutral, or negative to a specific individual. Often, it is necessary to consider the culture in which the individual was raised. For example, some cultures require young adults to live at home until they marry; others expect the children to leave once they reach young adulthood. Thus, the act of leaving home and entering the adult world may be understood very differently in different cultures and dealt with accordingly.

An accumulation of factors indirectly or directly associated with poverty can place children at high risk for illness, yet many disadvantaged families are able to rear physically and emotionally healthy children. A variety of factors mediate stressors, including social support networks, a stable family environment, the availability of mental health services, and active intervention by teachers and school administrators (Rutter, 1979; Rutter, Maughan, Mortimore, Ouston, & Smith, 1979).

Minority Status as a Source of Stress: Prejudice/Discrimination

Gordon Allport (1954) defined ethnic prejudice as "an antipathy based upon a faulty and inflexible generalization. It may be directed toward a group as a whole, or toward an individual because he is a member of that group" (p. 10). The group or individual who becomes the object of prejudice most often experiences a position of disadvantage. Many groups have been victims of prejudice, and it is clear that the victims of one era or place often become the victimizers of another.

Prejudice against religious groups (e.g., anti-Semitism) and various other ethnic groups (e.g., the hostility toward Irish immigrants who settled in Boston) has been commonplace throughout the history of the United States. Today, rising emigration and undocumented migrant rates from Southeast Asia and Central America in conjunction with the economic slowdown in the United States have precipitated a wave of prejudice against these ethnic groups.

Children develop prejudicial attitudes from their parents and their culture. Parents communicate prejudicial convictions through the language they use, the attitudes and stereotypes they maintain, and the behaviors they display. Parents may, for example, direct their child not to play with children they deem undesirable because of their color or the language they speak; the child will begin to believe that those whose race or linguistic background differs from his or her own possess negative characteristics. Moreover, the broader society may reinforce the parents' prejudicial attitudes. Porter (1971) noted that children often overhear their parents and other adults expressing prejudicial attitudes during conversations and in the telling of ethnic jokes. Not infrequently, parents assume that when their young children appear to be preoccupied with their play, they are not tuned into such exchanges, or they assume that a young child does not have the capacity to understand the discussion.

Prejudicial attitudes also are transmitted through the behavioral cues of parents. Lillian Smith (1944) provides a vivid illustration in her book *Killers of the Dream*.

> Neither the Negro or sex was often discussed at length in our home. We were given no formal instructions in these difficult matters but we learned our lessons well. We learned the intricate system of taboos, of renunciations and compensations, of manners, voice modulations, works, and feelings along with our prayers, our toilet habits, and our games. (pp. 27–28)

Unfortunately, it is not uncommon to observe intraethnic as well as interethnic discrimination among minority groups themselves.

Prejudicial attitudes are often reinforced by members of the dominant group who are in leadership positions and by social institutions. Japanese-Americans felt the brunt of such attitudes during the early 1940s. The ostensible reason for stripping this group of citizens of all their rights and properties and relocating them to camps was the fear that they might commit acts of disloyalty during World War II (Yamomoto & Iga, 1983), yet there was no factual basis for the expectation that Japanese-Americans would be involved in sabotage or espionage (Conrat & Conrat, 1972). Prior to the 1940s, federal and state legislation excluded and/or isolated people of color, as exemplified by Jim Crow laws, the Chinese Exclusion Act of 1882, and legislation mandating boarding school education for American Indian children.

Norton (1983) reported that African-American children, not unlike other children, evaluate themselves as individuals within their family and immediate environment. Thus, they often are immune to the negative perception that the broader society has about their blackness (Rosenberg & Simmons, 1972; Taylor, 1976). Such immunity to the values of the broader society has been observed in children of other minority groups as well.

However, the potential to experience the social stressors of prejudice and discrimination exists for most minority children as they move into the broader society (Spurlock, 1986), especially when a change of residence relocates them into a predominantly nonminority community. For example, an African-American family known to one of the authors encountered these stressors when they moved to an Anglo-American community in southern California. Daniel, age 11, was the first victim: Upon his return home on the afternoon of his first day in his new school, Daniel reported hearing comments by teachers and students that implied that the African-American students and those of Mexican heritage had lesser abilities than the Anglo-American children. Daniel's parents became still more concerned when later that evening they heard Daniel, lamenting his racial identity, conclude, "If I were white, I'd be smart."

Numerous examples come to the attention of those who work with minority children. Jamal, age 8, reports, "My teacher says black people can't follow instructions; that's why I didn't do the right assignment." An African-American teacher overheard talking to an African-American colleague provides an additional example: "These black kids from the projects don't want to learn; they're dumb and might just as well drop out of school." Her colleague was observed to nod in affirmation. Other minority groups share the brunt of similar comments.

Prejudice often is reinforced by labels that originally were unrelated to race. The label becomes an epithet that provokes psychological pain for those children on the receiving end. For example, the labeling of Asian-Americans as "bananas," of Mexican-Americans as "potatoes," and of American Indians as "apples" implies in many circles a tendency toward weakness in members of these groups; they are perceived as yellow, brown, or red on the outside and white on the inside, that is, as ambivalent about their cultural heritage and guilty of identifying with the dominant group. Williams and Moreland (1976) cite examples from religion.

> In Judeo-Christian religion, the conflict between the powers of good and evil is portrayed as a struggle between the powers of light and the forces of darkness. On a more personal level, the wayward soul is urged to repent of his black sins, to be cleansed, and to become as "white as snow." (p. 39)

Despite efforts in the mass media to eliminate disparaging images of minority group members, negative stereotypes continue to surface from time to time (Arias, 1982; Iiyama & Kitano, 1982; Powell, 1982). Television reruns, a common source of entertainment for a large percentage of television viewers of all ages and ethnic groups, dilute the positive impact of recent changes undertaken to eradicate negative images of minorities. Attneave (1979) wrote of the television programs of yesteryear.

> The media reinforces negative stereotypes of American Indians, as well as the problems experienced by Indian children themselves. These derive in part from films, from television westerns, and from vestigial animosities that remain between the conqueror and the defeated. (p. 241)

Clinicians need to assess the impact of prejudice and discriminatory practices on a minority child's self-image, self-esteem, and identity and also must be cognizant of their own prejudices. Frequently, a clinician's prejudices, which may be subtle, can interfere with evaluative and therapeutic interchanges. Moreover, clinicians may over-identify with children of their own cultural background and consequently may lose the objectivity necessary for effective interventions.

A number of clinicians (Bernard, 1953; Calnek, 1970; Oberndorf, 1954; Rosen & Frank, 1962; Spiegel, 1976) have considered various issues related to prejudice that have not been generally addressed in the training of therapists, as well as the impact of such inattention on the future work of therapists. Bernard (1953) made the following observation:

> If an analyst has insufficiently analyzed his own unconscious material pertaining to his own group memberships and those of others, he and his patients may be insufficiently protected from the interference of a variety of positive and negative countertransference reactions stimulated by the ethnic, religious and racial elements that are present in the analytic situation, the patient's personality and in the specific content of the patient's material. (p. 259)

Thomas (1962) described his psychotherapeutic work with an African-American adult male. The patient had had a previous but unsuccessful experience with an Anglo-American therapist. This therapist had commented that the patient's problems were rooted in his lifelong experiences with racial oppression and had given him the impression that he could not expect any relief from his emotional distress.

Norris and Spurlock (1992) call attention to the likelihood that therapists who have had no earlier direct experience with African-Americans may begin psychotherapy with these patients with an "unrecognized fear of the impulsivity and potential dangerousness of the patient. These factors may impact on the psychotherapeutic process evidenced by the therapist's paralysis and inability to become appropriately active in the therapy." Barbarin (1984) also addresses this pattern in terms of therapists who distance themselves by passively accepting a patient's termination. These same patterns have been known to occur in other kinds of biracial or bicultural therapy dyads.

"White guilt," experienced at times by minority therapists also, provokes certain countertransference reactions in psychotherapy work, which may cause a therapist to oversimplify the causes of a patient's distress, and even overlook the more specific but salient psychotherapeutic issues. An Anglo-American clinician's evaluation of an African-American male adolescent who had been ordered by a juvenile court judge to receive psychotherapy illustrates this phenomenon: The clinician's evaluation emphasized the patient's family history of emotional deprivation and poverty and suggested that the "long history of discrimination of African-Americans [was] being enough to understand the patient's behavior" (Norris & Spurlock, 1992).

Acculturation as a Stressor

For many minority and immigrant children the process of acculturation is studded with stressors. This is especially so when they are not fully rooted in either culture. The children struggle over appropriate behavior and values as they try to adhere to two, sometimes contrasting, sets of standards. Moreover, the mass media present images of a middle-class Anglo-American culture that often is unattainable by minority group members and immigrants (Katz, 1981). And those who achieve competence and acceptance in the dominant culture may find that this involves a loss of their original culture; in this sense, acculturation involves a loss that threatens personal identity (LaFromboise & BigFoot, 1988).

Yamamoto (1978) described the acculturation issues for three generations of Japanese-Americans. Instead of the fulfillment of their cultural expectation of ongoing care within the warmth and protection of their families, an increasing number of the *issei*, the first generation, experience exclusion and/or a life in separate quarters from their adult offspring. *Nisei*, the second generation, achieve high educational and occupational levels. The *sansei*, the third generation, become more

Americanized and suffer the problems that most young Americans encounter.

To assure an accurate assessment of culturally different patients, it is useful for clinicians to know the cultural compatibility between the individual's country of origin and the "host community" (Lee, 1988). For example, most Filipino and Singaporean immigrants speak English whereas rural Chinese from the People's Republic of China and rural Japanese are less likely to acquire a full command of English. Linguistic incompatibility has a long-term impact for the family: Owing to the loss of a shared language, non-English-speaking grandparents and parents become less able to communicate with the younger generation.

The issue of biculturalism poses a particular problem for American Indian youth:

> To grow up as an Indian child is to grow up as a member of an extraordinarily disadvantaged minority. The pervasive emotional, physical, and social disabilities create a legacy of hopelessness and helplessness from which Indian youths must struggle to emerge. (Yates, 1987, p. 1137)

American Indian youths, like those of other minority groups, often struggle to make a successful adjustment to both cultures. They may value the heritage and nurturance of their own people but may also experience pressure to assimilate to an ultimately rejecting society. One of the authors has observed this pattern among many African-Americans: Despite having achieved academic success and earned well-deserved promotions in the workplace of the dominant culture, they nevertheless encounter racial discrimination on a daily basis.

Minority parents who are immigrants are not immune to developing a pattern of restricting the Americanization of their children, for the marked difference between American ways and those of the country of origin can make for pronounced strains in the parent–child relationship. Canino and Canino (1980) call attention to aggression as a source of contention in Puerto Rican families who live on the mainland. Assertiveness, competitiveness, and independence, which are valued by American parents, contradict the core values of Puerto Rican culture, especially that of *respeto*, which literally means respect and which implies a special consideration for older people. The more acculturated Puerto Rican children may be too assertive in the eyes of their parents, who perceive them as *presentao*, that is, as crossing "the boundaries of respect and distance that govern new relationships and behavior in the presence of adults and older people" (p. 538). In many instances the Puerto Rican adolescent's struggle between *respeto* and aggressiveness leads to an inner conflict between self-effacement and expansiveness (Rendon, 1974).

Additional stressors in immigrant children stem from difficulties in adapting to migration itself and from the burden of functioning in a dominant society that frequently discriminates against them (Rutter, 1981). The following case vignette provides an example.

Clinical Vignette

Luis, a 9-year-old Colombian boy who had a previous history of separation anxiety and difficulties with transitions, was troubled by his family's impending move from Spanish Harlem to upstate New York. There he would be living in a neighborhood with few Latino children and attending a parochial school.

The therapist, fully aware of the move as a potential stressor for Luis, talked with the family about the child's concerns and helped them plan a gradual transition for Luis to his new neighborhood during the summer months prior to the move. The therapist also identified another Latino family in the new area with children in the same school.

Socioeconomic and Environmental Stressors

Some Demographic Facts

According to a 1991 report (*State of America's Children*), there are 12.6 million children living below the poverty line. In previous reports the greatest increase of the poor in metropolitan areas occurred in the inner city (Wilson, 1987). The sharp rise (23% in 1959 to 52% in 1989) in female-headed families is a major factor contributing to the increase in child poverty (State of America's Children, 1991). One-third of the homeless in the United States are families with children (*Homeless Families*, 1991).

These statistics reflect some demographic risk factors affecting minority youth, many of whom come from poor, highly stressed families. Obviously, not every minority child from a poor and highly stressed family becomes mentally ill. Yet for those vulnerable to illness because of genetic or psychological factors the added stress factors of poverty and homelessness can affect symptom manifestation, course of illness, and prognosis. A cursory review of the literature identifies social class and environmental risk factors that affect a child's development.

Area of Residence

Area of residence influences child psychopathology rates: Rates generally are higher in the inner city and lower in rural and small communities. Therefore, the area of residence may serve as either a protective or a high-risk environment for children (Wolkind & Rutter, 1985). Inner-city living may present children and their parents with multiple stressors, which if cumulative may be more damaging to healthy functioning than a single acute stressor would be. Residence in an inner city exposes a child to a lack of social cohesion and integration, to overcrowded and unsafe buildings, and to frequent environmental changes requiring quick adaptation. A marginal economic existence (even when the head of the household is employed) can lead to homelessness. These experiences influence family functioning profoundly.

Few studies examine the effects of a child's immediate environment on his or her mental health. Homel and Burns (1989) focused on the home, the street, and the neighborhood to determine the effect of each when controlling for other sociodemographic factors (e.g., parents' occupation, cultural background, number of children in family, etc.). They concluded that children who reside in commercial and industrial areas of inner cities "stood out from all others in their feelings of loneliness, dislike of other children, feelings of rejection, worry, fear, anger and unhappiness and dissatisfaction with their lives and with their families in particular" (pp. 152–153). On the basis of extensive interviews, these authors posited that the social disadvantage resulting from living in a nonresidential area effectively restricts children's social life, alienates them from school and classmates, and burdens them with worries about their family's welfare. Homel and Burns found that parents who reside in commercial areas were critical of the garbage in the street and the abandoned lots and buildings and were fearful of crime.

Such conditions are faced by Puerto Rican families who reside in inner-city communities of New York City (La Vietes, 1979). The children live in overcrowded conditions with little or no privacy, share beds, have limited play areas, and are subjected to an excessive degree of external stimulation. The following vignette illustrates the problems many of these families experience.

Clinical Vignette

Aimee, age 8, was referred to the clinic because of nightmares, worries, and concerns about her mother's safety. Her family had migrated recently from a rural area in the West Indies, where they had lived within a supportive extended family network. Aimee's father had remained in the West Indies. Her mother came to the United States in search of greater job opportunities and better education for her children.

Back in the West Indies, Aimee had enjoyed a large area to play in and had spent most of her free time outside. In contrast, she now lived in a crowded one-bedroom apartment and had to share her bed with her siblings. The apartment was in one of the worst crime-infested areas of the city; a crack raid had recently occurred in the next apartment. Aimee frequently heard shots at night and was often exposed to gang violence. Two older children in her school had been found dead in the previous 2 years, and she herself had been assaulted once. Aimee and her mother had become increasingly fearful, and Aimee was not allowed to go outdoors in the afternoons and on weekends.

Inadequate heat and electricity characterized the building in which the family lived. Because they had lived all their lives in a tropical climate, they were particularly sensitive to the cold weather.

Aimee met the diagnostic criteria for a separation anxiety disorder and was becoming school phobic. She also displayed symptoms of posttraumatic stress disorder. Hers was certainly a high-risk environment, and the number of stressful events she had experienced had overwhelmed her adaptive capacities.

Aimee's clinician was aware of the impact of these events on the family. He initiated the sessions by assessing the coping styles of the family in the past. He soon understood that Aimee's separation anxiety was precipitated by the dangerous neighborhood, the lack of the previously protective father, and the recent traumatic incidents. Aware of the added inability of this migrant family to access appropriate public resources, he consulted with a colleague from a social service agency. They orchestrated their efforts with those of a housing agency to locate an apartment in a more stable, safer community closer to a West Indian church. In a follow-up contact a year later, Aimee was free of symptoms and was adjusting well to her new school.

School and Learning Stressors

The School Setting

The inadequacy of community services for the poor extends to the educational system. In many communities, not only is there a lack of supplies and equipment but the buildings often are in poor repair, with broken windows, inoperable elevators or exits, inadequate air circulation, and plumbing difficulties in the lavatories. Many schools institute strict safety measures within their interiors. Others, overcrowded with high student–teacher ratios and frequent loss of control in the classroom, cannot address the problems of inadequate equipment and building disrepair; the total atmosphere is not conducive to teaching or learning. In such circumstances, school places children at greater risk rather than protecting them.

There are some inner-city schools, however, that provide a positive educational experience, and their success is rooted in the involvement of parents, educators and other professionals, and community residents. The participants set about to develop a sense of continuity between the home and school environment. The New Haven school program, developed by a psychiatrist and activist, James Comer, is outlined in some detail in the section on school programs in Chapter 5.

The Language Problem in the Classroom

Normal but underachieving minority students whose language at home differs from that used in school are often overrepresented in programs for the learning disabled (Ortiz & Yates, 1983). Behaviors directly or indirectly related to lack of linguistic proficiency constitute the most frequent reason for psychiatric referral of students whose primary language is not English (Ortiz & Maldonado-Colon, 1986). Many of the behaviors considered problematic by teachers are, in reality, characteristics of students who are in the process of second language acquisition. When students who are starting to acquire the linguistic abilities necessary to handle the complex language used by teachers and instructional materials experience achievement difficulties, a referral to special education is likely to follow. Unfortunately, lack of English proficiency is rarely considered as a possible cause for achievement difficulties, and frequently a child undergoing acquisition of a second language is diagnosed incorrectly as a learning-disabled child.

Assessing and determining a learning disability in a child is a difficult task. When assessment involves a student whose first language is other than English, another dimension is added to an already complex procedure. The language development of a bilingual child may or may not be similar to that of the monolingual child. Sound assessment calls for examiners to be knowledgeable about the child's language development and the interaction between the original and the acquired language, as well as about learning methods the child has developed (Miramontes, 1987).

A child becomes alienated from school when the classroom teacher sends the message that the child's linguistic style is inferior to Standard English. Hilliard (1983) makes specific reference to what he terms "African-American language" and suggests that while it may not be prestigious, it is not linguistically deficient. Heath (1989) makes a similar point: "Negative assessments of language abilities often underlie expressions of sweeping prejudicial characteristics of Black Americans, especially those living in poverty" (p. 369).

"Black English" (also referred to as "Black Non-Standard English" or "African-American English"), commonplace among African-Americans in urban communities and the rural South, has African and English roots (Hilliard, 1983). One of several non-Standard English dialects, it is characterized in part by the absence of past tense forms (Houston, 1971, p. 241). The tendency for some social service providers to equate the use of Black English with pronounced intellectual deficiencies is obviously not in the best interests of African-American children.

For the most part, educators fail to reinforce and cultivate bilingualism, which is a potential educational asset. This cultural and linguistic annihilation was legitimized by theories that posited that a child reared with two languages would be linguistically handicapped. More recent studies (Hakuta & Garcia, 1989) conclude that in situations where "the second language is added as an enrichment to the native language and not at the expense of the native language" and where bilingualism is not a social stigma "higher degrees of bilingualism are associated with higher levels of cognitive attainment" (p. 375). Increasing evidence suggests that a second language does not compete with the first language during language acquisition but that both languages build upon a common cognitive base that is the same for all languages.

Hakuta and Garcia (1989) report a lack of consensus as to the effectiveness of bilingual education owing to inadequate evaluation research that has been compromised by poor measurement and design. They further caution policymakers and social science researchers against expecting bilingual education to be the panacea for linguistic minority groups whose members face numerous other problems.

Special Education Placement/Misplacement

Certain groups of children are at higher risk for low self-esteem as a result of their school experiences. These groups include learning-disabled children, retarded children, language-deficient children, and disruptive-behavior children.

Clearly, it is important in clinical work to explore the child's school experience. For example, if the child is in a special education class, the clinician should inquire about the child's experience in, response to, and feelings about the program. A downward cycle of low self-esteem, delinquent behavior, and/or a sense of alienation may occur. The learning-disabled child may also be an object of ridicule. A special education placement should be implemented only with knowledge of the effectiveness of the particular program the child will enter. This may be accomplished by arranging for the child and parents to observe the class or by exploring other available alternatives.

The long-term effects of a special education placement on a student's social, academic, and vocational future necessitate a critical look at the effectiveness of referral, assessment, and placement procedures. Placement committees mistakenly refer a number of children on the basis of their interpretation of certain behavioral, linguistic, cultural, and economic characteristics as deviant. Those behaviors that do not conform to expectations should not necessarily be viewed as deviant; they may be normal behaviors within an individual's reference group. The situation of the American Indian illustrates this point.

The issue of whether Indian boarding schools contributed to the mental health problems of American Indian children has been hotly debated. Established to provide a better education for Indian children, the teaching format was based on the American mainstream curriculum with little awareness of the cultural uniqueness of American Indian nations. Criticisms leveled against these schools commonly cite the poor quality of the education, the impersonality of the facilities, the lack of qualified and properly trained staff, the absence of appropriate American Indian role models, the separation of the children from their families and native culture, and the consequent loss of important developmental ceremonies, such as the naming ceremony among the Navajo (Berlin, 1986; Kleinfeld & Bloom, 1977).

An important study of the effects of boarding schools on the mental health of Eskimo adolescents provides another example (Kleinfeld & Bloom, 1977). Almost one half (49%) of the freshmen developed school-related social and emotional problems; 25% of these problems were judged to be serious. Different cultural expectations proved to be the source of many of the problems these Eskimo youths encountered. Such differences were also apparent when the youngsters attended public city schools and were housed in boarding homes with Anglo-American families: "Many boarding home parents prevented students from eating whenever they were hungry as they did in the village and limited their intake of costly meat, a staple of diet in a hunting culture" (Kleinfeld & Bloom, 1977, p. 416).

Expectations and School Performance

In the literature there are reports that school performance varies by ethnic group. Ogbu (1978) has developed a classification of minority groups in the United States that he believes explains differences in academic performance. He classifies minorities as autonomous, immigrant, or caste-like. Autonomous minorities, like Jews, Mormons, and the Amish, are relatively small in population size, are not oppressed by a dominant group, but may be victims of prejudice. These groups, which possess distinctive cultural, linguistic, or religious traits and often have cultural models of success, do not exhibit a disproportionate amount of school failure.

Ogbu's second minority group classification has been represented in recent years by Chinese and Koreans, among others, who immigrated to the United States voluntarily to improve their political, economic, or social status. The mainstream may view them negatively, but they do not necessarily hold this view of themselves. They perceive their living and occupational conditions, as compared to those of their country of origin, as much improved, and they often have the option to return to their homeland if they are dissatisfied with their lives in the United States. The children perform well in school and on standardized tests, even though their culture differs from that of the majority middle class.

On the other hand, caste-like minorities experience a disproportionate amount of school failure. Their members have been "incorporated into the country more or less involuntarily and permanently and then relegated to menial positions through legal and extralegal devices" (Ogbu, 1986, p. 27). African-Americans are an example, but Mexican-Americans, Puerto Ricans, Native Hawaiians and American Indians also possess some caste-like attributes. These groups are ascribed an inferior status by the dominant group, and they experience economic subordination. As a result, caste-like minorities develop a "collective institutional discrimination perspective," which does not view individual effort, academic success, and acculturation toward the mainstream as the path to advancement:

> They believe that their chances are better through collective efforts and manipulating the system. This perspective leads the minorities to channel their time and efforts into collective struggle, i.e., to activities intended to change the system as a way of getting ahead or as a prerequisite for getting ahead. (Ogbu, 1986, p. 28)

The children of caste-like minorities view academic success, according to Ogbu (1986), as "acting white." For example, African-

American children realistically perceive the differential rewards African-American and Anglo-American adults obtain as a result of education. They perceive that African-Americans lag far behind and feel they need to work twice as hard as their Anglo-American counterparts for the same recognition. Many children decide to give up in the face of such inequality and choose instead to adopt behavior that is in opposition to that of the Anglo-American mainstream. To achieve academically and acculturate to the Anglo-American norm is viewed as "Uncle Tom" behavior.

Trueba (1986) questions whether historical events far removed from the students' current social context provide an adequate explanation for school failure. He believes that current social conditions may contribute to the problem and argues that there "is abundant empirical evidence and personal experiences of academic mobility among Blacks, Chicanos, and Native Americans in response to well-planned and culturally meaningful educational activities on their behalf" (p. 257).

Motivation to succeed academically also varies by ethnic group. Many recently immigrated Hmong, Vietnamese, and Korean children achieve academic success, owing to their family's high educational expectations, despite language and cultural differences and prejudice. Often, immigrant families place a burden on the child to succeed for the entire family or ethnic group. For example, parents of many Central American refugee students may remind their children of the extreme risks the family took to migrate to the United States. The academic achievement of the child is perceived as the reward for assuming these risks.

Several researchers propose that the difference in values between teachers and parents also affects school learning among lower-income minority group children. This discontinuity in values between home and school has been attributed to ethnic differences between parents and teachers (Howard & Scott, 1981), social class differences (Leacock, 1969; McCandlers, 1967), or both (Lambert, 1979). Teachers and parents differ especially on specific values such as self-direction or conformity in children. Further, value disparities may affect the quality of the relationship that develops between parents and school staff and may increase the likelihood of interpersonal conflicts between teachers and students (Eggleston & McFarland, 1975). These, in turn, may result in lower school achievement (Hess, 1969), a lower self-concept (Guildford, Gupta, & Goldberg, 1972), and, possibly, higher school dropout rates among these groups (Matluck, 1978).

Individual minority children who have the opportunity to participate in special culturally sensitive programs achieve success, but these programs are very much an exception. As a whole, the education of inner-city children is not comparable in quality to that of middle-class children who live in economically stable neighborhoods. One can attribute such inequity to institutional racism, which has its roots in the historical relationship between the Anglo-American mainstream society and caste-like minorities. Further, one can speculate that socially and culturally sensitive programs, taught by good teachers with good instructional materials, would be implemented in a vigorous and expert manner if the dominant society were as concerned about caste-like minority children as it is about Anglo-American children.

For some minority children, academic achievement often is sought in the context of family or peer group identity rather than through individual success. In this case, the children can realize optimal academic performance if teachers can successfully link the need for affiliation with the need for achievement. Conversely, Navajo children are satisfied to work independently, and a teacher who encourages their group interaction would be violating cultural norms.

The Successful Education of the Minority Student

Several issues must be considered when examining the educational opportunities provided to inner-city children. Public schools often are overwhelmed by such problems as limited budgets, unresponsive bureaucracies, large classroom size, and limited staff. Violence and blatant substance abuse in the corridors and recreational areas are frequent. Many schools hire security officers to monitor their building's entrances and exits and to check for weapons among the student body. Some install a complex system of locks and alarms in doors and windows. Under circumstances such as these, culturally sensitive services cannot be expected to flourish. Only in the context of an adequate and responsive school system can culturally congruent teaching approaches reduce the high dropout rates and potentially increase student achievement and motivation.

Research suggests ways in which schools can address problem behaviors. Wolkind and Rutter (1985) cite studies that demonstrate that schools in London differ markedly in delinquency rates, attendance, and examination success. These differences remain after statistically controlling for the student population's sociodemographic characteristics and previous delinquent behavior, indicating that the schools themselves emerge as frequent contributors to the dysfunctional behavior of students. Wolkind and Rutter conclude that "schools that foster high self-esteem and that promote social and academic success reduce the likelihood of emotional and behavioral disturbance" (p. 83).

Clinicians who work with minority populations need to be particularly aware of the impact of schools on children and adolescents in inner cities. Symptoms that suggest the possibility of a depressive disorder, school phobia, learning delay, or emotional disturbance must be fully and carefully evaluated. Many symptoms may be reactions to an inadequate school system.

Many organizational, systemic, and economic variables affect the ability of an individual school to provide a good education in a nurturing and disciplined environment. The clinician should assess the degree to which the child's school provides positive role models, high expectations for work and behavior, adequate discipline and praise, and a cohesive staff with a common goal. "To the extent that a child's school deviates from these criteria, academic and emotional development are compromised" (Wolkind & Rutter, 1985, p. 83).

A school visit often is necessary because school cooperation and intervention is crucial. Frequently, limited budgets do not allow schools to provide appropiate supportive services or to teach children in a safe, stimulating, and culturally sensitive environment. Clinicians often need to identify the one teacher or school officer who is willing to make an extra commitment and thus modify the child's experience. In some cases the clinician must be willing to recommend a school change.

In sum, the successful education of the minority child requires the collaborative effort of many disciplines. Policy changes are needed as well. First, the inferior quality of the educational services rendered to children in low-income areas must be addressed. The physical space, the quality of books and equipment, and the experience level of teachers should be similar to those of model and successful schools. Further, the definition of cultural sensitivity must be expanded. The attributional and cognitive styles of the children's native culture should be addressed and incorporated into classroom teaching, and portrayal of the cultural and racial diversity of our society should be included in the curriculum. Finally, the school should provide children an opportunity to learn skills that are not part of their native culture but that are necessary to achieve practical success in the United States. The following vignettes illustrate the impact of school experiences and the educational system on the individual child.

Clinical Vignette

Richard, a 14-year-old African-American male with an unusual talent for music, had recently transferred from a suburban public school, where he had been performing well, to an overpopulated inner-city school with no art or music program and few resources.

A gentle, well-spoken adolescent, Richard developed symptoms of depression and withdrawal and manifested multiple fears in his new environment, a large school infested by crime and drugs that offered no supports for his special talents.

A week after Richard's arrival a student fight erupted. One of his classmates was shot and seriously wounded. Because there was little likelihood that Richard's family would move to a new area, the therapist used some connections in the community to negotiate a transfer for the youngster to a smaller school with a resourceful and caring principal and a different type of student body. To facilitate Richard's transition to his new environment and help him recapture his self-image, his social science teacher involved him in a study group with other youngsters. The group focused on the impact of the urban experience on African-American music. Richard's symptoms soon abated.

Many readers will realize that the results of the therapeutic intervention with Richard are atypical and that the therapeutic work with him certainly extended beyond the therapist's office. (This case also illustrates the role of the clinician as an advocate, an issue discussed in some detail in the last chapter.) Most clinicians do not have this therapist's connections; even so, it is difficult for a clinician to penetrate the bureaucracy of a public school system and arrange for the transfer of a student. There are probably many Richards in the inner-city public schools, and each could benefit from a transfer to a school that has a nonthreatening environment that is conducive to learning.

Clinical Vignette

Tony, a 13-year-old bilingual Latino adolescent, was referred to the Committee on Special Education because of his truancy, lack of motivation, and attitude problems manifested toward his teachers. Because of his bilingualism, the school staff placed him in an (overcrowded) bilingual class that included children with low motivation and poor skills; Tony had been experiencing difficulties ever since. Although he continued to perform well scholastically, his frequent and unexcused absences suggested to his teachers that there were problems. One teacher voiced the following opinion: "He is like all these poor children—no interest, no discipline, and no motivation."

The testing finally performed by the Committee on Special Education revealed an unusually bright child who had been bored in the classroom. Tony was placed in another school, one sensitive to his special talents. His behavior changed dramatically. In a 2-year follow-up, Tony's record showed no absences, and he had become the best student in his class. He was involved in a college-bound program.

The Inaccessibilty of Health Care

Disparities in health care delivery for minority versus Anglo-American children persist and may account for the health problems frequently observed in the former as they grow older. Problems related to access of care and the severe shortage of primary care physicians in inner-city and rural areas prove to be of considerable significance for children and families of the lower socioeconomic levels in general and for multiproblem families in particular. A number of factors serve as barriers to adequate health care for children, ranging from eligibility rules of a service program to a parent's financial and time limitations. Further, access to several needed services for a multiproblem child or family is blocked by the service system practice of providing specialized, rather than comprehensive, programs. For example, a 10-year-old boy has become a juvenile court system statistic because of repeated episodes of stealing from the neighborhood grocer. He now is confined to a juvenile residential facility, which is not addressing his learning disability (dyslexia), the fact that he continues to mourn the loss by murder of his 14-year-old brother, the desertion of his mother by way of substance abuse, and his need for ongoing, rather than symptomatic, treatment for his asthma.

Economically disadvantaged minority families often lack good health maintenance care. Mostly, they access health care only during emergencies or after the disease has progressed. This certainly affects the evolution and prognosis of their illnesses. The following vignette is illustrative.

Clinical Vignette

Juan, a 5-year-old Latino child, came to the outpatient clinic with a history of impulsivity, overactivity, frequent angry outbursts, immaturity, and severe language and speech delays. His parents, already experiencing considerable stress due to poor housing and unemployment, had reacted to his symptoms with severe punitive measures. They had been aware of some difficulties since the child was 2 and had attributed his speech delay to issues of bilingualism. The child was addressed in Spanish at home and had attended an English-speaking preschool program. His frequent ear infections had been treated only partially: The family was unable to fully pay for the prescribed antibiotics, so home remedies were instituted. A health provider in an area clinic considered most of Juan's behavioral problems to be transitory and due solely to family and social stressors. Because the family's culture taught them to respect and not question people in authority, they had not, despite some ongoing doubts, pursued further exploration of Juan's problems.

Juan's difficulties persisted. Because he was having additional learning problems in school, the family was advised to return to the health clinic. They were told that Juan might be retarded. The schoolteacher disagreed with this diagnosis and referred the family to a mental health evaluation center.

A bilingual clinician concluded after a comprehensive evaluation that the child had serious speech and language delays in both Spanish and English. Juan was referred for speech and hearing evaluations. He was then diagnosed as having a moderate bilateral hearing loss secondary to his ear infections. An early intervention and rehabilitation program could have been implemented by a competent clinician, and Juan's secondary social, emotional, and severe cognitive and communication problems could have been avoided. Factors associated with poverty, stress, poor health care, and a minority culture had complicated the clinical picture and placed this already vulnerable child at high risk.

Internal Stressors

Murphy and Moriarty (1976) call attention to vulnerabilities in children such as sensory motor deficits, deviant body morphology, unusual sensitivities, integrative and adaptive difficulties, insufficient impulse control, inhibitions, and incapacity to read a caretaker's cues, which can place them at risk to develop behavioral problems and tax their abilities to cope adequately with stress. A vignette illustrates the complexity of such difficulties.

Clinical Vignette

Mario, a 6-year-old Mexican-American boy was referred to the clinic because he was explosive, irritable, fidgety, and overly reactive. He was particularly sensitive to rejection and very attached to his mother. The school expressed concern because Mario had difficulty with frustration tolerance and became overly attached to his teachers. He cried easily and became anxious and overwhelmed when stressed. He required an unusual amount of teacher attention and support.

Mario's history suggested that he was one of those children who easily succumb to ordinary and expectable life stressors. As an infant he was overly sensitive to noise and adjusted poorly to change. It was difficult for his mother to reassure and comfort him. When he grew older, Mario had problems reading the social cues of his peers and adapting to new situations. His temperamental vulnerabilities had been compounded by the family's cultural style of overprotection and prolonged attachment and dependency on the maternal figure. This style of care had served to protect him from many stimuli and demands but had also prevented him from developing an efficient adaptive style of his own. The child's poor coping style had been further taxed by a series of other difficulties, including several family moves and frequent financial reversals.

The therapist's intervention addressed the environment, the mother, and the child himself: she first recommended an environment that was structured, consistent, and not too stimulating, such as a quiet school setting with clear behavior expectations and teachers trained in special education. The therapist then implemented treatment based on a psychoeducational model. In view of Mario's strong attachment to his mother, the mother was asked to participate in the treatment. Fully aware of the cultural nuances of childrearing and sex-role behavior and of the importance of the extended family in this group, the therapist began with efforts to diminish the intensity of Mario's attachment to his mother. She suggested that the child spend more time with an uncle who seemed to be an independent, sociable, and highly motivated individual. The therapist also saw the child individually, and through drawings and play techniques she helped foster the child's sense of personal control, independence, endurance, verbal expressiveness, and self-esteem.

As a consequence of these interventions there was a significant decrease in symptoms on a 6-month follow-up.

RISK FACTORS

Prenatal and birth complications are risk factors associated with poor outcome (Field, 1980). The findings of a 20-year longitudinal study (Werner & Smith, 1982) in Kauai, Hawaii, illustrate an association between socioeconomic status and birth complications. The multiethnic and multiracial sample included Japanese, Chinese, Filipinos, Portuguese, Puerto Ricans, Koreans, and Anglo-American participants, as well as subjects who were part- and full-Hawaiian.

Environmental risk factors were found to correlate with the occurrence of central nervous system damage but to also influence its subsequent development:

> Perinatal complications were consistently related to later impaired physical and psychological development only when combined with persistently poor environmental circumstances (e.g., chronic poverty, family instability, or maternal mental health problems). Children who were raised in more affluent homes, with an intact family and a well-educated mother, showed few, if any, negative effects from reproductive stress, unless there was severe central nervous system impairment. (Werner & Smith, 1982, p. 31)

It should be noted that poverty alone was not found to be sufficient to cause problems in development. Research documents the significance of the child–caretaker relationship. In the Werner and Smith study, mothers with low levels of education were found to often interact inappropriately with a child they perceived as unresponsive. Consequently, by the second year "caregiver and child appeared caught in a vicious cycle of increasing frustration, characterized by parental behavior that was perceived as 'careless,' 'erratic,' 'indifferent,' 'ambivalent,' or 'overprotective'" (p. 33). In the same study, infants with biological risk factors often had difficult temperaments. They were reported to have the worst prognosis for developing learning disabilities when their caretakers were stressed and the home environment was chaotic. In short, Werner and Smith found that those children

> with learning and/or behavior problems that persisted into late adolescence had higher rates of moderate to severe perinatal stress, low birthweight, and "chronic conditions leading to minimal brain dysfunctions" noted by pediatricians in infancy. They tended to live more often in chronic poverty or amidst parental psychopathology than children whose problems were transient. (p. 35)

Unfortunately, Werner and Smith did not include acculturation or generational status as variables in their equation. Consequently, it is difficult to determine the extent to which socioeconomic status information is spuriously related to immigrant status and/or sociohistorical caste-like status; that is, to some extent the variables of socioeconomic status and immigrant status may be confounded.

In addition, some ethnic groups seem to be at particular risk. African-Americans and Puerto Ricans have a higher incidence of very low birth weight infants than do Anglo-Americans (Public Health Service, 1990, p. 376). In the case of African-Americans, a lower prevalence of involvement in comprehensive prenatal care may explain these findings.

PROTECTIVE FACTORS

Researchers have identified various personality traits that act as internal mediators to stress. These include locus of control, self-esteem, social orientation, achievement motivation, and cognitive style. One of the internal mediators, social comprehension, has been more fully described as being a protective factor in children. Social comprehension includes interpersonal understanding; problem-solving ability; and the capacity to comprehend, appreciate, and produce humor (Rutter, 1987). Researchers have also explored such variables as perceived competence, behavioral styles (Fontana & Dovidio, 1984), and various temperamental characteristics such as activity level and quality of withdrawal (Plomin, 1983).

Preschool children who have been labeled invulnerable in studies of the high-risk offspring of psychotic parents were characterized as appearing socially at ease, actively trying to master their environment, developing a high degree of autonomy, and knowing how to attract and use the support of adults (Anthony, 1978). In an earlier study, Werner (1961) found sociability, dominance, endurance, high activity level, and demonstrativeness to be associated with invulnerability.

Competence in the social, school, and cognitive dimensions is requisite for resiliency in children (Garmezy, Masten, & Tellegen, 1983). Resilient adolescents have been found to possess an internalized set of values and are more socially perceptive and mature, more responsible, and more appreciative and nurturant than those who succumb to stress; they also have been observed to possess better verbal communication skills (Werner & Smith, 1982).

Competent children in inner cities have been characterized as demonstrating reflectiveness and impulse control (Garmezy, 1981). Resilient adolescents scored higher on California Personal Inventory scales of Responsibility, Socialization, Achievement, and Communality than adolescents who had developed learning or behavioral problems. Werner and Smith (1982) observed that positive self-esteem and internal locus of control discriminated between good and poor outcomes only when considerable stress was involved. Positive sense of self, sense of personal power, and internal locus of control were found to be important factors of resiliency in disadvantaged African-American children (Garmezy, 1981). Parents and teachers identified competent children as friendly, well liked by peers and adults, interpersonally sensitive, socially responsive and cooperative, and emotionally stable (Garmezy, 1981).

Rutter (1987) proposed four specific coping mechanisms in children that act to protect against stress, namely, the ability to (1) reduce the impact of stress, (2) avoid negative chain reactions, (3) establish self-efficacy and self-esteem, and (4) seek new opportunities.

Adaptability and malleability in children have been described as characteristics necessary to protect them against psychiatric disorders (Rutter, Yule, & Quentin, 1975). Caplan (1964) noted that those individuals who cope effectively are likely to come away with their coping abilities enhanced; those who deal ineffectively are likely to experience future pathological outcomes (Felner, 1984). In assessing the impact of a particular event on a child's development, it is important to determine whether the event and its consequences were predictable or not and whether the event caused more than one consequence (Compas, Davis, Forsythe, & Wagner, 1985).

Anthony (1987) has described a vulnerability–invulnerability spectrum on which he locates those children who succumb to ordinary and expectable life stresses; those who are vulnerable but who are blessed with an overprotective environment and do well as long as they are not challenged; those who bounce back after each stress and become increasingly resilient; and those who are nonvulnerable, that is, who are robust from birth onward.

THE RELATIONSHIP BETWEEN
SOCIAL CLASS AND PSYCHOPATHOLOGY

The interest of social scientists in social class stems from the belief that variables such as wealth, occupation, and prestige help to explain human behavior (Farrington, 1986). Thus, members of the same social class are thought to share "attitudes, values, and patterns of life" (Hollingshead & Redlich, 1958, p. 86), and socioeconomic status is believed to affect individual behavior. Certainly the conditions under which people live vary by socioeconomic status, and these may well influence the behavior of individuals.

Research has been conducted to investigate the correlations between psychiatric disorders and socioeconomic status. Two theories continue to be discussed: (1) the social selection theory, which proposes that individuals with emotional disabilities or dysfunctions sink to the lower socioeconomic groups, and (2) the social causation theory, which posits that poverty and its difficulties can cause mental illness. It has been proposed that schizophrenia fits the social selection model whereas major depression, substance abuse, and antisocial personality are consistent with social causation theory (Dohrenwend et al., 1992). An association between child psychopathology and socioeconomic status has not been demonstrated as clearly as it has been for adults (Dohrenwend et al., 1980). Three possibilities for this difference have been cited (Wolkind & Rutter, 1985): Disorders in which social class is a factor are much less frequent in children; social conditions affect children and adults differently; and social class holds a different meaning for adults and children. Family discord or disruption has been found to influence a child's mental health more than socioeconomic status (Wolkind & Rutter, 1985).

Associations between childrearing practices, social class, and educational pursuits have been established: For example, working-class parents are less likely than middle-class parents to make use of reasoning in disciplining their children and to promote curiosity. Middle-class parents encourage their children to ask questions and are more likely to provide detail in their explanations (Wolkind & Rutter, 1985). Some blurring of these distinctions has been observed: Middle-class parents who have hectic work schedules are at times too harried to respond to their children's curiosity with detailed explanations, at least at the time of questioning, and many working-class parents do encourage their children's curiosity.

A more profound association between low socioeconomic status and delinquency exists, but only in cases of serious crimes and for repeat offenders at the lower extreme of the socioeconomic scale (Wolkind & Rutter, 1985). However, other factors, such as criminal background of parents, the extent of family discord, and residence in overcrowded or dilapidated housing, contribute more to predicting delinquency than does parental occupation.

Rutter (1979) describes six familial risk factors that appear to correlate with childhood psychiatric disorders: severe marital distress, low social status, overcrowding or large family size, paternal criminality, maternal psychiatric disorder, and admission of child to foster care placement. And it is the cumulative effect of these factors, more than the existence of any single one, that increases the possibility of negative outcome.

THE DIAGNOSTIC CHALLENGE

✦

The intent of this section is to identify the sociocultural factors critical to the diagnostic process in the clinical evaluation of minority children and to integrate these factors with a creative and sensitive use of the available diagnostic tools, namely, history taking, assessment tests, and classification schemes. This section provides guidelines to enable the clinician to elicit comprehensive, relevant, and culturally pertinent historical information; to consider cultural influences when choosing and interpreting assessment tests; and to use the current multiaxial evaluation system of the American Psychiatric Association's (1993) *DSM-IV Draft Criteria* as an effective diagnostic tool. Clinical examples illustrate the diagnostic challenge facing the mental health clinician who chooses to work with African-American, Asian-American, American Indian, and Latino children.

Once a diagnosis is made, the clinician's focus turns to understanding the parts of the environment that contribute to exacerbations or remissions of the illness and to assessing whether previous treatment failed because of the nature of the illness itself or because of inadequate, uncoordinated, or inappropriate service delivery systems. Frequently, clinicians encounter the challenge of evaluating children who were previously misdiagnosed and whose treatment, though prolonged and possibly well intentioned, proved ineffective.

CHAPTER 2

History Taking

✦

THE INFLUENCE OF CULTURE ON DIAGNOSIS

A number of clinicians and researchers document the need to take culture into account if an accurate diagnosis and effective treatment plans are to be made (Giordano, 1973; Opler & Singer, 1956; Papajohn & Spiegel, 1975; Yamamoto, James, & Polley, 1968). More recently, Foulks (1982) has reminded the clinician that culture determines, to a large extent, how one "experiences, identifies, interprets, and communicates psychic function" (p. 240). Leighton (1982) emphasized the need to understand behaviors that make up clinical syndromes in relation to the setting in which these behaviors occur and provided a vivid illustration:

> If a 35-year-old middle-class Episcopalian physician complains that someone is making him ill by witchcraft, a mental disorder is probably indicated. The same complaint from a 50-year-old Italian immigrant laborer, by contrast, might have no relationship whatever to any kind of mental disorder. The same would be true of persons of Spanish, Mexican, Pennsylvania Dutch, Nigerian, Eskimo, Navajo, Haitian, and many other cultures where belief in witchcraft is common. (p. 202)

The following vignette illustrates the importance of understanding belief patterns within the context of a particular family.

Clinical Vignette

Dylan, an 11-year-old Irish boy, was hospitalized for suicidal ideation. He expressed a wish to die and be reincarnated as a more

39

advanced and better person. During the mental status examination Dylan admitted to visual and auditory hallucinations of spirits telling him to kill his father.

During a family interview the clinician learned that Dylan's previously Catholic family practiced Hinduism and *santería*. Furthermore, they had been Jehovah's Witnesses and had participated in several other religions in the past. Upon evaluation the mother had received a diagnosis of manic-depressive illness and the father a diagnosis of unspecified psychotic disorder.

Family history included a chaotic home environment and past sexual abuse perpetrated against the patient and his siblings by both parents. The clinician assigned to Dylan sought consultation to facilitate understanding of the impact of the family belief systems on the child.

Belief Systems and Diagnosis

Dylan's case illustrates several important issues: First, clinicians must be alert to a belief system that seems somewhat dystonic to the culture. Many healthy individuals adopt other cultural patterns to enrich their own; however, frequent occurrence of such behavior may reflect underlying problems. Dylan's family had borrowed other cultural patterns to express, make sense of, and discharge very disorganized behavior. They did not attend any of the recognized services in their community of the religions they adopted and practiced these beliefs only within the confines of their family circle.

Second, symptoms often are expressed within a family's belief system. Dylan believed in reincarnation, but his wish to die was a response to his low self-esteem and poor self-image, brought about by his disturbed and abusive parents. This vulnerable child used religious language to express a high level of psychopathology within himself and his family. Many people believe in reincarnation, yet few want to commit suicide in order to reincarnate. Dylan's hallucinations of spirits, which were subsequently identified as deities of the *santería* religion, were the product of the severe and distorted indoctrination of these beliefs by his abusive father.

Third, clinicians need to be informed about belief systems other than their own to be able to differentiate between the nuances of normal and dysfunctional patterns. Such knowledge proved a great help in approaching Dylan and his family inasmuch as these religious beliefs had become the conduit and expression of mental illness.

A clinician's cultural misunderstanding or reliance on stereotypes can lead to the development of a faulty diagnosis. Adebimpe (1981)

has suggested that in the past psychiatrists were not inclined to diagnose depression in African-Americans because they believed them to
be too impoverished or too happy-go-lucky to be depressed. In other
instances the actual diagnosis may be accurate but not the meaning
attributed to the symptoms. Bender's (1939) analysis of the meaning
of the behavior patterns of "Negro children" diagnosed with a psychiatric disorder illustrates the problem created by a reliance on stereotypes:

> There has appeared to be a special pattern in behavior disorders of Negro
> children that displays itself in several ways. This is related to the ques-
> tions of motility and impulse. Two features which almost everyone will
> concede as characteristic of the race are: the special capacity for lazi-
> ness is the ability to sleep for long periods of time, when it fits the needs
> of the situation. The dancing represents special motility patterns and ten-
> dencies. (pp. 217–218)

Culture-Specific Syndromes

Some syndromes have been identified as unique to specific cultures or
as occurring with particular frequency among a defined group of
people (Griffith & Young, 1988). For example, American psychiatrists
who encounter West Indian, Haitian, or Puerto Rican patients should
have some knowledge of the syndromes of "falling out" and *ataque*.
The former, referred to as "blacking out" by Bahamians and "indis-
position" by Haitians who have settled in Miami, is characterized by
a collapse during which the individual cannot move or speak but is
able to understand what others say (Griffith & Young, 1988). The
syndrome Puerto Ricans call "*ataque*" is characterized by bizarre sei-
zure patterns, usually psychogenic in nature (Gomez, 1982). These two
syndromes are similar in that the length of episode may be very brief
or may extend to several days. The accompanying hallucinations and
violent behavior may lead a clinician to consider diagnoses such as
acute shizophreniform reaction or atypical psychosis (Griffith &
Young, 1988).

A prevalent condition unique to the Japanese, particularly among
adolescents and young adults, is *taijin kyoto sho* (TKS), or "fear of
facing or interacting with other people." These patients experience a
profound fear, at times reaching psychotic proportions, of hurting the
feelings of others owing to imagined shortcomings within themselves
(Kitanashi & Tseng, 1988, cited in Prince, 1989). Shore and Manson
(1981) described the *Windigo* psychosis, a condition observed among

the Ojibwa Indians of southern Canada. Melancholia and a delusion of the transformation of the victim into a monster who eats human flesh characterize this syndrome. *Irijua* is a children's disorder prevalent in Peru; the symptoms appear after the birth of a sibling or after weaning and are characterized by sadness, melancholy, irritability, hypersensitivity, anorexia, loss of weight and tearfulness. *Mal ojo* is a Spanish term (translated into English as "evil eye") that refers to a syndrome that includes the following: fitful sleep, crying without apparent cause, diarrhea, vomiting, and fever (in a child or infant this syndrome is believed to be caused by a fixed stare from an adult; Hughes, 1985).

It is unfortunate that the literature on these syndromes is so lacking, especially for children, that we do not know whether their causes are psychogenic, physical, or both, or how their symptoms correlate with Western diagnostic criteria. Nevertheless, the syndromes are important cultural idioms of distress and/or illness, and the clinician must be aware of them in order to communicate effectively with patients.

The clinician must also be aware of certain indigenous practices in order not to misdiagnose some cases as cases of child abuse. The Cambodians and Hmong (a mountain-dwelling people of China, Vietnam, and Laos), for example, use "cupping" as a healing practice; this consists of placing a small heated cup on the skin and allowing it to cool, which causes a circular reddened area to appear (Buchwald, Panwala, & Hooton, 1992; Reinhart & Rhus, 1984). The Vietnamese, Chinese, and Cambodians use *cao cio* or coin rubbing, a practice that involves rubbing the skin with a coin to alleviate common symptoms and that can result in symmetrical and linear petechiae (Golden & Duster, 1977; Yeatman & Dang, 1980). The Mien (people from the Mien-Yang area in the north central Szechwan province of China) use a healing practice called "moxibustion," which consists of the application of heat to the skin in a specific pattern by means of a burning object, such as something that produces incense (Buchwald et al., 1992; Reinhart & Rhus, 1984).

The literature suggests that the same basic patterns of psychopathology exist around the world and that culture-bound syndromes are folk categories for behaviors (Westermeyer, 1987). A distinction is made between the emic (intracultural) and the etic (universal) aspects of cross-cultural diagnosis.

The clinician must consider the possibility that a particular diagnosis may have different behavioral manifestations according to the ethnicity of a patient. These cultural differences, which may be evident in the severity and frequency of the concomitant symptoms, must be considered in the diagnostic process and in the formulation of a patient's prognosis (Westermeyer, 1987).

Canino (1988) provides a summary statement addressing the issue of culture-specific disorders and the effect of these disorders in children.

> The whole area of culture-specific disorders, nevertheless, continues to be controversial. Some researchers feel that these disorders are unique to some cultures, while others feel that they are variants of disorders seen around the world or simply idiomatic expressions of distress. This issue becomes more complicated in this country because the expressions of these disorders may be correlated to the levels of acculturation of the particular cultural subgroup. Of more interest, though, is that nothing has been written on the effect of these disorders in children. . . . Familiarity with the disorders may facilitate a more reliable family history of mental illness and offer better assessment of cultural syntonicity or dystonicity of the child's presenting symptomatology. (p. 1028)

To prepare for the initial interview with a minority child and his or her family, clinicians need to acquire knowledge about the potential influence of culture on mental health and the development of disorders and to prepare a set of pertinent questions to ask. It is particularly important for clinicians to identify differences as well as similarities within and between cultural groups. Failure to do so may contribute to their perceiving a difference as an emotional problem or a mental illness. This chapter emphasizes and illustrates issues relevant to a family's cultural background in the context of taking a history. It begins with a clinical vignette:

IDENTIFYING INTRAGROUP DIFFERENCES

Clinical Vignette

Grace, a withdrawn and overly shy Asian-American 10-year-old, was accompanied to the clinic by her parents for the initial evaluation session. The clinician, who addressed the parents to obtain a full clinical history, made the following assumptions: The family is Chinese because their address is near Chinatown. Their dress and demeanor indicate that this is a first-generation, traditional family. The family's belief system is based on Confucianism. Although the child is withdrawn, she is probably doing well academically.

A comprehensive history revealed the family to be a third-generation, nontraditional Korean Catholic family who suspected their child had a learning disability on the basis of her poor school performance. If it had not been further explored, the clinician's initial impression clearly would have affected his interview style, the focus of his questioning, and possibly his diagnosis and the eventual effectiveness of his interventions.

Asian-Americans emigrate from various Asian nations and represent different cultural groups, which share many commonalities but are also characterized by differences among themselves as well as from Western populations. The differences and commonalities extend to family units within each group as well. Some groups seek political refuge in the United States; others come voluntarily. Asian-Americans may experience severe and overt prejudice, but not all suffer such indignities.

Wong (1982), who argues that there is no typical Chinese family, advocates the study of Chinese family structure and functioning with a focus on the history of its formation, development, and modification. Significant changes have occurred in the Chinese family over time. For example, the Chinese who had been tillers of the soil and who immigrated between 1920 and 1943 differ considerably from the highly educated Chinese who have come to the United States since the mid-1960s.

Many individuals of Asian background were born in America. However, this does not negate the importance of the clinician's collecting information about patients' geographical place of birth (rural vs. urban or suburban, coastal vs. inland, Hawaii vs. mainland) and exposure to members of their ethnic group and about their generational stage (i.e., first-generation American, second-generation American, etc.). Asian-Americans range from the recently arrived to those who have lived in the United States for four or five generations (Sue & Chin, 1983).

Among American Indian people, too, there are diversities. Clevenger (1982) calls attention to these:

> There are differences in social patterns, dialects, economic and living conditions. There are some 800,000 of us living within the boundaries of the United States, composing more than 200 tribes or bands, and speaking one or more of over 200 living language groups. We reside on large reservations, such as my reservation, the Navajo, which extends from northern New Mexico into a large portion of Arizona and parts of Utah. Some reservations are quite small. The Tewa tribe lives on a small portion of land completely surrounded by the city of El Paso, Texas. Some tribes are recognized by the Federal government. Others, such as the Alabama-Conchiti who live near Houston, Texas, are not federally rec-

ognized. Some of us live in rural circumstances, such as the Jicarilla Apaches. Perhaps 50% of us, however, are now living in the urban centers, such as Los Angeles and Seattle. (pp. 149–150)

Ideally, the clinician should be aware of the diversities and similarities among Latino groups as well. Like Asian-Americans and American Indians, Latinos represent different cultural backgrounds:

> It is common practice to lump together all Spanish-speaking peoples, as if they constituted one huge homogeneous mass, while glossing over the multiple differences among and within Hispanic subgroups. All share a common language and Spanish heritage, as well as a set of cultural values which are based on cooperation and mutual aid; on the strengths and supports provided by the family and the community; on the status and prestige ascribed to the person because of what he/she is rather than what he/she has achieved; on the recognition of a person's dignity and respect regardless of station in life; and on the interpersonal sharing of emotional aspects of life. However, beyond these parameters, the similarities diminish. Hispanic groups also differ in the amount of influence from African, Native American and non-Hispanic European traditions. Each group has maintained its autonomy and is clearly distinguishable from the other. (Arce, 1982, p. 139)

The heritage of Latino children varies: A child from Buenos Aires may have a German or Italian heritage, a child from Guatemala a Mayan heritage, and a child from the Caribbean an African heritage. Latinos, like other minority groups, are represented at all socioeconomic levels, but inner-city Latino children and adolescents—primarily Mexican-Americans, Cubans, Puerto Ricans, and an increasing number of Central Americans and Dominicans—mostly belong to families at the lower socioeconomic levels. These children experience a variety of simultaneous and sequential stressors that increase their vulnerability to disorders (Canino & Canino, 1980; Vega, Hough, & Romero, 1983).

Clinicians should also be alert to cultural differences, as well as similarities, among those identified as black or African-American. Immigrants from the Caribbean islands and West and East Africa may bear some similarities to American-born blacks, but for many the differences are much greater. Identified as African-Americans, they hold various beliefs about death and illness, some of which lead some to choose their traditional practitioners (e.g., Yoruba and voodoo priests) to alleviate their symptoms.

It is essential that the clinician determine how patients identify themselves rather than assume, for example, that English-speaking persons with dark skin and kinky hair are African-American or that those with olive skin, straight hair, and a Spanish surname are Latino. Persons fitting the first description may be proud to be Trinidadian and may identify themselves as black but not American. Those fitting the second description may be equally proud of their American Indian heritage.

DETERMINING THE PRESENTING PROBLEM AND COLLECTING DEVELOPMENTAL INFORMATION

Determining the Nature of the Problem

The clinician's first task in taking a history is to clarify from the family's perspective the nature of the problem that brings them for help and to explain the assessment process. Ideally, the clinician is aware that it is inappropriate in some cultures, particularly for strangers, to ask personal questions. The clinician should also keep in mind that some items of necessary information may have a special cultural meaning: For example, some cultures view the child as a year of age at the time of birth.

Primary Complaints

The interviewer should inquire about the immediate reasons for the referral as well as the situation specificity of the complaints. Differences in opinion on the part of caregivers, teachers and other referral sources, and the child about the severity or frequency of the behavior should be identified in the history and explored further. Misunderstandings about the reason for referral should be addressed. An evaluation of a child or adolescent who may be viewed as "culturally different" requires the clinician to explore possible cultural influences that may have precipitated the referral. The following vignette is illustrative.

Clinical Vignette

Maria, a 13-year-old Latino girl, was referred to the clinic for disrespectful behavior at home. Described by her parents as confrontational, assertive, and too autonomous, Maria demanded more freedom and openly talked about boys and sex. Her parents' traditional beliefs and childrearing attitudes were in direct opposition to their child's behavior.

The differences in her parents' and teachers' perceptions of Maria were clear. Her teachers perceived her as an assertive and independent young woman who felt comfortable exploring difficult issues. They regarded her behavior as an indication of strength. Maria's parents, on the other hand, viewed her behavior as deviant.

During the history taking, the clinician learned that the parents had sent Maria to a progressive liberal school to achieve their goal of a good education for their daughter. At school Maria had been told to speak up, know her own mind, question what she heard, and be independent. The evaluating clinician arranged a meeting between the teachers and the parents to clarify the mixed messages given to Maria. After a series of meetings directed by the biculturally sensitive clinician, misunderstandings were resolved and the family felt better able to direct their daughter through a healthy adolescence. For their part, the teachers became more aware of the family's cultural beliefs and values and helped Maria integrate both philosophies.

Present Illness

Details on the duration and degree of the child's impairment should be explored within the context of his or her environment. Chronological details of the problem behavior, from the onset of the first symptoms to the characteristics of the presenting problem, should be identified and recorded. The clinician should try to distinguish the extent to which the behavior is endogenous or reactive to recent stressors in the child's environment.

It is crucial to assess the child's behavior in the context of the family's social class and culture and to examine its meaning to the child and the community. Information needs to be gathered about any previous mental health treatment of the child for the presenting problem—the frequency of sessions, the length of treatment, and the child's and family's response to it. If no previous professional mental health treatment has been sought or provided, the interviewer should inquire if the family has approached others within the community for help, for example, priests, ministers, community leaders, godparents, or healers. Such information provides a good sense of the family's health-seeking behavior and their previous experience in resolving their problems. Any inconsistencies in the reporting of the chain of events that led to the present illness among the various informants should be explored further and recorded.

Developmental History

The greater the amount of time that elapses between an event in the patient's past and an inquiry about that event, the less reliable and more distorted the information provided. Stressful events often are forgotten or revised. Consequently, it proves helpful to offer the informants relevant anchor points. The child's pediatric chart, dated photographs, videotapes, or baby books can enhance a caretaker's memories of the child's developmental stages.

In cases in which documents have been lost or were never acquired, a clinician may ask about the ways the family celebrates or recognizes a particular holiday or about the happenings at a significant event, such as a wedding, a wake, a birthday party, or a religious or cultural gathering. One follows such inquiries with questions about the child's level of skills at the time: "Please tell me a story of what your child was like then. What did she do, how did she behave, and how did she compare to other children?" If other family members cared for the child during particularly crucial developmental stages, one should request permission to contact these individuals to learn their impressions.

A basic component of the developmental history is its assessment in terms of the normal behavioral patterns of childhood. The range of individual variation should be noted. It helps to ask caretakers if they have observed any areas of precocious development or any delay, interruption, or setback in the child's progress as compared to other children or siblings.

Clinicians must be particularly sensitive to possible caregiver bias. Contradictions, sudden lapses of memory, and frequent revisions of previous information should alert the clinician. Informants may overreport or exaggerate the child's problems, thus distorting the developmental history and alarming the clinician, or they may deny or conceal the problems and act overly cautious, fearing that the mental health worker can read their minds or will discover a terrible, unsolvable, and stigmatizing illness in the child. Thus, it facilitates information gathering if the clinician repeats certain key questions once the family feels more comfortable with the process.

Pregnancy and Delivery

To obtain a comprehensive history of the mother's pregnancy with and delivery of the child being evaluated, the clinician must inquire about sociocultural attitudes toward pregnancy and motherhood and evaluate their consequences and meanings for the mother and other family members. Feelings about prenatal health care, obstetricians, and midwives also should be explored. Data need to be obtained about any special diets and medications the mother was on during pregnancy, as well as about cultural attitudes about diet and food cravings. Several specific questions need to be asked.

- Who in the immediate community, besides health personnel, supported and advised the mother about ways to ensure a safe pregnancy?
- Did the mother understand the risks of smoking, taking drugs or alcohol, and ingesting medicines during pregnancy? Did she engage in any of these practices during her pregnancy?
- Was the child's father available and supportive, and if not, who was available to provide support?
- What, if any, preparations were made in advance of the birth, and what familial or financial stressors were anticipated or created by the pregnancy and birth of the child?
- Was the mother undergoing any particular stressful life events during the pregnancy, and if so, what were these events and how did the mother resolve them?
- Who was present at the child's delivery?
- How many hours did the delivery take, and how painful was the delivery for the mother?
- Were there any complications in the delivery?

Infancy

The United States ranks 19th in the world in infant mortality, behind such nations as Spain, Singapore, Japan, and Germany. In 1987 about one in four babies nationwide was born to a mother who did not receive early prenatal care (*SOS America*, 1990).

Recent studies suggest that, compared to Anglo-Americans, Mexican-Americans have higher neonatal mortality rates at any birth weight (Williams, Binkin, & Clingman, in press). The infant mortality rates for Puerto Rican children born in the United States are less favorable than those for Mexican-Americans (*Black and Minority Health*, 1985). These findings emphasize the need to ask carefully about previous infant losses in minority group mothers. The clinician also must assess the impact of such losses on maternal attitudes and expectations toward the patient.

Following the usual inquiry for birth weight and postnatal complications, the clinician should attempt to determine if the mother had had a preference for the sex of her baby, how the baby's name was selected, what process was followed in naming the child, and whether the mother experienced any period of postpartum depression. If possible, information should be obtained from those persons who helped the mother care for the infant during this period. Shifts in family attitudes and roles also need to be explored.

One also inquires about cultural attitudes toward breast- or bottle-feeding, weaning practices, physical arrangements in the household for the baby, and decisions about the primary caretaker for day and/or night. In many cultures the grandmother comes to assist the mother for a period after the child is born and often lives with the family for a short time. For other cultures the role of caretaker falls totally on the mother, who cares for the baby during the day, breast-feeds, and is expected to get up at night. The importance of eliciting a patient's early developmental history is exemplified by the following case.

Clinical Vignette

Enrique, a 7-year-old Latino child from a recently immigrated family, was referred to the clinic with symptoms of separation anxiety and inmature behavior. When the clinician elicited a history, it was learned that the child still slept with his parents and was not yet weaned from the mother.

The parents came from a rural Central American town and informed the clinician that in their culture the decision to leave the parental bed and to be weaned was always made by the child. In further questioning it was learned that the older children in the family had made this decision at a much earlier age.

Prior to the birth of Enrique the mother had lost two infant children. On arriving in this country the parents were still mourning these losses and in addition had to mourn the loss of their community of family and friends. Enrique had been born soon after their arrival. The parents had become overly attached to the child and in their overprotection of him had exaggerated cultural norms. They had been unable to cue into Enrique's earlier readiness to become more independent.

Medical History

The family history of medical illnesses and the impact of these illnesses on the children must be explored. Dates and times of caregivers' hospitalizations or injuries should be sought. It is critical to ask for any history of somatization. Inquiries should be made about aches and pains, stress headaches, mild gastritis, tiredness, and other "pseudo-medical" illnesses experienced by the caretakers. The child's presentation of psychological symptoms may mimic the caretakers' style of expressing distress through physical complaints.

Parents often fail to seek appropriate health care because of insufficient funds, system or language barriers, or lack of knowledge (Van Oss, Marin, & Padilla, 1983). In 1986, 22% of Hispanic-Americans, 10.1% of African-Americans, and 7.7% of whites were not covered by any form of public or private health insurance (U.S. Congress, 1989b). Finally, a child may have received second-rate care in a large, financially troubled, and understaffed institution.

CULTURAL EXPECTATIONS OF CHILD DEVELOPMENT AND BEHAVIOR

Expectations concerning children's development and behavior vary across cultures. Key attributes such as passivity, dependence, and the acquisition of language and motor skills acquire different meanings in different cultures. A particular culture (or family) may tolerate poor motor skills but not delayed verbal acquisition. Another culture may show acceptance of dependent and cooperative behaviors but not autonomous and competitive behaviors. In some cultures a child who manifests learning difficulties may be shown more tolerance than a child who demonstrates anxious behaviors. Cultural norms are influenced by socioeconomic level and the level of acculturation of a given family. Cultural influences may delay referral and identification of a problem or may precipitate a premature or inappropriate referral.

Language and communication need to be assessed within the framework of familial and cultural expectations as well. Some cultures highly value and reinforce early verbalization and fluency. Others show primary concern about early socialization skills and affective expression. Bilingualism and the use of idiomatic expression in the household also require examination.

Minority group communication patterns differ from those used in the dominant culture. Latino Caribbean children are taught to be physically and emotionally expressive. They are comfortable in close proximity with others but are taught, as are many Asian-American children, not to look directly into the eyes of authority figures (considered to be a sign of disrespect). American Indian, Latino, Asian-American, and African-American children in general are taught to share. Competitive striving is generally inhibited whereas cooperative behavior is encouraged.

The American Indian culture emphasizes nonverbal communication. Feelings, particularly anger, are not openly expressed verbally or nonverbally (Katz, 1981). Self-control, independence, and social responsibility are valued (LaFromboise & BigFoot, 1988).

For American Indian children, and often for other minority children as well, allegiance is to the family and community rather than to the self (Yates, 1987). These cultures place value on not being singled out or striving to be better than others for individual gains; rather, individuals struggle to be equal to others or to be better for the family or clan (Berlin, 1986; LaFromboise & BigFoot, 1988). The following case, cited by Yates (1987) is illustrative:

> At 17 years of age, Charlie was about to graduate from high school. He was an excellent boxer and had become the state boxing champion. During a school assembly, the principal gave Charlie a special award accompanied by a long, impassioned congratulatory address. On the way out of the auditorium, a group of American Indian boys jumped on Charlie and pummeled him soundly. Charlie dropped out of school even though there was but one month to graduation. (p. 1137)

The endeavor for which Charlie achieved recognition involved individual gain, rather than gain for the group or community. His Indian classmates may have perceived his achievement as a betrayal of the group.

American Indian parents view children as autonomous and equal individuals with their own unique developmental pace. They tend not to interfere with what they consider to be the natural unfolding of development. Specific developmental tasks may be encouraged and rewarded but are seldom taught. This parental perspective has profound implications for the clinician who is trying to involve the family in treatment plans. Noninterfering parents may be mistakenly viewed as detached, uncaring, or uninvolved (Yates, 1987). Although the parents may care deeply for the child's well-being, they consider it the child's decision to participate in or withdraw from treatment and to comply with or reject a medication regimen.

CULTURAL ATTITUDES TOWARD HEALTH PRACTICES

The family's cultural attitudes about and previous experiences with doctors and hospitals should be explored, as should their feelings about the quality and availability of services in their community. Cultural beliefs about the effectiveness of medication need to be understood. Physicians must educate parents about the benefits and side effects of the medicines prescribed and must be sensitive to the child's and family's beliefs and expectations. To be more effective, a clinician often needs to integrate folk beliefs into treatment interventions. The following vignette illustrates this approach:

Clinical Vignette

Pauline, a 16-year-old Navajo adolescent was hospitalized after emergency surgery for a ruptured appendix. Her surgeon requested a psychiatric consultation after discovering that Pauline had spent two nights in a stiffened posture, claiming her eyes could not move and crying for her mother. Pauline had also experienced an episode of hyperventilation and palpitations and had expressed a fear of death. The day nurse, a male, reported that Pauline had failed to change her menstrual pad.

Pauline admitted to strong feelings of guilt and shame because she had seen a medicine man a week before and had ignored his suggestion to visit a physician. She attributed her nighttime difficulties to her failure to heed this advice. According to Navajo taboo, men cannot be exposed to menstruating females, which explains Pauline's difficulties with the male nurse. A female nurse was subsequently substituted.

Reglan, which had been administered to Pauline postoperatively, explained some of her symptoms, and another medication was administered. Permission was granted to allow a medicine man to conduct a ceremony in the hospital to restore harmony and negate Pauline's failure to heed the first medicine man's directives. At the time of discharge, all symptoms had abated.

THE INFLUENCE OF CULTURE ON CHILDREARING PRACTICES

The clinician needs to frame a family's childrearing practices within the context of the immediate environment and the child's stage of development. It is particularly relevant to compare and contrast a family's attitudes with those of the community and the larger society.

Sex Education

Views about sexual education vary among cultures. Many cultures believe sexual education should be taught at home. Others delegate this task to the children's peers and teachers. Some families use humor and short stories to teach their children about sexuality; others choose more intellectual, informational approaches.

One needs to ask questions about the family's attitude toward open nudity; masturbation; and erotic movies, magazines, and books and to determine any other form of sexual expression to which the child is exposed. Sample questions include the following: What are the sleeping arrangements at home? Who sleeps with whom? Do adolescents or young adults live in the household? Are any other persons besides the parents involved as child caretakers? How old are other caretakers? Are they male or female? Is there any history of sexual abuse in siblings, parents, or neighbors?

Sex Roles and Expectations

A clear (and at times rigid) demarcation of sex-role behavior occurs in certain families and cultures. It is important to learn about gender-role expectations for each cultural group. For example, some traditional Latino families grant men greater and earlier independence than women. They expect men to achieve well outside the home and women to devote themselves to the family and to construct their lives around their husband and children (Senour, 1977).

In some families sex roles may be ambiguous or interchangeable. Gender expectations in the home culture may differ significantly from those in the new culture. A change in gender role as a result of immigration creates considerable conflict in some families. It also is important to understand the particular role of gender and age in the family setting. For example, the firstborn son may be expected to assume tremendous responsibilities, regardless of his age, if the father is absent.

Discipline

The clinician needs to assess the family's attitudes toward authority and their ability to determine an adequate punishment for rule infractions, maintain consistency, and follow through with discipline. The childrearing practices of some cultures are characterized by both indulgent affection and harsh punishment (Szapocznik, Scopetta, & Tillman, 1979). Others support severe maternal restriction of peer-directed aggression (Minturn & Lambert, 1964). Families assign different members to the various roles of judge, police officer, or jailer.

Cultures vary in their styles of discipline, which may be short-term or long-term and may involve physical punishment, embarrassment or shame, withdrawal of love, suspension of social and recreational activities or deprivation of toys and television time. Physical punishment has become a highly charged issue in communities where physical abuse is prevalent and has to be reported. The clinician must be able to assess when the cultural norm of physical punishment becomes abusive and dangerous and must help parents find alternative and effective approaches that are culturally sensitive and effective. (It is common for West Indians and Puerto Ricans, for example, to include physical punishment as part of their disciplinary repertoire.) Furthermore, families may use disciplinary styles consistently or haphazardly: Boys may be punished differently than girls and adolescents differently than elementary school children. Siblings may be punished differently, according to their particular response style or role in the family.

Sleep Patterns

The clinician needs to gather information about sleep patterns and any sleep-related problems and to learn about the family's view of adequate sleeping arrangements and their interpretation and approach to nightmares, night terrors, and fear of the dark. Some Puerto Ricans, for instance, attend nighttime social activities with their children and may be lax about the children's sleeping habits. In some cultures children's dreams and nightmares may be interpreted in accord with religious beliefs. At this point in the history taking it is appropriate to inquire about nocturnal bed-wetting as well as about bedtime routines and rituals.

Development of Social Skills

Generosity, mutual support, and reciprocal assistance are often valued in the Mexican culture (Kunce & Vales, 1984). In Anglo-American cultures children are taught to be assertive, outspoken, and highly individualistic. It is important to determine if the child is gregarious, shy, or withdrawn. Several questions are appropriate in the effort to obtain information about the minority child's social skills:

- Does the child get along with older children, age-mates, and younger children?

- Does the child have a preference for playmates of the same sex or the opposite sex?
- Have there been any changes in the child's social interactions, peer interests, or position in class?
- Is the child a leader or a follower, a conformist or a rebel?
- Is the child selfish or generous? Defiant or easygoing?
- Is the child moody, impatient with others, appropriately responsive, labile or explosive?
- How does the child get along with teachers, parents, and other adults?
- Does the child play the clown in class? The scapegoat?
- Is the child a member of the "in" or the "out" group?

Clinicians also need to ask questions to facilitate their understanding of the family's social style and expectations regarding the child's social skills.

- Is the family isolated or active in their community?
- Does their culture expect frequent and intense social interactions in an extended network, or does it respect privacy and a nuclear family orientation?
- Is the family living in a socially and culturally homogenous community or in a heterogeneous setting?
- Is the community viewed as safe?
- Who are the models or teachers of socialization skills in the family?
- Do the skills taught at home converge with or differ from those required at school, in the park, or on the playing field?

Habits and Fears

One next inquires about a child's habits and fears, their frequency, severity, and intensity. The myriad of possible habits ranges from thumb sucking, nail biting, and grinding teeth to rocking, hair pulling, head banging, fire setting, and animal cruelty. Possible fears include fear of insects, heights, animals, the dark, elevators, subways, and airplanes. Threats of attack by the boogeyman among African-Americans (or among Puerto Ricans, by *El Cuco*) may be used to instill discipline and compliance. Puerto Rican mothers tend to report fear and anxiety symptoms in their children more frequently than do others (Canino, Gould, Prupis, & Shaffer, 1986).

Once again, it is necessary to understand the family's response to certain behaviors in their child. A parent who is afraid of insects or heights, for example, is barely able to help a child with the same symptoms. For children who are irritable, fearful, and anxious about getting hurt when they leave home and/or school, a realistic assessment must be made, particularly in crime-infested inner-city areas. Their fears may be well founded.

Adaptive Behaviors

Finally, to assess the child's strengths and adaptive behaviors, the clinician inquires about malleability; frustration tolerance; and his or her ability to delay gratification, adjust to new situations, and learn through experience. One asks the family to recall vignettes about times of stress in the child's life (e.g., the birth of a sibling, a move to a new neighborhood or school, parental separation or divorce, the loss of important caretakers). Answers to questions regarding the intensity, length, and type of response give the clinician a good sense of the child's adaptive or coping style.

The coping styles of the children of the many families who experience stress related to discrimination or poor housing and other environmental conditions may be taxed. If additional and chronic stressors persist, such as exposure to violence, these children may develop coping styles that frequently are misunderstood by clinicians to be maladaptive or indicative of psychopathology. For example, a high degree of isolation of affect, denial, displacement, and hyperalertness may be necessary for these children to survive their environment. They often present as distractable and unmotivated, and school performance frequently becomes their lowest priority.

Further, children in inner-city areas frequently are exposed to adult models who experience high levels of stress and are irritable, explosive, impulsive, and unable to implement good parenting. Frequently, these adults become cautious and suspicious, and expect the worst in their efforts to cope with their dangerous and unreliable neighborhoods. Children in the process of learning coping skills and seeking role models will develop similar strategies in order to survive.

FAMILY HISTORY

There is no ideal approach to family-history taking and diagnosis. However, it is pertinent to identify family roles, alliances, and dynamics. Malone (1979) describes the importance of family interviews, which enable clinicians to observe the child's behavior as it is influenced by and influences the family system; the capacity and motivation of family members to change the problem behavior; the family's nonverbal communication patterns; their patterns in the expression of affect, the assignment of roles, problem solving, and conflict resolution; and any structural imbalances in the family (e.g., splitting, alliances, collusions, and scapegoating).

Additionally, it is important for the clinician to recognize the importance of the family in forging and communicating social and cultural attitudes, beliefs, and biases in their children. The clinician needs to evaluate the relative sense of security on the part of parents and caretakers regarding ethnic and racial identity, financial status, and religious and traditional beliefs. The family's level of acculturation and adaptation to their community and the degree of involvement in their immediate neighborhood can provide information about the extent of their support network.

The Role of the Extended Family

Typically, the extended family functions as a source of support for many minority groups, as the matrix of collective sharing and interdependent loyalty, and as the means by which cultural and religious values are communicated. A review of the role of the extended family for a sampling of minority groups illustrates its importance.

For traditional Mexican-American families, the family structure is characterized by formalized kinship relations to the godparent system and by loyalty to the family. Often, the extended family takes priority over other social institutions (Palacios & Franco, 1986).

American Indian families usually include parents, children, aunts, uncles, cousins, and grandparents in an active kinship system (Red Horse, 1983). This lateral extension to include multiple households may be further broadened to incorporate unrelated individuals. For example, a person significant to the family may be inducted into the family system by formal rituals and would then assume a family role within that system.

The extended family also is of considerable significance to African-American families. Many children who live in single-parent families belong to some variation of an extended family (Norton, 1983). The clinician should not assume that an African-American child referred for services comes from a fatherless home. Ideally, clinicians who are aware of the negative stereotypes of the African-American family should conduct their evaluation of a particular family with a commitment to seek information about its actual structure and functioning. Such an approach should enable the clinician to determine a given child's self-concept, the presence of positive role models in the family or community, and family strengths.

The expanding definition of what constitutes a family requires the clinician to ask not only about caregivers living within the household but about those outside it as well. Important extended family members may include grandparents, godparents, friends, teachers, and ministers. Additionally, a parent's significant other may not initially be considered a formal family member yet may prove to be an excellent substitute for the absent parental figure.

A Family's Values

It is particularly important for clinicians who work in health delivery systems in large heterogenous communities to be aware of the values of their socioeconomically and culturally diverse client populations. Client populations may differ from professionals in their perceptions of mental health and disease and may consider symptomatic what the clinician may not and vice versa. Thus, it is important to specify a family's particular style and cultural allegiance, concepts of socially desirable and undesirable behavior, and perception of psychological distress in their children. Clinicians perform better when they assume a learning position and acknowledge their need to know more about the family's culture.

The family values component may be easily incorporated into family history taking; most families are willing to share information about their style of living and do so more comfortably than they divulge personal information or details about areas of conflict. One facilitates the process by asking about religious practices and major holidays, dietary habits, community activities, and recreational and musical interests. The clinician may use a focus on family history as an opportunity to repeat, if necessary, previous inquiries pertaining to the particulars of childrearing and parents' attitudes toward teaching, disciplining, and playing with their children (Canino, 1985). In determining a family's values, awareness of cultural differences again proves helpful. For example, familiarity with the impact of the Baptist church on southern African-Americans, of Pentecostalism and Catholicism on Latinos, and of Confucianism and Buddhism on Asians and with the value of nature to American Indians can facilitate information gathering and interpretation. Questions about a particular group's sexual role expectations, attitudes toward authority figures, and degree of respect toward the elderly are important to ask, as these values also may vary among cultures.

A family's culture may also influence its perception of time and the physical and social environment. For example, American Indians and Latinos share a present time orientation. Asian-Americans and American Indians see themselves as reaching a certain harmony with their environment, whereas many Latinos consider themselves to be subject to it. Latinos, American Indians, and Asian-Americans do not openly express disagreement and aggressiveness. Traditional Mexicans and Asians appear formal, polite, and reserved in initial encounters, but other groups, such as Caribbean Latinos, tend to be more open and expressive (Jones & Korchin, 1982).

Other Family History Data

Family history data to obtain include the following: parents' age, place of birth, educational status, type of employment, religion; number, age, and educational status of the patients' siblings; work habits and level of motivation of parents and siblings; parental responses to the different developmental stages of their children; and parents' ability to be intimate and offer empathy. The family's history and values provides a contextual basis important to the clinician and to the diagnostic process. It is critical that the clinician also inquire about any previous psychiatric history or hospitalization in the family and its impact on the child. The influence of acute or chronic stressors, incarcerations, and legal problems—and of catastrophic events like war and torture—must be assessed.

The examiner needs to be aware of the possibility of changes in family dynamics in response to the move to a different cultural setting. Typically, relocation means a shift in the roles of the parents. Children may be exposed to long separations from their parents. In some cases, the parents migrate first, leaving the children in their country of origin. In others, owing to periods of stress, children are sent for various periods of time to live with relatives in another country or state. Women may find employment more quickly than their spouses, although their jobs may be low level and low paying. The high rates of unemployment or underemployment of the men in the new community may trigger shifts in intrafamilial relationships: The mother gains a new role as breadwinner, and the father must adjust to household chores. When such shifts within the family structure are coupled with bewildering demands and expectations from the broader environment, children may be overwhelmed (Canino & Canino, 1980).

Age and Language Fluency

The age of family members at the time of immigration is an important piece of information to collect from foreign-born patients and their families. In some instances parents may have immigrated first in an effort to obtain stability before the children arrive. The age at immigration may contribute to an individual's difficulties in learning the culture and language of the new society.

Asian children who experience language problems in grammar school usually learn English in about a year unless they live within a cultural enclave (e.g., Chinatown). Asian adolescents take longer to learn English, and some do not shed the accent of their culture of origin. As with Latino immigrants, linguistic problems in Asian immigrants tend to occur in the area of fluency and grammatical accuracy rather than with vocabulary acquisition.

The clinician also should identify any discrepancy between grade placement of foreign-born children and adolescents and their chronological age and should ask about their reactions to the grade placement.

Religion and Belief Systems

Religion and belief systems prove potentially important sources of information. Clinicians should ask about the religion and belief systems of the patient and parents and about the family's religion of origin to determine how culturally based beliefs may relate to a child's symptoms (and subsequent diagnosis and treatment interventions).

For the purposes of this discussion we will focus on belief systems and will not address the well-documented, established religions that are more familiar to clinicians. Clinicians who work with children from culturally diverse backgrounds should obtain information about the child's and family's exposure to the many belief systems that may be prevalent in their culture. For example, a Puerto Rican or Dominican family may trust in *espiritismo*—a belief that the spirits of the dead communicate in various ways to human beings, usually through a medium—and may turn to an *espiritista* (practitioner) even while involved in the traditional psychotherapy process (Vega et al., 1983; Gomez, 1982). (In a study by Bird and Canino [1981] a significant number of Puerto Rican children attending a public psychiatric clinic were reported to have been taken by their parents to *espiritistas*.) Clinicians who treat Cubans and Brazilians should know about *santería*, a belief system based on the syncretism of African religions and Catholicism, in which Catholic saints represent African deities. Those who treat Mexicans and Latin Americans should understand *curanderismo*, a system of folk healing that utilizes medicinal herbs and potions. Shamanism (observed in American Indians, Koreans, and others) is practiced under the assumption that inanimate as well as animate objects are endowed with spirits; human misfortune is thus caused by incorrect relationships with these spirits. "Root work," seen frequently in African-American communities in the South, consists of the use of plant roots to prepare potions for both good and evil purposes.

Although American Indian tribes are characterized by the importance and richness of their religious beliefs, these beliefs vary from one tribe to another (Beauvais, Oetting, & Edwards, 1985). Some American Indian tribes believe that reciprocal influences exist between the human and the spirit worlds and that reincarnation is a journey between these two worlds (LaFromboise & BigFoot, 1988). Medicine men and women hold honored positions in many tribes. Usually, these are mature persons who have demonstrated social responsibility and economic success (Berlin, 1987; Topper, 1987). Only such highly qualified members of the tribe are allowed to learn the complex healing ceremonies and traditions.

If a family has sought help from the ethnic group's spiritual healer, it is preferable that the mental health professional collaborate with that person. In the case of a Mexican-American family, for example, collaboration would be with the traditional healer, the *curanderos* (Vega et al., 1983). The *santeros* is the healer sought by some Cuban-Americans. With Asian-American families, it is important for the clinician to assess exposure of the Japanese to Shinto and of the Koreans to shamanism. For the Chinese patient, an inquiry into the practice of *qi-gong* is indicated; this practice, based on the importance of *qi* ("vital energy"), recommends a series of exercises to improve physical and mental health (Lin, Kleinman, & Lin, 1981).

It is the custom after a brief period of questioning for practitioners of traditional healing methods to make a diagnosis and give a prescription. Patients accustomed to this practice frequently fail to understand the purpose of lengthy evaluations and the lack of treatment in the initial diagnostic process. Consequently, they may be disappointed and may even drop out of treatment.

Protective Family Factors

Many studies describe the value of protective family factors. All cultures have wihin them norms that enhance growth and development in their young and that serve as additional sources of support and strength when families are exposed to adversity. Clinicians must assess these factors carefully in order to utilize them wisely during their interventions.

Resilient adolescents come from homes in which rules are consistently enforced (Werner & Smith, 1982); good supervision and well-balanced discipline are available (Rutter, 1979); a good relationship with and between the parents exists (Werner & Smith, 1982); there is a high level of warmth and an absence of severe criticism (Rutter, 1979); and an adequate identification figure is present in the household (Garmezy, 1981). Parents of more resilient children clearly define their own role in the family as well as the roles of the children, give their children more opportunities for self-direction (Garmezy, 1981), and are highly perceptive (Garmezy, Mastern, & Tellegen, 1984) and less possessive and anxious (Anthony, 1974).

Other studies indicate that family interactional variables such as maternal warmth (Kauffman, Grunebaum, Cohler, & Garner, 1979) and healthy and benign parental attributions toward the child (Yu, 1979) appear associated with greater competence in high-risk children. These family factors correlate with other variables: For example, the intelligence quotients of children and their parents often correlate (Bonchard & McGue, 1981), as does internal locus of control with a warm and protective family environment (Garmezy, 1983). African-American children within the lower socioeconomic group are more likely to achieve when they live in households that are cleaner, have less clutter, and are less crowded (Garmezy, 1983). Parents influence the child's social milieu and support networks (Hauser, Vieyra, & Jacobson, 1989), and high self-esteem in children is linked both to emotional stability in mothers and to good parental interaction (Coopersmith, 1967).

Cauce, Felner, and Primavera (1982) found in their study of the differential impact of specific support systems in highly stressed adolescents that family supports are related to high scholastic self-concept but that peer supports are negatively related to school grades and school attendance. The study findings thus suggest that under some circumstances social supports may be related to negative outcomes and that peers may hold pejorative attitudes toward scholarly pursuits.

SCHOOL HISTORY

Children spend a large portion of their time at school. Once the clinician gains the trust of the child and the parents, he or she should request permission to call the child's teachers and guidance counselor. Both the child and the parents should be reassured that any inquiries will be part of the evaluation and that all information obtained will be kept confidential. The clinician also should reassure the parents that no information about the child will be released to the school unless they grant permission and until a sense of the school's potential reaction to the information has been assessed. The clinician is encouraged to arrange a school visit upon approval of all parties involved, as such visits may prove enlightening.

A school history taken from a knowledgeable caretaker should include a list of the different schools the child has attended and specify both the reasons for and adjustments to each school change. Many children in the inner cities may be kept out of school to assist their parents in the home or to serve as negotiators or translators between their parents and government agencies. Others miss school owing to extended visits to their country of origin.

The clinician should assess the degree of cultural sensitivity of the school by determining if it has a multicultural curriculum and, if so, how effectively it is implemented. A review of old school report cards or tests may prove helpful in addition to the child's and parents' recollections about individual teachers, classmates, and special class events. Caregivers should be advised that a perusal of class pictures with the child may serve to trigger significant memories of school experiences. Clinicians need to address particular achievements, grade failures, and special class placements; the use of boarding schools, resource rooms, or disciplinary actions; and the presence of school phobias or truancy; they also need to determine the extent to which a child's problems are related to language difficulties or cultural differences. Parental attitudes about education, teachers, and the school provide significant information.

The child should be asked which teachers, subjects, and classmates he or she likes most and least. This information should then be compared to grades and teacher reports. If the child has attended several schools, the clinician should ask about the school liked best (and least) and why. The child's answers to questions about his or her participation in and reaction to extracurricular activities, bilingual programs, and enrichment programs should be noted. The child also might be questioned about any experiences that singled him or her out for ridicule or praise. The following vignette illustrates the contribution of a child's cultural background to such an experience.

Clinical Vignette

Ramon, a 10-year-old Latino boy, was referred by the school guidance counselor for his cross-dressing, a habit that was ridiculed by his classmates. When asked about wearing a girl's white winter coat, Ramon had refused to answer. Teachers expressed concern about an underlying sexual identity problem. Ramon's mother had been uncooperative in her efforts to change Ramon's behavior, and her secrecy had intensified the school's concerns.

Ramon and his mother were referred to a bilingual, bicultural outpatient service. The "problem" was immediately identified by the evaluating clinician. Ramon, a very bright youngster, was in the process of becoming a priest in *santería*. This required him to wear white clothes for a period of time. No boy's white winter coat had been available to the family. Due to previous experiences in which their beliefs had been criticized and thought of as ritualistic, magical, and primitive, the family had decided to conceal their beliefs from school personnel, although it was well known in their own community.

Ramon was well adjusted and gave no evidence of true cross-dressing. With the permission of the family and Ramon a school consultation/education session was implemented, and the problem was resolved.

If the child attends an inner-city public school plagued by overpopulation, violence, and rapid teacher turnover, this should be recorded in the history as a potential stressor. In multiethnic areas, questions about the ethnic composition of the student body as compared to the teaching and administrative staff can be revealing. In the following vignette the experiences of a 9-year-old Latino boy illustrate the difficulties likely to arise when a child's ethnicity makes him highly visible in the school setting:

Clinical Vignette

Mario, a 9-year-old new arrival from Central America, had moved with his family to a homogeneous neighborhood in which they were the first Spanish-speaking family. Consequently, Mario was one of the few Latino children in his classroom. He soon developed symptoms of school phobia and was referred to an outpatient mental health clinic.

A clinician sensitive to cultural issues chose to work very closely with the school, a decision that facilitated access for Mario to a bicultural, bilingual program. The clinician also realized that Mario was a target of racial slurs and physical attacks by other children on his way to and from school. The school responded to the clinician's request to address these issues at the next parent–teacher conference. With the ongoing support of a dedicated principal, Mario's symptoms abated, and he was able to adjust to his new environment.

Finally, information from teachers about the child's cognitive skills and social behavior is crucial. Questions should address the child's cognitive strengths and weaknesses in particular subjects and in terms of his or her ability to focus, frustration tolerance, motivation, and organizational abilities. A child's response to structure, attitudes toward authority, and ability to follow rules can be revealing. In determining the nature of the child's pattern of social interaction, clinicians must focus on class composition and cohesion as well as on whether the child stands out for either positive or negative behaviors. Questions such as the following can guide the clinician's inquiry:

- Is the child a leader or a follower?
- Is the child studious or a clown, quiet or rowdy?
- Who are the child's friends?
- Is the child respected or a scapegoat of other children?
- Is the child sensitive, immature, moody, cruel, bossy, or given to bullying other children?
- Is the child overactive? If so, when?
- What are the child's behaviors during lunchtime, recess, and gym?
- Is the child the teacher's pet or the teacher's thorn?

The next group of questions should be asked if the youth has dropped out of school; it is important to determine the reasons for this action.

- Was there a particular motivating or precipitating factor?
- What experiences preceded dropping out of school (e.g., poor grades, an episode of dismissal, peer pressure)?
- Is the action regretted?
- What does the youth do now during school hours? Are there any recreational facilities in the area?

THE MENTAL STATUS EXAMINATION

The Setting and Process

Minority children and their families, especially recent immigrants or new arrivals to the community, may perceive a mental health facility or hospital as alien territory. Some may view the facility as another bureaucratic institution staffed by persons who are intimidating, if not openly hostile. Others may equate clinics and hospitals with long waiting periods to see doctors and other health professionals who will not or cannot answer questions or who always seem to be in a hurry and often are patronizing.

Such perceptions and fears can have an impact on the way the child or the parents respond to the mental status examination. Many parents may be unfamiliar with the nature of a psychiatric examination or treatment and may be uncomfortable with the process. Thus, at first contact the clinician must explain the process.

In some cultures disturbed behavior may be viewed as related to a physical disorder or willfulness; thus, talking about the behavior is not expected to cure it. The examiner should recognize the possibility that the parents may hold this point of view and should suggest to them causes of disordered behavior other than physical illness or willfulness (e.g., stress, separation from one's homeland). Furthermore, particularly among Asian cultures, it is unacceptable to discuss family and personal matters with someone outside the family. Therefore, the examiner needs to assure the family of confidentiality.

Some experts suggest home visits as a means of alleviating discomfort about the evaluation process. The family at home may be more comfortable, but if the clinician's attitude is that of a distant professional this may dilute any feelings of ease in the family experiences. If family visits are not possible, the physical aspects of the clinic setting should reflect the multicultural characteristics of its patient population.

The space in which the child is to be examined should be sufficient to allow for some freedom of movement but not so large as to encourage the child to distance himself or herself from the examiner. Since most young children are more likely to communicate nonverbally through play, it is essential that play materials be available for them. Toys that facilitate creativity and promote verbal communication are preferable to more structured toys. For example, wooden blocks of various dimensions make a better examining tool than a dollhouse does—especially when working with inner-city children who are more familiar with apartment buildings than with houses.

Since the child therapist cannot keep up with the myriad of new toys and games that appear on the market and is probably unfamiliar with toys and games used by children in different cultures and at different socioeconomic levels, several basic concepts may provide some guidance: Puppets and small dolls that can be used to represent members of a family are diagnostically useful and should be racially heterogenous. For those cultures in which extended families are significant, enough dolls to represent grandparent, aunt, uncle, and godparent figures in addition to parents should be available; dolls should represent adults and children of both sexes. The child should be encouraged to name the figures and to describe each in terms of likes and dislikes.

For young children, toys such as cars and trucks, animals, soldiers, and community figures (e.g., police officer and fire fighter) help to elicit clinically rich information. Figures or toy materials that can be made to represent cops and robbers, police cars, fire trucks, and ambulances should be available. Superheroes and heroic figures belong in the toy cabinet. A detective kit that includes a plastic gun, badge, identification card, and handcuffs is always popular. Play money and plastic jewelry can elicit considerable information about a family's financial difficulties and can become the objects of robberies or the means of expressing extreme deprivation.

Recognizing that some youngsters may belong to a homeless family, examiners can elicit such information by asking children to draw a picture of the building in which they live and also one of their room or by offering to assist them in making a diagram of the facility and locating important pieces of furniture in it. A set of blocks and dollhouse furniture will enable very young children to construct and furnish a building similar to the one in which they live. As children perform these tasks, clinicians can ask them to describe their neighborhood and to identify the features that make it special and those that make it unattractive. A request for neighborhood stories or events often further clarifies the circumstances under which a child lives.

Two play syringes should be available for those children reared in neighborhoods or families in which drugs may be present; one should be labeled MEDICINE, for playing doctor, the other POISON. The small bottles of whiskey and wine available on airplane flights can be useful tools in eliciting significant information when alcoholism is a family problem. The clinician can provide play food or Play-Doh to make food items when assessing a child who has eating difficulties or who is seriously deprived. This will facilitate information gathering and future interventions.

One may ask children who have emigrated from other countries or who belong to a minority culture to bring pictures, magazines, or newspapers from their country or culture of origin. One can ask these children what similarities and differences they perceive between themselves and their peers at school, thus obtaining a better sense of the stress they are experiencing in the process of acculturation. The clinician also may get a sense of a child's cultural background by asking about holidays and how the family celebrates:

- What foods are served for special occasions in your home?
- How are birthdays celebrated in your family?
- Who are your favorite heroes and heroines?
- What type of music do you like best and least?
- What was the best party you ever attended?
- What do you like to do at parties?
- What turns you off at parties?

The Child's Separation from the Parent

Multiple factors impinge on the manner in which a child separates from the individual who has brought him or her to the examination. In this volume the focus is on ethnic factors.

Young children—even those who have been described as outgoing—who have recently immigrated to this country may be startled by the appearance of an examiner from another culture and may be reluctant to leave their mother. And despite explanations to the contrary, some youngsters may persist in perceiving the clinical setting as the site of an examination that will involve various kinds of physical probing and thus may experience difficulty separating. Children also are sensitive to the mispronounciation of their names and may hesitate when asked to accompany a clinician who fails in this way to reassure them.

Physical Appearance and Behavior during the Interview

A number of clinical observations are possible immediately: Upon encountering the child in the waiting room, the clinician should note any resemblance or dissimilarity to the parents. This may be of particular significance in a biracial or bicultural family. Other physical characteristics of the child—stature, weight, nutritional state, gait, mannerisms—can be observed in the waiting area and en route to the clinician's office. Initial observations may suggest the need for closer scrutiny during the course of the examination. For example, the slight build of a 12-year-old African-American boy appeared in marked contrast to his tall and muscularly built father; however, this difference paled in significance when bruises were observed on the child's forearms.

Shades of color and the shape of facial features may be of particular significance for some minority group children, especially if these factors are important to their families and others in their immediate environment. African-American children of fair complexion may be teased by their peers who have darker skin. Other African-American families may view dark skin, a broad nose, or thick lips as a negative feature. Fair coloring and Caucasian features in Amerasian youngsters provoke jeering from others in their country of birth; this stigma is not necessarily erased when they immigrate to the United States. Exploration of self-image is an important aspect of the examination of all children. Inquiries into their feelings about the way they look and how they would like to look are likely to yield significant information.

The clinician should be alert to signs of malnutrition. In addition to appearing underweight and stunted in growth, malnourished children may display lethargy, limited attention span, and eyes that lack luster.

Dress can also be assessed immediately upon meeting the child. Although cleanliness and neatness are important to take note of, the designer jeans and expensive footwear a youngster wears may be of greater significance in understanding family dynamics, especially if the family is beset by financial problems. Cultural factors may play a role in determining how a child is dressed for the examination: For some minority group families an appointment with a doctor means dressing in one's best clothes, and if the proper clothes are not available, a parent may even cancel the appointment.

Throughout the interview, the examiner should be alert to signs of anxiety (e.g., nail or lip biting, tics, hyperalertness, or impaired attention span). Brief gaps in attention suggest the possibility of anxiety, epilepsy, or hallucinatory experiences and warrant further exploration. Any gross motor activity should be recorded, as should observations about a child's considerable fidgeting, pacing, hypoactivity, or rigidity. Information previously obtained during history taking about sleep patterns, dietary habits, and highly stimulating experiences may help clarify some of these observations.

Affect

In assessing the child's affect the examiner should be alert to various cultural influences. One may observe, for example, the restrained, non-verbal approach of Chinese-Americans who have not acculturated fully, the quietly observant manner of an American Indian child, the expressive and open quality of the Caribbean child, and the defiant stance of an inner-city adolescent.

The clinician needs to know how the bilingual child best expresses certain feelings. The expression of affect may be more intense in settings where it is permitted. If cultural patterns inhibit the expression of anger or demand a compliant and respectful stance toward adults, the clinician can utilize such play materials as puppets and play weapons to elicit spontaneous feelings in the child. A child may be more comfortable expressing certain feelings when peers are present and often needs explicit permission from the family to express feelings in public. During the interview the examiner should observe the child's ability to express verbally or nonverbally a full range of feelings and should determine if these feelings are appropiate to the topic under discussion and well modulated. An inhibited or shy child can be asked to pictorially represent different feelings and to then tell the examiner some stories about when these feelings arise. This segment of the evaluation should include questions about the youngster's experiences of feeling sad or happy, mood swings, thoughts about hurting others, wishes to be dead, and feelings about the referral.

Speech and Communication Style

Examiners must be alert to the impact of culture, as well as of physical and psychological difficulties, on speech and style of communication. The following questions may help direct their observations: Does the child make considerable use of body language (shaking the head or nodding to imply negative or affirmative responses and shrugging the shoulders to imply that he or she does not know or is uncertain) instead of verbal communication? Is code switching present (e.g., when an African-American child slips into use of non-Standard English after using Standard English during most of the interview)? Does a high rate of repetition of misconstructed sentences represent schizophrenic language, or is it simply the use of English by a minority group child who has not completely internalized Standard English? Does the child stammer or stutter? Are there signs of delayed speech or of defective speech associated with deafness? Is there a misuse of pronouns? Is the child's speech echolalic?

The Use of "Feeling Scales"

Once the examiner has some sense of the child's strengths and primary mode of communication, he or she creates a "feeling scale." For the child who likes music, the feeling scale is a set of notes from soft to loud; for the child who is primarily visual, it is a color scale of pale to intense colors. With these scales children can respond to questions about how happy, angry, sad, or worried they are. Or the examiner can ask children to express their feelings with a special walk or facial expression. Once the child responds, it is helpful to ask for a story about when the child was happiest, saddest, angriest, and most worried and then to inquire about the response of family, friends, and teachers at those times.

The Thinking Process

According to Lev Vygotsky (1978), cognitive development is specific to the sociocultural milieu in which it occurs. Vygotsky's premise is that all cognition is mediated by the technical and psychological tools of the culture; thus, it contrasts markedly with the Piagetian emphasis on biologically based autoregulative processes.

In evaluating the thought processes of culturally diverse children, the examiner should be alert to whether blocking and the retardation of thinking and speaking occur. The examiner should consider the possibility that a minority child may be responding slowly because he or she is thinking in his or her own language first and then translating that response into English. The use of neologisms may have different meanings at different ages: Their use by young children may relate to their interest in playing with words and may have no pathological significance, as may be the case with adolescents. Examiners must evaluate a child's accuracy in comprehending a question when they assess the irrelevancy of the answer and must consider the possibility that a language barrier is the source of the misunderstanding.

The presence or absence of paranoid ideation and disordered perception must be explored. Here, too, certain cultural factors must be considered in determining the normalcy or pathology of the response. For example, "hearing the Lord speak" may be a culture-specific impression and therefore nonpathological for some religious groups. An inner-city African-American adolescent's statement "All whites are out to get us" may actually represent the thinking of the community in which he lives rather than qualify as a sign of paranoia. The examiner must be careful in making the distinction between a youngster's hyperalertness or cautiousness and paranoid thinking.

Evaluation of Central Nervous System Functioning

An evaluation of central nervous system functioning is especially important in an examination of children who may have a history of exposure to drugs in utero, premature birth, poor nutrition, lead intoxication, and head traumas. Such evaluation is appropriate for many inner-city children. Although referral for a complete neurological examination may be indicated, a psychiatrist should examine for the presence or absence of soft neurological signs and should assess the child's gross and fine motor coordination. The clinician examines perceptual motor capacities by asking the child to copy specific geometric designs and by observing the way the child handles the pencil in performing this task and in taking dictation of simple sentences.

INTRAPSYCHIC AND INTERPERSONAL FACTORS

The Child's Self-Image

Examiners must determine what view the children they assess hold of themselves. Questions may be asked to assess whether the children perceive themselves as good or bad and to determine their impression of how others see them. To obtain additional information clinicians may ask children to identify their strengths and vulnerabilities. Examiners need to be aware that many minority group children differentiate between the way the dominant society and those in their immediate community view them (Rosenberg & Simmons, 1971).

Examiners might ask youngsters to identify what they like most and least about themselves and what changes, if any, they would make in themselves if they could. Clinicians should keep in mind that children do not necessarily perceive themselves to be a member of the group specified on their birth certificate or of a group identified by others. This becomes particularly important when working with bicultural and/or biracial children.

Clinical Vignette

Mary Beth, a 9-year-old Mexican-Indian girl, was brought for an evaluation by her adoptive Anglo-American father. During the first interview the clinician asked her what she liked about herself. She mentioned her shiny, long black hair and her long eyelashes. She did not like her brown skin color. On pursuing this further, the clinician learned that this dislike reflected her peers' assessment of her. Mary Beth was the only Latino child in a Protestant school with an all-Anglo-American student body.

The Child's Relationships with Family Members and Others

Information about important others can be obtained by questioning children about the structure of their family and asking them to identify those members with whom they get along best and least. After drawing a family diagram clinicians may ask children to indicate the family members they love, fear, and dislike the most, as well as the one they worry about the most and the one they fight with most frequently. Clinicians also may pose similar questions about peers and others, such as teachers, with whom the children have considerable contact.

Insight, Judgment, and Coping Skills

Questions addressing children's understanding of the reasons for the referral and of the basis of their problem and how it might be corrected will provide some information about their insight and judgment. To elicit information about the child's coping skills, the examiner might select one of the following hypothetical scenarios as appropriate for exploration:

Scenario 1: You are the only [Puerto Rican or African-American or Asian-American or American Indian] in your class. Your classmates tease you and call you dumb. How does this make you feel? What do you do?

Scenario 2: A 15-year-old girl and her family (parents and five siblings) emigrated from Southeast Asia a year ago. The girl now wants to be identified as a typical American high school girl, but her parents object to her dating and her disregard for the customs of their homeland. If you were this girl, what would you do?

Scenario 3: Eight-year old Ruben, the oldest of five children, has grown afraid to go to school because of the reported violence in his neighborhood. There are no adults available to accompany him to school. What would you do if you were Ruben?

Fantasy Material

To elicit fantasy material, clinicians can have children draw pictures—of a person, their family, their neighborhood, and their classroom—and tell stories about them.

Once children have drawn a picture of a person and told a story, clinicians can ask them to color the picture and add items of clothing they wish the person to wear. At this time children can be asked if the person looks like other people in their family, and their response to this question can be pursued further. Asking children how they would change the person physically if they could often elicits feelings about racial or ethnic differences within the family.

Once children have drawn a picture of their family and have discussed with the clinician their stories about the family, they can be asked to draw other people they feel should be part of the family—as well as those that should be excluded—and to color all the family members with crayons and to tell a little about each one as they do so, including both positive and negative details. Suggestions can be made to children that they draw love and anger and worry lines on each member of the family, as appropriate. At this time, clinicians might ask what language is spoken at home and whether family members are from "the old country."

Clinicians can ask children to draw a map of their immediate neighborhood and to point out and tell about play areas and neighbors' houses as well as dangerous places. These can be marked with special symbols or colors.

It might also be helpful for clinicians to ask children to draw a diagram of their classroom and discuss the contents of the room. Children can be asked if the desks are comfortable, if the room temperature is just right, and if the classroom is quiet or noisy. Then they can be encouraged to list their favorite friends; the bullies, jocks, leaders, and bookworms in their class; and the ugliest and most attractive classmates; special stars can be provided to the children to enable them to identify favorite teachers, classes, and subjects. Finally, children can be asked to specify the ethnic identity of their classmates and to tell about any incidents of discrimination or show of preference on the basis of age, sex, race, or social class.

Issues of Identification

The examiner should ask the child to identify persons both within and outside the family circle whom he or she wants to be like and to explain why. The focus in follow-up questions should be on gathering more information about these individuals. Should the child and the nonfamily members so identified be of different ethnic groups, the examiner might ask if the child has a heroine or hero who is of his or her own group. Ideally, the examiner should know the names of a few persons of the same or similar background as the child who are well known to the general public and should ask the child what he or she knows and thinks about these persons. Clinicians also should ask children if they ever wish for things they do not have and should encourage them to elaborate on these wishes.

CONCLUDING COMMENTS

A comprehensive history, one that is sensitive to the cultural background and ethnic identity of the minority child and family, is critical to the diagnostic process. Once this information is collected, the clinician is prepared to proceed with the diagnostic process and to make use of assessment tests and the multiaxial evaluation system of the *Diagnostic and Statistical Manual of Mental Disorders* (American Psychiatric Association, 1987, 1993), as indicated and appropriate.

CHAPTER 3

Assessment Strategies

✦

Assessment strategies are available to assist the clinician with the diagnostic process. However, the clinician who works with African-American, Asian-American, Latino, and American Indian children and their families needs to choose assessment approaches wisely; to consider, both in choice of strategy and in interpretation, the cultural background of the child; and to guard against any bias in the assessment or in his or her interpretation of the results. A discussion of the clinical relevance of assessment techniques precedes a review of the literature, which identifies and elaborates on both current progress and problems.

CLINICAL RELEVANCE OF ASSESSMENT STRATEGIES

Clinicians need to understand and to be familiar with the indications for intelligence and psychological testing. Competent testing can facilitate the diagnosis, identify problems difficult to assess during a regular evaluation, and provide information on the child's cognitive style, neurological status, and psychological well-being. Administered by experienced professionals, psychological tests facilitate the assessment of symptoms and the extent to which they are entrenched or reactive. A profile of the child's strengths and vulnerabilities helps the clinician plan his or her treatment interventions.

Clinicians also must understand tests results that may be found in case charts and may be used to facilitate a child's diagnosis and placement. Further, they must keep pace with the literature that identifies and critiques instruments utilized to assess and diagnose minority children.

There are few reports in the literature that address the cultural validity and reliability of assessment instruments and that identify the limitations of test results in certain contexts, a dearth of culturally sensitive and competent testing professionals, and an overwhelmed system of care with minimal testing resources. Some typical responses by overworked or stressed evaluators to a clinician's request for testing illustrate this:

> "This is all we have to test them with; take it or leave it. These children live in the real world and are expected to compete in it; they must be measured by the same norms. No wonder the results are poor; the parents never stimulate them at home. All they do is watch television."

> "Our load of cases is too large. We have no time to do the full battery."

> "Sure he scored poorly in verbal abilities. What did you expect from a bilingual home?"

Unfortunately, as testing professionals become more and more overwhelmed by paperwork and by the stress of testing children with a mutiplicity of serious problems, they have less and less time to explain test limitations and results to parents and teachers. This further complicates the process and precipitates an undue amount of distress and miscommunication. The consequences are numerous and serious: For example, a child may be kept unnecessarily in a special education class, missing the opportunity to be mainstreamed, or a child may exhibit a severe conduct disorder because his or her learning disability and attention deficit disorder was not diagnosed in a timely way.

When discussing test results with a family, the clinician should always introduce the topic by identifying and describing the different types of intelligence, namely, social, scientific and mathematical, creative, linguistic, mechanical, and motor intelligence. The clinician should first focus on the child's strengths; when identifying a child's vulnerabilities, he or she should provide suggestions for intervention. The clinician also must respect and address the family's expectations and explore thoroughly the meaning of the test results to the family and any possible misinterpetations. Test samples should be available to demonstrate to parents how a particular skill was measured, if they request such information. Such demonstrations often help parents feel more comfortable in asking questions.

ASSESSING INTELLECTUAL FUNCTIONING IN MINORITY CHILDREN

Cultural Bias

Efforts to counter cultural bias in assessments of intellectual functioning (e.g., Raven's Progressive Matrices and the Cattell Culture-Fair Intelligence Test; Williams, 1987) have failed to achieve their goal of culture-free or "culture-fair" tests. Further, the absence of adequate norms and the use of nonstandardized translations make it difficult to obtain reliable information on which to interpret results.

Taylor and Payne (1983) identified four cultural biases evident in instruments developed for intellectual assessment, biases based on situation, direction, value, and language. A mismatch between examiner and child takes place in a situational bias: The examiner may assume a child is motivated to guess in order to achieve a high score; in actuality, the child may be motivated to avoid responding incorrectly and will thus be inhibited about answering questions when feeling uncertain.

A direction bias involves the way questions and instructions are phrased. Some instructions are syntactically complex and seem to discriminate against minority groups. A test that asks for an imaginary story may discriminate against Mexican-American children, who find this task culturally incongruent and consequently remain silent or respond in short sentences.

A value bias occurs when a question centers on what a child would do in certain situations. The "correct" answer reflects the response that is acceptable in the dominant culture.

Linguistic bias is apparent when an examination assesses the child's knowledge of a particular language or dialect rather than his or her general linguistic development. A child whose first language is not English but who is judged by standard norms is discriminated against. Moreover, some children achieve a flexible linguistic repertoire, which is missed by examiners who alter an assessment battery to take into account a presumed dialect that may not be the pattern used by the child.

Tests Designed to Counter Bias in Intellectual Assessment

The Culture-Fair Intelligence Test, a paper-and-pencil test developed by R. B. Cattell (1959), is available on three levels: Scale 1 for ages 4 to 8 and mentally retarded adults; Scale 2 for ages 8 to 13 and adults of average intelligence; and Scale 3 for ages 10 to 16 and adults of superior intelligence. This test attempts to be fair regardless of the cultural background of the subject by avoiding the use of language. The Cattell tests have been administered in several European countries, in North America, and in certain African and Asian cultures. Norms tend to remain unchanged in cultures moderately similar to the one in which the tests were developed, but performance falls considerably below the original norms in other cultures (Anastasi, 1988).

Several tests do not require literacy, such as the Porteus Maze, Draw-a-Person Test, Bender–Gestalt Test, Rorschach Test, Thematic Apperception Test (TAT), and parts of the Wechsler Adult Intelligence Scales (WAIS) and the Wechsler Intelligence Scale for Children (WISC). It is unclear if these tests consider the issue of cultural influence on a child's response. Further, the validity and reliability of some of these tests remain questionable. Norms for the WISC-R (revised), published in 1972, include a 10% sample of African-American, Mexican-American, and other minority children, but it is unclear if this sample is representative of the variety of minority groups in the United States (Padilla & Wyatt, 1983).

Mercer (1979) developed the System of Multicultural Pluralistic Assessment (SOMPA) in an effort to achieve nondiscriminatory or nonbiased intellectual assessment. SOMPA supports its nondiscriminatory goals by (1) adjusting IQ scores according to social and cultural characteristics to prevent overrepresentation of minority groups in special education; (2) providing for the language needs of Latino children and their parents by including Spanish versions of most of the tests; and (3) offering a variety of models of assessment on which to base decisions about the propriety of special programs for Anglo-Americans, African-Americans, and Latinos. A longitudinal study (Figueroa & Sassenrath, 1989) of members of these three groups was conducted over a 10-year period to evaluate the predictive validity of SOMPA. Anglo-Americans achieved higher scores on the achievement test than the Latinos, who had slightly higher scores than the African-Americans. The data suggest that IQ, as measured by SOMPA, or Estimated Learning Potential (ELP) can contribute to the prediction of school achievement. The need persists, however, to question the appropriateness and sufficiency of diagnostic inferences based predominantly on IQ.

Jones and Thorne (1987) caution that culture-specific tests, such as the Black Intelligence Test of Cultural Homogeneity (Williams, 1970), are an ideological reaction of minority social scientists who consider "a given ethnic group as homogeneous without consideration of geographical, religious, generational and social status differences" (p. 490). They advocate an "emic exploration" in which the clinician, after conducting a formal structured clinical interview, gathers more information by probing responses that seem to point to psychopathology. The clinician conveys respect for the patient, who is accepted as a collaborative partner, and trust and rapport are established. Jones and Thorne (1987) conclude:

> By failing to include the subject's (i.e., patient's) viewpoint in various aspects of assessment and psychological inquiry, we have often obscured the meaning of our findings and have promoted the attitude that cultural differences are boundaries to be crossed rather than relationships to be entered into. (p. 494)

Helms (1992) argues that the assumptions inherent in implicit biological or environmental philosophical perspectives and used to explain differences in performance on cognitive ability tests (CATs) by African-Americans and Anglo-Americans are based on different conceptualizations of culture. She maintains that neither approach has been defined adequately to allow valid interpretations of racial and ethnic group differences in CAT performance or to justify the extensive use of such measures across racial and ethnic groups other than for research purposes. To create a more viable alternative for examining the comparative meaning of CAT scores when respondents' race or ethnicity is an issue, Helms (1992) proposes a culturalist perspective, which calls for specification of those race-related or ethnicity-related psychological characteristics that are hypothesized to describe and possibly differentiate racial or ethnic groups.

C. L. Williams (1987) states that intelligence test results are influenced by an individual's past learning history, which may be impossible to separate from his or her own culture, and that cultural unfamiliarity can have an impact on test results. Williams offers appropriate guidance when he advises clinicians to be culturally sensitive and to describe the individual's level of functioning rather than give only numerical scores.

A clinician must be fully aware of the effect of the quality of the child's education on intelligence test results. Some inner-city schools are unable to meet the needs of increasing numbers of children in their classrooms; the schools often are understaffed and their teachers overworked. Further, in addition to reviewing a child's pediatric chart to rule out impaired vision or hearing difficulties, the clinician needs to consider the limitations of measuring only academic skills, the impact on the child of high levels of chronic stress, the lack of an intellectually stimulating and motivating environment, the child's frequent exposure to endless hours of television viewing, and the absence of encouragement of the child from adults to be studious and diligent.

Standardized measures to evaluate both intelligence and learning difficulties must be sensitively administered. Most importantly, assessment tests must be interpreted sensitively when used with inner-city children if they are to contribute to the diagnostic process.

Helms (1992) urges practitioners to challenge social scientists to produce culturally sensitive psychological explanations (e.g., culture-specific attitudes, feelings, or behaviors) for the differences in children's performance on cognitive ability tests rather than continue to use such measures until better assessment tests are available. She calls for a modification of existing tests to include more cultural variety; the development and standardization of new types of cognitive assessment instruments; and the presentation of explicit principles, hypotheses, assumptions, and theoretical models for investigating such factors as attitudes and environment instead of race or ethnicity.

DIAGNOSTIC TESTS FOR MENTAL DISORDERS

The Recognition of Cultural Factors in Diagnostic Tests for Mental Disorders

Lopez and Nunez (1987) assessed the degree to which cultural factors are considered or referred to in 11 widely used diagnostic criteria and interview schedules for schizophrenia and affective and personality disorders. Overall, the diagnostic instruments they selected minimally recognize the influence of cultural factors on the expression and definition of the aforementioned disorders. Although 8 of the 11 instruments refer to cultural influences in psychopathology, these are limited primarily to the identification of delusions and hallucinations in schizophrenia. The diagnostic instruments for affective and personality disorders include few cultural references.

Lopez and Nunez (1987) call for a general statement that specifies the influence of cultural values, beliefs, and practices in each set of diagnostic criteria and interview schedules. Further, they recommend that references to specific cultural factors be made for specific disorders and symptoms. Such consideration of cultural factors may prompt evaluators to consider seriously the cultural background of each patient.

Some ecologically sensitive instruments have been developed despite the ongoing controversy about culture-free tests. Tell Me A Story (TEMAS; Malgady, Costantino, & Rogler, 1984) provides one example: This projective technique consists of 23 colorful cards that depict African-American and Latino characters in an urban setting. Each card presents a conflict that needs to be resolved (e.g., stealing versus helping). A quantitative scoring system rates children on several personality dimensions. African-Americans and Latinos were found to be more verbally fluent on the TEMAS than on the TAT. No significant differences emerged among Anglo-American students. The results are consistent with the belief of Miller-Jones (1989) that cognitive processes may remain untapped and thus may be assumed not to exist if the task presented is not in keeping with the child's social-ecological environment.

Several diagnostic tests are available in various languages for minority groups. The Zung Scale for Depression and the 90-item Symptom Checklist (SCL-90) have been translated into Hmong script (Westermeyer, Vang, & Neider, 1983). Hwu, Yeh, Chang, and Yeh (1986) utilized the Diagnostic Interview Schedule with a Chinese population. Kinzie et al. (1982) developed the Vietnamese Depression Scale upon finding that the Beck Depression Inventory is neither reliable nor valid for the Vietnamese population. The Psychiatric Status Schedule, available in Chinese, Japanese, Korean, and Vietnamese (Yamamoto et al., 1982), has been standardized using an adult population. Chu, Lubin, and Sue (1984) studied the reliability and validity of the Depression Adjective Checklist that was translated into Chinese. They found interlanguage reliability and high correlations between the Chinese and the English versions of the self-reported state depression.

A small number of studies focus on the use of the Minnesota Multiphasic Personality Inventory (MMPI) in the assessment of Asian-Americans (Marsella, Sanborn, Kameoka, Shizuru, & Brennan, 1975; Sue & Sue, 1974; Tsushima & Onorato, 1982). The predictive and concurrent validity of many of these diagnostic tests have yet to be established independently for other ethnic groups (Leong, 1986).

The issue of language dominance is of central importance in assessing the appropriateness and validity of psychiatric instruments for Latino populations in the United States. The limited and tentative data available suggest important effects of language on the psychiatric assessment of Latinos: Feelings are reported with more emotion in the native language (Phillipus, 1971); symptoms appear to be less bizarre (Ruiz, 1975) and disclosure of feelings significantly greater when reported in the native language for Spanish-dominant bilinguals (Price & Cuellar, 1981); and interpreters have a definite effect on the diagnosis of Spanish-speaking patients (Marcos, 1979). The effect of the language of assessment on reported symptomatology (among Spanish-dominant and English-dominant bilinguals, particularly children) in structured clinical interviews has not been fully researched and remains another important task to be undertaken.

Assessment of Diagnostic Tests for Mental Disorders for Appropriateness, Validity, and Reliability

The Child Behavior Checklist (CBCL), developed by Achenbach (1978), is a self-administered scale designed to record in a standardized format the behavioral problems and competencies of children ages 4 through 16 (Achenbach, 1978, 1979; Achenbach & Edelbrock, 1981). Spanish translations of the instrument have been tested in Puerto Rico (Bird et al., 1987). Bird, Gould, Rubio-Stipec, Staghezza, and Canino (1991) recommend higher cutoff points in the total score of the Puerto Rican population. Their results also show that the CBCL—which is a screening instrument for the American Psychiatric Association's revised third edition of its *Diagnostic and Statistical Manual of Mental Disorders* (1987), or DSM-III-R, diagnoses alone—effectively identifies in Puerto Rican children the presence or absence of psychopathology, as well as the severity of disturbance, the presence of impairment, and the need for service.

The Inventario de Ansiedad Rasgo–Estado Para Niños (IDAREN) is the Spanish translation of the State–Trait Anxiety Inventory (Spielberger, Gonzalez, Martinez, Natalicio, & Natalicio, 1971). The scale consists of 20 items that measure relatively stable individual differences in anxiety proneness. The IDAREN has been tested widely with Puerto Rican children. The internal consistency, test–retest reliability, and concurrent validity of the instrument, as well as its equivalence to the English version, have been established adequately (Bauermeister, Villamil-Forastieri, & Spielberger, 1976). The IDAREN can be used for research purposes to identify children varying in anxiety proneness and as an evaluation tool for measuring the effectiveness of clinical treatment to reduce neurotic anxiety in children.

The Children's Global Assessment Scale (CGAS) was devised by Shaffer et al. (1983) to reflect the lowest level of functioning for a child or adolescent during a specified time period. Scores on the CGAS range in value from 1 for the most impaired child to 100 for the healthiest. Interrater reliability has been documented for use of the CGAS with Puerto Rican children (Bird et al., 1987). The results of this study are similar to those reported by Shaffer et al. (1983) on a New York sample of Anglo-American children. This suggests that the CGAS may have cross-cultural applicability. Excellent interrater agreement was found for both samples: psychiatrists agreed on 83.5% of the subjects that were doubly rated, for an overall kappa of .65. The CGAS also was found to be useful in discriminating between the more impaired, the less impaired, and the unimpaired in both clinical and community samples (Bird et al., 1987).

Psychological tests to assess American Indian youths use norms based on representative samples from the majority population. Work has been done to provide normative data for minority populations and foreign language editions of instruments have appeared, but thus far little research has focused on the applicability of traditional psychological tests to the American Indian population. Manson, Ackerson, Dick, Baron, and Fleming (1990) suggest caution in using the Center for Epidemiologic Studies Depression Scale (CES-D) with American Indian adolescents. They report major gender differences in the endorsement pattern of certain items as well as in the prevalence of depressive symptoms. Ackerson, Dick, Manson, and Baron (1990) investigated the use of the Inventory to Diagnose Depression (IDD) with American Indian youths. Similar to the CES-D, the IDD was constructed for adult populations. Preliminary findings suggest that the IDD would be suitable for use with an adolescent population: The group found high internal consistency (.94–.96), relatively few gender effects for test items, and prevalence estimates of depression that were comparable to epidemiological studies.

CONCLUDING COMMENTS

Generalizations are not yet possible, but some studies suggest an influence on test performance by the examiner's race (Barnes, 1969) and by the examiner's language (Padilla & Garza, 1975). Furthermore, other subtle factors affect motivation and performance in children, for example, their ability to identify failure or success within the testing situation, their ability to perform under stress, and their understanding and familiarity with the testing materials (Padilla & Garza, 1975).

Some suggest that the tasks on which children are tested be made more relevant to both the cognitive process and to the behavioral repertoire of inner-city children. Others recommend that the clinician assume the role of anthropologist and enter into the culture of the minority child to more fully understand the meaning the young patient ascribes to his or her own behavior.

Ultimately, the mental health worker must make a clinical judgment as to whether a behavioral or emotional attribute is a culturally syntonic way of manifesting distress, a behavior adopted to survive a particular sociocultural milieu, or a universal symptom of psychiatric disorder. These judgments can be sound only if clinicians are knowledgeable about the culture of their patients.

CHAPTER 4

Diagnostic Categories

✦

Few studies address the correlation of type of mental disorder with cultural factors. Despite the paucity of cross-cultural research, clinicians cannot dismiss the importance of sociocultural (in addition to biological and psychological) factors in the course of making a diagnostic assessment. As our knowledge of these factors increases, and existing information and changing cultural patterns are reassessed, diagnostic practices and classification will have to change. With further research, diagnostic categories may become more applicable to children and adolescents across cultures and social class levels; for now, clinicians must at least be knowledgeable about current diagnostic criteria, whatever their limitations. In this chapter we will outline those criteria and show how cultural differences can affect a clinical diagnosis.

DSM-IV: BASIC FEATURES

There have been major changes in the description and classification of diagnostic categories since publication of the first edition of the American Psychiatric Association's (APA) *Diagnostic and Statistical Manual of Mental Disorders* (DSM) in 1952. The manual, which has evolved from early classifications reflecting theoretical etiological influences to the International Classification of Diseases (World Health Organization, 1992), currently utilizes a multiaxial approach, integrating recent methodological and research developments.

Several basic features of the forthcoming DSM-IV are particularly relevant to the clinical evaluation and treatment of minority children. According to *DSM-IV Draft Criteria* (APA, 1993),

> Whatever its original cause, it [mental disorder] must currently be considered a manifestation of a behavioral, psychological, or biological dysfunction in the individual. Neither deviant behavior, e.g., political, religious, or sexual, nor conflicts that are primarily between the individual and society are mental disorders unless the deviance or conflict is a symptom of a dysfunction in the individual, as described above. . . .
>
> Non-clinical decision makers should also be cautioned that a diagnosis does not carry any necessary implications regarding the causes of the individual's mental disorder or its associated impairments. (pp. A:8–A:9)

Particularly important to clinicians who work with minority children is DSM-IV's caveat (as noted in *DSM-IV Draft Criteria*) about its use in different cultures. The caution is particularly appropriate in the context of this volume's proposed use of DSM-IV as a diagnostic tool.

> Special caution must be exercised when a clinician from one ethnic group uses the DSM-IV classification to evaluate an individual from a different ethnic or cultural group. A clinician who is unfamiliar with the nuances of an individual's cultural frame of reference may incorrectly judge as psychopathology those normal variations in behavior, belief, or experience that are particular to the individual's culture. For example, certain religious practices or beliefs (e.g., hearing or seeing a deceased relative during bereavement) may be misdiagnosed as manifestations of a psychotic disorder. Applying personality disorder criteria across cultural settings may be especially difficult because of the wide cultural variation in concepts of self, styles of communication, and coping mechanisms. (APA, 1993, p. A:10)

A lack of consensus persists as to the most valid definitions of childhood psychopathology and the boundaries between mental disorder and normalcy (Bird et al., 1990). Needed are more comparisons between the rates and correlates of psychiatric disorders in different cultures to determine which patterns are influenced more strongly by social forces and which are shaped by genetic or biological processes (Weisz et al., 1987). There is a need for caution in the process of diagnosing minority children: Findings suggest that many children who meet diagnostic criteria for mental disorder but who are not severely impaired are not necessarily in need of mental health services (Bird et al., 1991).

THE MULTIAXIAL SYSTEM FOR EVALUATION IN DSM-IV

The multiaxial system for evaluation in DSM-IV provides a biopsychosocial approach to assessment. The system requires assessment of the individual on several axes, each of which refers to a different class of information. As noted in *DSM-IV Draft Criteria* (APA, 1993), "the use of the multiaxial system facilitates comprehensive and systematic evaluation with attention to the various mental disorders and general medical conditions, social and environmental problems, and levels of functioning that might be overlooked if the focus were on assessing a single presenting problem" (p. D:1).

The clinician uses the multiaxial system to evaluate a person on each of the following five axes: Axis I, clinical syndromes and other conditions that may be a focus of clinical attention; Axis II, personality disorders; Axis III, general medical conditions; Axis IV, psychosocial and environmental problems; and Axis V, global assessment of functioning. This classification system, in addition, allows for a special section called disorders usually first diagnosed in infancy, childhood, or adolescence. Many clinicians who are adept in diagnosing in terms of Axes I, II, and III fail to consider Axes IV and V diagnoses, which frequently are of enormous importance in helping to assess prognosis and future treatment approaches.

MENTAL DISORDERS CLASSIFIED UNDER AXIS I AND AXIS II OF DSM-IV: CULTURAL FACTORS AND INFLUENCES

In view of the exposure to a multiplicity of physical, social, and psychological stressors, the population of minority children in our poorest communities are often quite difficult to diagnose. Sometimes they indicate behaviors that do not meet any one diagnosis, but whose severity demand therapeutic intervention. Other times their behaviors are solely a reflection of the exposure to continuous environmental stressors, and perhaps the "diagnosis" should be reserved for unresponsive social and political institutions. Finally, these children may truly suffer from emotional disorders, arriving at our clinics with chronic symptoms and overlapping or multiple diagnoses.

In light of these complex variables the clinician should indicate in his assessment any diagnostic uncertainty, address exclusionary criteria, and comment on the severity, significance, and course of the symptoms.

We have selected several of the mental disorders classified on Axes I and II for particular focus, along with traumas and psychosocial stressors that may serve to precipitate or predispose a child to certain disorders. Our discussion identifies and directs attention to the sociocultural factors and influences a clinician needs to consider when attempting a diagnosis on a child who is a member of a minority group population. When a child meets the appropriate diagnostic criteria, attention to his or her special circumstances and to context-relevant factors is crucial in determining future treatment approaches.

Depressive Disorders and Symptoms

Frequency

Depression in childhood no longer is viewed as a rare phenomenon. Children and adolescents who have been victims of sexual abuse frequently experience depressive symptoms (MacVicar, 1979; Sansonnet-Hayden, Haley, Marriage, & Fine, 1987). Other reports document the occurrence of depression in child and adolescent patient populations: 23 of 100 pediatric inpatients admitted for orthopaedic procedures (Kashani, Venzke, & Millar, 1981) and 28% of child psychiatry clinic patients (Carlson & Cantwell, 1980).

Depressive Symptoms in Minority Children

Although depressive features are not necessarily specific to any ethnic group, Pierce (1988) notes that "regardless of site or social variables, all Blacks in any workplace suffer special added stress as a result of threatened, perceived, and actual racism" (p. 27). The reported subdued expressiveness of emotionality of some Asian-American groups must not mislead clinicians to underestimate or underdiagnose mood disorders in this population. Somatization of depression often is observed in those of Asian background (Araneta, 1982; Gaw, 1982; Yamamoto, 1982), as well as in African-Americans and some groups of Latinos. For example, a child's inattentiveness in the classroom or clowning and disruptive behavior may accompany other symptoms of depression.

The chronic stresses, frustrations, and violence and the multiple losses that inner-city minority children and adolescents experience may predispose them to depressive symptoms and often to a presentation of dysthymic disorder or a depressive disorder not otherwise specified. Many have suffered the loss of their own peers to violent death. As one adolescent reported, "That was later. The first ones to die were the boys; friends like Butch and Pig and Charles who became caught up in what seemed to be the easy money and adventure of street life. In all, I have seen eight friends die" (Lee, 1993, p. B6).

Claude Brown (1965) provides a vivid illustration of despair in his autobiography, *Manchild in the Promised Land*:

> Man, Sonny, they ain't no kids in Harlem, I ain't seen any. I've seen some really small people actin' like kids. They were too small to be grown,

and they might've looked like kids, but they don't have any kids in Harlem, because nobody has time for a childhood. Man, do you ever remember bein' a kid, Sonny? Man, you lucky. I don't ever remember bein' happy and not scared. I don't know what happened, man, but I missed out on that childhood thing, because I don't ever recall bein' a kid. (p. 295)

Latino, American Indian, Asian-American, and African-American children all encounter numerous assaults to their self-esteem, exacerbating their vulnerability to depression. In school, a child's place of work, assaults to the self-esteem of many children of color may emanate not only from children of the school's dominant ethnic group but from prejudiced teachers as well: Third graders of mostly Mexican-American heritage overheard their white teacher announce in a stage whisper to visitors, "These students are not very smart; most of them are on welfare."

Myers and King (1983) identify the particular vulnerability of African-American children to depression "because of the attack on their self-concept in school, the threat or actuality of abandonment due to the destruction of family, and the insurmountable obstacles of society" (p. 291).

Clinical Vignette

Billy, a 10-year-old African-American boy who had just transferred to a new school because of a family move, was referred to the clinic by the school nurse because of a teacher's concern that his behavior differed markedly from the behavior reported in the school transfer papers. The transfer note described Billy as an interested and alert student and emphasized his intellectual curiosity and excellent grades. In his new school Billy was observed to be apathetic, and he was failing in his work.

Information gathered during the evaluation process revealed that the family had become dysfunctional several months prior to the referral. Billy's family had fallen on hard times. After nearly a year of unemployment (with the exception of odd jobs), Billy's stepfather, a recovering alcoholic, had several bouts of drinking. He eventually left the mother and child. The mother was fearful of losing her job owing to a pronounced drop in sales at her place of employment. From Billy's perspective, a role reversal had occurred; he was now in the position of parenting his mother.

Billy admitted to frightening nightmares (apparently triggered, in part, by the physical battles between his mother and stepfather prior to his stepfather's departure), visions of his abandoning parents, and suicidal thoughts. The mother reported a history of "periods of the blues" since adolescence and a similar "spell" on Billy's part 5 years earlier, when the family moved to the city from a small southern town.

The clinician decided to focus on the mother's observation that Billy related well to others and possessed considerable strengths in addition to his presenting symptoms. Billy's history revealed a healthy start to his development. His mother, who was willing to accept help for her son and herself, had already sought assistance from her minister for direction to an Al-Anon program. The clinician, aware of the issues related to the "culture" of unemployment and the stressful ripple effects of joblessness, followed Billy and his mother closely for the possibility of depressive episodes.

Dual Diagnoses

A child's fear of abandonment also may be rooted in a family's move to the United States from a distant land. If harrowing experiences occurred en route, the fear is compounded. Since such experiences obviously prove traumatic to entire families, parents are likely to be emotionally unavailable to their children because of their own bereavement and depressive symptoms. This leaves many children emotionally orphaned at a very young age.

A large number of Southeast Asian children encounter frightening experiences in the course of migrating to the United States. The stress accompanying efforts to acculturate to a new environment tends to exacerbate the problem for many of these children, who are given the dual diagnosis of dysthymia and posttraumatic stress disorder (PTSD).

The abuse of alcohol and other addictive substances by minority group youth seeking a high sometimes reflects the dual diagnosis of substance use disorder and mood disorder. A detailed discussion of this pattern appears in a subsequent section; however, the following case vignette is presented to illustrate the problem among minority youth.

Clinical Vignette

Josefina, a 16-year-old, perceived herself as unattractive. The third of five children in an inner-city Latino family, Josefina could not recall ever feeling good about herself. Truant from school for most of the year, she was ashamed of her poor academic standing. She was also ashamed of her family's living conditions.

Josefina recalled drinking wine coolers by age 12. She explained, "[They] lifted my spirits and made me feel better about myself." But, she added, the elevated mood was short-lived; she soon found herself willing, if not eager, to accept other drugs offered to her by both peers and strangers. Describing herself as a drug addict, Josefina was now asking for help.

Josefina's earlier history, as reported by her mother, was replete with signs and symptoms of a depressive disorder: depressed mood, sleep disturbances, early morning awakening, poor self-esteem, poor appetite, and fatigue. Josefina received the dual diagnosis of depressive disorder and substance use disorder.

Depression is not always an underlying factor in suicide, but it certainly is a serious antecedent (Husain & Vandiver, 1984). The increase in the reported incidence of suicide among African-American teenagers and young adults has been alarming in recent years (Gibbs, 1989). The compounding of stressors, including limited resources and supports, accounts for some of the difficulties these young people experience in establishing healthy connections. Their resulting isolation tends to reinforce negative feelings about the meaning and essence of life and may intensify feelings of hopelessness and despair and pave the way to suicide (Myers & King, 1983).

Thompson and Walker (1988) cite reports linking suicides of American Indian youths to an underlying depression as well as to excessive drinking. The literature provides more than a hint that depression and drinking are not necessarily separate entities, as reported in *Suicide and Ethnicity in the United States* (Committee on Cultural Psychiatry, 1989). American Indian youths experience not only the personal identity crisis of adolescence but also the additional burden of the adaptational crisis of their culture. The psychological helplessness and increased feelings of hopelessness engendered by such circumstances sometimes make self-inflicted death seem like an acceptable solution.

The alarming increase in substance abuse among young Latinos (including pregnant women) and their neglect or abandonment of their children contributes to the development in the children of a poor sense of self and to increasing their vulnerability and susceptibility to depressive symptoms. The high incidence of alcoholism observed on many American Indian reservations and in inner-city American Indian communities results in child neglect, which makes it difficult for the children to develop a positive sense of self and paves the way for depressive symptoms as well as problems related to neglect. Their experiences as refugees also make Southeast Asian families, including their children, particularly vulnerable to depressive symptoms, which often exist in combination with posttraumatic stress disorder (Sack, Angell, Kinzie, & Rath, 1986).

Many case examples reveal a specific pattern of symptomatology for clinical depression. Some cultures express depression with frequent somatic symptoms (Kleinman, 1977), others with substance abuse or concomitant disruptive behaviors. Abdul, an African-American boy, displayed the latter symptom.

Clinical Vignette

Abdul's referral to a child psychiatry clinic had been initiated by a teacher who described herself "at wit's end" in her attempts to handle the child's clowning and acting-out behavior in the classroom. The clinician learned that Abdul had been exposed to multiple incidents of domestic violence in his chaotic family setting and had also been subjected to repeated experiences of threatened and actual abandonment.

Now 10, Abdul initiated his clowning behavior as a much younger child. He was irritable, could not concentrate, had insomnia, and suffered feelings of worthlessness. His clowning had garnered some response from adults, although the attention was not sustained. Subsequently, Abdul learned that disruptive behavior elicited a similar response. The responses may have been studded with annoyance, if not anger, yet they served to acknowledge his presence.

At one point during the initial diagnostic session the clinician challenged Abdul's declaration that he did not care about getting into trouble, a declaration that suggested that he had already experienced trouble in the short span of his life. Abdul's verbal response of denial contrasted sharply with his facial expression and tear-filled eyes.

Adjustment Disorders

Five indications of adjustment disorder are listed in *DSM-IV Draft Criteria* (American Psychiatric Association, 1993, p. S:1):

[1] the development of emotional or behavioral symptoms in response to an identifiable stressor(s); [2] the fact that the symptoms or behaviors are clinically significant as evidenced by either of the following: marked distress that is in excess of what would be expected from exposure to the stressor; significant impairment in social or occupational (academic) functioning; [3] the stress-related disturbance does not meet criteria for any specific Axis I Disorder and is not merely an exacerbation of a preexisting Axis I or Axis II disorder; [4] does not represent bereave-

ment; [5] the symptoms do not persist for more than six months after the termination of stressors (or its consequences). (p. S:1)

All children and adolescents experience stressors that may precipitate an adjustment disorder. Common stressors that have a negative impact on children across all cultures include divorce and custody battles, illnesses that necessitate hospitalization, and accidents. Minority group children also experience stressors rooted in racist practices. In a recent newspaper series the following comment was made by an inner-city adolescent: "Sometimes I think, how far am I going to be able to go being female and black—two things against me" (Lee, 1993, p. B6).

The resulting problems are likely to be exacerbated for immigrant youngsters and their families, who are exposed to multiple other stressors, such as learning a new language and customs. Le (1983) describes the many adjustment problems recently transplanted Vietnamese children experience in the United States: They must learn English to be able to communicate with teachers and classmates; they must learn new ways of behaving, thinking, and learning; and they must sort out and decide which parts of their cultural heritage to retain and which aspects to modify or replace in order to function effectively in their new country (p. 379). Le (1983) notes that those psychiatric disorders of the Indochinese that are situational or reactive often appear to clinicians to be severe disorders and are misdiagnosed as such.

The stressors that stem from transitions from one culture to another are not limited to the most recent immigrants to these shores, however. American Indian youths who move to urban communities from their Indian nations encounter stressors related to racist practices of authority figures as well as to cultural differences. Inner-city minority children who move with their families to suburbia may face similar stressors. Smith (1988) cites a typical case of a middle-class African-American child who encountered multiple stressors.

Clinical Vignette

Randy, a 9-year-old African-American boy, was referred for psychiatric evaluation because of school failure despite an above average IQ. He demonstrated sad, withdrawn behavior that alternated with random attacks on schoolmates and frequent vomiting, which appeared to be self-induced. The clinician learned in an interview with this sad young fellow that he was clinically depressed in response to several losses in his life.

Randy had moved with his mother to a sparsely integrated neighborhood that offered plenty of green grass but no children who knew or liked him. He left behind, in a less prestigious African-American neighborhood, friends and a continually present grandmother and grandfather who talked to him. The old neighborhood also provided many opportunities for Randy to see his father. In contrast to this full social life, Randy's daily routine now meant that he was alone in his new house from 4 to 7 P.M., at which time his mother rushed in, prepared a quick meal, and went to sleep. Randy was diagnosed to have an adjustment disorder with mixed disturbance of emotions and conduct.

Clinical Vignette

Jack, an 18-year-old African-American, attempted suicide during his freshman year at a prestigious Ivy League college. Jack had attended white private preparatory schools on scholarships, but he felt isolated in the college setting and longed for the familiar social contacts with members of his extended family and church. His discontent with college life was reinforced by his perception of a racist atmosphere in some of his classes and in his dormitory. Jack vacillated between intense anger and despair. Poor grades in two examinations in a required course intensified his feelings of despair.

In recounting the incidents that led to his ingesting sleeping pills along with a couple of drinks, Jack stated that he had not intended to kill himself even though he was aware of feelings of despondency and a desire to end his current situation. Acknowledging that there are better ways to resolve his conflicts, Jack accepted a referral for treatment.

The examiner identified several losses that triggered Jack's depressive symptoms and suicide attempt. In addition to the loss of important family and social contacts, Jack, who had previously earned superior grades, experienced a loss of academic standing when he met with keener competition in college and was no longer the consistent star of the class. He also experienced the loss of a significant ideal, namely, acceptance regardless of race. Like many African-American youths who have made some progress in the dominant culture, Jack was psychologically unprepared for the subtle racist practices he encountered in the college setting. He was diagnosed with an adjustment disorder with depressive features.

Disruptive Behavior Disorders

She ran with a gang of girls who beat and robbed other girls of their jewelry and cash. She struggled alone to take care of her two younger sisters, Lakisha, now 13, and Latreece, 5. She was more often absent from school than not. Her first job was holding drugs and cash for a major neighborhhood crack dealer. (Lee, 1993, p. A2)

In evaluating minority youngsters, especially those from the inner city, it is crucial to obtain information on the family and neighborhood. Often, there is a history of child abuse and/or neglect. It is crucial to ask about the possibility of lead intoxication and malnutrition. Other predisposing factors to disruptive behavior disorder in children include parental abuse of alcohol or other substances and antisocial personality disorder in a family member. The presence of such factors often makes it impossible to determine the extent to which symptoms—even those that resemble behaviors associated with attention deficit disorders—are externally induced or reflect the child's own psychopathology. The following vignette reflects some of these issues:

Clinical Vignette

Larry, an 11-year-old American Indian, was referred for psychiatric evaluation by a social service agency because of complaints by his foster mother of his lying, stealing, fighting with his foster siblings, and aggressive outbursts in the classroom. Family members believed Larry was deliberately destroying the belongings of his foster siblings.

This was the third foster placement for Larry. He was first placed at age 8, following his mother's psychiatric hospitalization for depression and attempted suicide and charges of child neglect by a maternal aunt who had been designated as a caretaker by the family. Larry complained of sexual and physical abuse in his first foster placement, but his charges—unlike those he made about his second foster placement—were not substantiated.

Larry's history illustrates the multiple vulnerabilities that may contribute to a conduct disorder. It was incumbent upon the examiner to investigate the possibility of neurological damage, in view of Larry's history of physical abuse, as well as to probe the psychiatric and social roots of his difficulties.

Frequently, inner-city children live in crime-infested areas where survival skills demand physical strength and aggression. Social and economic pressures create an environment where lying, stealing, truancy, and early drug abuse and sexual behavior are common. Families often are unable to offer consistent caretaking; consequenly, there is frequent institutional living and a shifting or absence of parental figures. Unfair, discriminatory, and abusive behavior on the part of institutions and authority figures complicate these issues. Thus, the clinician needs to consider conduct disorders and oppositional defiant disorders carefully within the context in which they occur.

Anxiety Disorders

In view of the frequent real dangers of inner-city living and the high crime rates, many families are apprehensive about letting their children out of their sight. Parents themselves may feel unsafe and often are anxious about the real dangers in their communities. For parents who are immigrants, ignorant of the new culture and language and with limited social support, normal apprehension may turn to real fear, which is then communicated openly to the children. The child's anxiety may increase in instances of actual harm or sudden separation from a parent or parental figure. A diagnosis of anxiety disorder is appropriate only when the child's worries are unrealistic and persist. In planning a treatment approach the clinician must carefully evaluate and address the parents' level of anxiety.

Clinical Vignette

Alfred, a verbal and engaging Mexican-American 7-year-old, presented to the clinic with recurrent nightmares and worries about his mother's safety. He had become a bed wetter, seemed anxious and irritable in school, and complained frequently of stomachaches and headaches. These symptoms had lasted over 8 months.

The clinician learned that Alfred's mother often went out dancing in a community she frequently described to the child as "full of muggers and drug addicts." When her boyfriend was not around, she often slept with Alfred because she feared the dark and being alone. She frequently talked to her own mother about how much safer it was in Mexico, at the same time exposing Alfred, who overheard these conversations, to tales told in graphic detail of the most recent crimes in the area.

When Alfred's mother developed a panic disorder, his grandmother recounted her severe nightmares in the child's presence. Family counseling sessions focused on facilitating a move for the family to another community and on developing a safer social network. Alfred's symptoms abated.

The frequent but chronic level of psychosocial stress often makes it difficult to differentiate anxiety disorders from adjustment disorder with anxious mood. Social withdrawal also needs to be assessed within the culture and the family. Some groups tend to oversocialize their children; others teach their children to be reticent, withdrawn, and suspicious of social interactions.

Posttraumatic Stress Disorder

Posttraumatic stress disorder (PTSD) is characterized by the following symptoms, which occur after the experience of an emotionally disturbing event: reexperiencing the traumatic event, avoidance of stimuli associated with the event, and increased arousal. The initial event may be any one of a broad range of traumas, including natural disasters and those caused by humankind. The witnessing of violence, especially homicide, rape, and suicide, may trigger symptoms of posttraumatic stress disorder. Children uprooted by a natural catastrophe also experience a trauma that may precipitate PTSD. Clinicians should not minimize the untoward effects of parental separation or divorce on children. As noted previously, PTSD often emerges as a component of a dual diagnosis.

Clinical Vignette

Johnny, an 8-year-old Mexican-American boy, was referred to a child psychiatry clinic by a general pediatric clinic for evaluation of neurovegetative symptoms and somatic complaints subsequent to the violent shooting death of his biological father 2 weeks earlier. Johnny was suffering from frequent nightmares in which this event was reenacted, and he had become overreactive to any sound that resembled a gunshot. His mother also was concerned about Johnny's reaction to having witnessed her severe beating by his stepfather, for which she was hospitalized and the stepfather incarcerated. These events occurred 5 months prior to the referral.

Johnny told the examiner that he thought about killing himself but added that he would not because it would be too hard on his mother. He talked about feeling anxious and eating a lot at such times. He also mentioned feeling "mad and sad at the same time" and experiencing trouble falling asleep at night and concentrating in school. The latter comment followed his statement that he had been on the honor roll.

During the course of the interview Johnny made several references to finding the person who had killed his father. He had made a pact with his friends to pursue this goal, and he was making weapons with them to protect his mother and himself in the event that someone broke into their home.

Johnny's history parallels that of many inner-city youngsters exposed to chronic violence. He was diagnosed as having a posttraumatic stress disorder.

Catastrophically Uprooted Children

Arroyo and Eth (1985) provide a comprehensive review of the literature focusing on children traumatized by war. Burlingham and Freud (1943) concluded in their study of children exposed to bombings during World War II that children are more likely to be affected by their parents' (or caregivers') responses to the traumatic situation than by the actual trauma. Papanek (1942) and Burt (1943) confirmed this finding; however, Burt also described symptoms in children that are similar to those experienced by soldiers. Carey-Trefzer (1949) described PTSD in children during World War II and identified a pre-existing psychological factor, rather than the actual trauma, as a major etiological agent of this disorder in the majority of children. Other studies of European children who were exposed to the traumas of war also reported signs and symptoms of PTSD (Brander, 1943; Cormina, 1943; Dunsdon, 1941; Mercier, 1943). More recently, in their study of Southeast Asian refugees, Williams and Westermeyer (1983) found no cases of PTSD and conjectured that the most prominent symptoms of the disorder had diminished sharply prior to the study.

Arroyo and Eth (1985), while noting the limitations of various studies of children who have been subjected to terrorist attacks (Allodi, 1980; Ayalon, 1983; Cohn, Holzer, Koch, & Severin, 1980), concluded:

> War and extreme civil strife can adversely affect the local children and adolescents psychologically and disrupt their normal development, and the more intimately and catastrophically the youth are victimized, the greater is the risk of developing seriously disabling psychiatric symptoms. (p. 107)

The impact on children of civil unrest is the major focus of Arroyo and Eth's (1985) study of 30 youngsters from Central America. The premorbid background of many of these children included profound poverty, domestic violence, and separation from parents who had emigrated to the United States long before the children's arrival here. Since many of the youngsters and their parents were undocumented aliens, it is likely that the symptoms of PTSD identified in them by the researchers were compounded by anxieties stemming from the threat of deportation. Harding and Looney (1977) and Looney (1979) have called attention to the fact that conditions in refugee camps often reinforce in children and their families the symptoms previously precipitated within the war-torn country from which they have fled. The close living conditions in the camps often tend to potentiate feelings of despair and hopelessness, and unaccompanied children are at highest risk for severe psychological impairment. In her study of refugee children from Southeast Asia, Carlin (1979) noted that the children's traumas were compounded by the overwhelming hardships of the refugee camps. Like adults, the children developed various symptoms of traumatization, including recurrent nightmares about traumatic events, psychic numbing, and excessive autonomic arousal; associated symptoms of anxiety and depression were commonplace. Kinzie, Sack, and Angell (1986) found that war trauma in Cambodian children related strongly to resettlement stress and to the diagnosis of PTSD and that PTSD and depression co-varied as diagnoses. Latino children from the war-torn countries of Central America have experienced similar difficulties.

Other Conditions

Child Abuse

Focus shifts now to child abuse, not a disorder itself but, rather, a trauma that may precipitate posttraumatic stress disorder. The physical injury of the child by a parent occurs within a pathological family structure; that is, the physical attacks are "superimposed upon a harsh and punitive childrearing climate" (Green, 1983, p. 231).

A report circulated by the U.S. House of Representatives Select Committee on Children, Youth and Families (1989) identifies 2.2 million cases of abuse filed in 1988, an increase of 83% from the 1.2 million cases filed 7 years earlier. The same report notes that fatalities stemming from child abuse rose by 5% (to an estimated total of 1,225 cases) from 1987 to 1988. The rise of substance abuse in the adult and youth population has been identified as a major cause of the increase in abuse and neglect of children.

> In the District of Columbia, almost 25% of the 6,000 cases of abuse and neglect reported to the Child and Family Division in 1985 involved alcohol abuse and emotional problems, generally related to other forms of substance abuse. . . . In 1988, crack use was identified in over 8,521 cases of child neglect in New York, over three times the number of such cases identified in 1986 . . . over 73% of New York's neglect-related child fatalities in 1987 resulted from parental drug use; in 1985 this figure had been 11%. (pp. 28–31)

Clearly, child abuse is not limited to any one ethnic, racial, or socioeconomic group, but Garbarino (1975) reports that parents in the lower socioeconomic groups are more likely to use physical means to punish their children. This finding may relate, in part, to the stressors that conditions of poverty generate, such as overcrowded housing that is poorly heated in winter and poorly ventilated in summer and the absence of essentials.

A child's need for intensive parenting because of premature birth or a chronic illness may overwhelm the mother, who may view the child as demanding and may become increasingly depressed, overtly angry, or out of control. No age group is immune to such a reaction, but it commonly is observed among adolescent mothers who are ill prepared for the responsibilities of parenting.

Multiproblem families in which disorganization reigns set the stage for the development of child abuse. In such families the abuse of alcohol and other substances contributes to child neglect, which often is a forerunner of child abuse. The high rate of alcoholism among American Indians, especially those who reside on reservations, most likely accounts for the child abuse, including sexual abuse, that is prevalent in many of these communities. Dorris (1989) highlights the frequency of alcoholism among American Indian women. His book describes the problems experienced by his adopted son, who was diagnosed as having fetal alcohol syndrome, and the resulting difficulties for the adoptive family. Two cases described in a newspaper report are typical:

> Aubreyon, 3, whose mother stabbed her crack-dealer father to death in self-defense, displays the classic signs of a child who has been physically abused or witnessed violence, both of which were the case. She flinches at sudden movements or loud noises and is overly occupied with the most minor injuries of others in the house. Earl, 8, shows signs of fetal alcohol exposure and, counsellors say, has been severely beaten by his mother. He has stopped up the house toilets in the treatment facility, smashed furniture and hit the other children for no apparent reason. (Boodman, 1990)

Piasecki, Manson, and Biernoff (1989) provide a comprehensive review of studies of child abuse and neglect in American Indian communities. Their findings highlight the enormity of the problem: There is wide variation in the prevalence of child abuse and neglect across different communities. In a small native community in Alaska, one-third of the children were described as neglected or abused and homeless. In that community cases of child neglect were reported to be much more numerous than abuse. Marital disruption, parental alcoholism, inadequate caregiver–child bonding, severe educational deficits, chronic physical illness, and interpersonal conflicts were identified as some of the underlying causes of child abuse and neglect, with shifts in family patterns, stemming from rapid sociocultural changes, recognized as contributing factors.

Jackson (1984) identifies children in foster care as particularly vulnerable to child abuse and neglect. Since African-American children are overrepresented in foster care, they may also be overrepresented among abused and neglected children. A study of African-American children in foster care (National Black Child Development Institute, 1989) yields some troublesome findings: (1) Most of the study population (75%) entered foster care because of abuse or neglect, but many foster care placements were also attributed to environmental stresses caused by chronic poverty. (2) In the five cities studied, the African-American children in foster care generally received no periodic health or educational assessment. (3) Children 5 years old or younger constituted the largest proportion of African-American children entering foster care and were at substantial risk for developmental delays, attention deficit disorder, and other consequences. (4) Older children often faced significant disruptions in their education as they moved from placement to placement.

Inner-City Catastrophes

I Had A Dream Repeatedly . . .

I am coming out of a supermarket and a man
is carrying a gun and tells me to give
him all my money. I give him my purse
and my jewelry, but he still shoots me.

And then I found myself in a funeral home. I
see my mom, my dad and my brother
crying and the rest of my family. I go up to
the coffin and see a person who reminds
me of me. I see myself. I start to cry and I
wake up.
　　　　—*Melanie* (in Plantenga, 1991, p. 27)

A number of conclusions drawn by Rutter (1982), who studied special stresses experienced by residents in sections of London, are applicable to the inner-city population of the United States. There are various sequelae of poverty and exposure to crime and violence. Life in the inner cities of the United States, as in London, "is associated with an increased susceptibility to a quite wide range of problems with different manifestations and different causes" (p. 356).

No community is immune from violence; however, it is more common in some areas than in others. Daily news stories report the high incidence of violent crime in inner cities—on the streets, in the corridors of public housing projects and privately owned apartment buildings, on public vehicles, and in the schools. The common occurrence of violent crime may blunt the reactions of some youngsters and their parents. However, many youngsters respond to the witnessing of a crime with sleep and eating disorders as well as behavioral changes, such as withdrawal and regressive or antisocial behavior. These children are not unlike the children in London described by Rutter, children whose most characteristic problems were "those beginning early, lasting a long time, and accompanied by many other problems in the family" (p. 357). As one adolescent resident of an inner city in the United States put it, "If you ain't careful, living around here can drive you crazy" (Terry, 1993, p. A16).

Catastrophic conditions within the inner cities, especially the increase in open drug abuse and violent crime, have multiplied continuously since the 1970s. Problems include unemployment and underemployment; increase in adolescent parenting, which is often coupled with child neglect and abuse; inner-city residents' increased dependency on welfare and an underground economy; and inner-city social isolation (Wilson, 1978).

Statements by inner-city children and adolescents express the alarm and pain generated by the violence that prevails in their neighborhoods. Kozol (1991) recounts a "chilling story" told by a group of children in East St. Louis, Illinois:

> Without warning, Smokey says, "My sister has got killed."
> "She was my best friend," Serena says.
> "They had beat her and raped her," Smokey says.
> "She was hollering out loud," says Little Sister.
> I ask them when it happened.
> Smokey says, "Last year."
> Serena corrects him and says, "Last week."
> "The police arrested one man, but they didn't catch the other," Smokey says.
> Serena says, "He was some kin to her."
> Smokey objects. "He weren't no kin to me. He was my momma's friend."
> "Her face was busted," Little Sister says.
> Serena describes the sequence of events. "They told her go behind the

school. They'll give her a quarter if she do. Then they knock her down and told her not to tell what they had did."

I ask, "Why did they kill her?"

"They was scared that she would tell," Serena says.

"One is in jail," says Smokey. "They can't find the other."

"Instead of raping little bitty children, they should find themselves a wife," says Little Sister.

"I hope," Serena says, "her spirit will come back and get that man."

"And kill that man," says Little Sister.

"Give her another chance to live," Serena says.

"My teacher came to the funeral," says Smokey.

"When a little child dies, my momma say a star go right to heaven," says Serena.

"My grandma was murdered," Mickey says out of the blue. "Somebody shot two bullets in her head."

I ask him, "Is she really dead?"

"She dead all right," says Mickey. "She was layin' there, just dead."

"I love my friends," Serena says. "I don't care if they no kin to me. I care for them. I hope his mother have another baby. Name her for my friend that's dead."

"I have a cat with three legs," Smokey says.

"Snakes hate rabbits," Mickey says, again for no apparent reason.

"Cats hate fishes," Little Sister says.

"It's a lot of hate," says Smokey. (pp. 13–14)

There is a lot of hate—some of it self-hatred—and there is fear and pain. There is no safe haven for these children. The violence engulfs them. Its ugliness and pain intrude upon them at intervals throughout the day and then again at night in terrifying dreams.

There is little, if any, immunity to the chronic pain and suffering for a large percentage of these children. For many, a pattern of violence is set for them to follow. This is captured in Hewlett's (1992) transcription of a poem dictated by an 8-year-old boy the day after his 10-month-old sister was found dead in the welfare hotel that had been the family's residence:

> When our baby die we start to
> sit by the window. We just
> sit an' sit, all wrapped up
> quiet in old shirts an' watch
> the pigeons. That pigeon she
> fly so fast, move so fast. She
> move nice. A real pretty flyer.
>
> She open her mouth and take in
> the wind. We just spread out crumbs.

Me and my brother. And we wait.
Sit and wait.
There under the windowsill.

She don't even see us 'til we slam
down the window. And she break.
She look with one eye.
She don't die right away.
We dip her in over and over,
in the water pot we boils on
the hot plate.
We wanna see how it be to die
slow like our baby die. (p. 4)

Substance-Related Disorders

Substance abuse emerges as a major public health problem among children and adolescents (Semlitz & Gold, 1986). A survey of 17,000 high school students conducted under the auspices of the National Institute of Drug Abuse (Johnston, 1985) revealed that drug use begins prior to the tenth grade. The use of illicit drugs by eighth graders increased from 8% in 1971 to 20% in 1978. Lifetime prevalence rates of drug abuse for high school seniors vary from drug to drug. Morrison (1991), suggesting that the figures most likely are underestimates since they fail to account for school dropouts or students who were absent at the time of the survey, reports the following rates: alcohol, 92%; cocaine, 17%; marijuana, 54%; stimulants, 26%.

No child or adolescent is immune to drug abuse, but the negative sequelae may be greater for minority group children who are isolated in inner cities and for American Indian youth on reservations. The number of drug-exposed infants has nearly quadrupled in the last 3 years in hospitals across the United States. Crack use was implicated in nearly 9,000 cases of child neglect in New York City in 1988, three times the number of such cases in 1986. In that same year more than 80% of the cases of child abuse and neglect reported in the District of Columbia involved substance abuse. Up to 60% of California's drug-exposed infants have been placed in foster care (SOS America, 1990). African-Americans accounted for 30% of the drug abuse deaths in males in 1984 (U.S. Congress, 1989a). Since all children and adolescents are at risk for succumbing to this disorder, clinicians must explore the possibility of substance abuse in the course of evaluating their young patients. This is particularly true for African-American, Asian-

American, American Indian, and Latino youth, who are at greater risk both for substance abuse and other forms of health impairment. Dual diagnoses are not uncommon. Chemical dependency often accompanies depression (a disorder frequently overlooked in minority group children), conduct disorders, and organic syndromes.

The use of drugs among adolescents need not necessarily lead to abuse of these substances. Farrow, Rees, and Worthington-Robert (1987) describe drug use and abuse as a continuum that begins with abstinence and progresses to dependency. In some settings adolescent use of alcohol and marijuana is viewed as typical, if not approved, adolescent behavior and is not regarded as a problem. However, the abuse of both legal and illicit drugs has reached alarming levels among children and adolescents in many communities nationwide.

The appearance and apparent ready availability of "designer drugs" compounds the physical and psychological problems that substance abuse generates for children and adolescents. Two of these, crack cocaine and "ice," have received considerable media attention. Crack cocaine, a combination of cocaine hydrochloride and baking soda, becomes highly addictive on the first try. "Ice," a form of methamphetamine that is smokable, provides a longer high than the brief high of crack cocaine (Smith, Ehrlich, & Seymour, 1991).

Utilizing a literature review as a frame of reference, Bailey (1989), who discusses etiology in terms of biological, psychological, and social factors, reports that recent studies indicate strong genetic roots in cases of substance abuse and emphasize the importance of obtaining a detailed family history in the course of evaluating a child or adolescent for this disorder. He cites Carroll (1981) and Kandel (1981) in identifying certain personality traits (anxiety, depression, poor self-control, and low self-esteem) that predispose to the development of substance abuse. Semlitz and Gold (1986) identified as etiological agents such psychological and social factors as predisposition toward nonconformity, parental and/or peer drug use and approval, low academic performance, and motivation.

Bailey (1989) also calls attention to substance abuse coupled with other psychiatric disorders. Substance abuse has been associated with affective disorders, including both unipolar and bipolar depression (Deyki, Levy, & Wells, 1987; Famularo, Stone, & Popper, 1985; Kashani, Keller, Solomon, Reid, & Mazzola, 1985), with attention deficit disorder (Gittelman, Mannuzza, Shemker, & Bonagura, 1985), and with antisocial behavior (Cantwell, 1978; Clayton, 1986; Robins, 1978). "Substance abuse may be a manifestation of psychopathology, an effect of psychopathology or unrelated to psychopathology" (Bailey, 1989, p. 155).

Literature focusing on substance abuse on the part of minority children and youth is scarce. The *Report of the Secretary's Task Force on Black and Minority Health* (1985) discusses prevalence of reported drug use:

> Prevalence of reported drug use within household populations is generally higher in urban areas than suburban or rural. Therefore, to the extent that minorities are most likely to reside in inner-city areas, they may be at greater risk of drug abuse and ultimately the negative social and health consequences associated with drug abuse. (pp. 134–135)

However, race differences in prevalence rates may be complicated by socioeconomic status and by living conditions (Miller et al., 1983).

Some studies of the 1960s and 1970s focusing on drug use and minority group youngsters associated drug use and abuse with delinquency. A team of investigators (Barker & Adams, 1963) identified different characteristics of glue sniffers and "other delinquents" admitted to a boys' school in Colorado; they reported that the majority of glue sniffers were Mexican-Americans, many of whom initiated the practice at age 13 or younger. Over one-half of child and adolescent glue sniffers admitted to a psychiatric service of a general hospital in Brooklyn were Puerto Rican (Brozovsky & Winkler, 1965).

Westermeyer (1974), in a reference to alcoholism among American Indian groups, stated that there appears to be no universal explanation for substance abuse in any one group or in the minority group population as a whole. The National Institute on Drug Abuse (Johnston, 1985) organized a workshop to review reports of studies and to generate discussions to identify factors that play a role in the use and misuse of drugs among minority populations. A literature review emphasized the paucity of data about epidemiology, treatment, and prevention and the need for research in these areas. The pressures of acculturation for some minority groups in the changing environment of their new surroundings produce major stresses that can and do lead to escapism through the use of drugs.

Hard data about drinking patterns of minority youth remain scarce, but the *Report of the Secretary's Task Force on Black and Minority Health* (1985) cites some significant findings:

> According to national surveys, black youth use alcohol less than their white or Hispanic counterparts. The use of alcohol in American Indian populations varies from tribe to tribe, but abuse has been reported to be high and accounts for a sizeable percentage of accidental deaths (i.e., driving while intoxicated). (p. 131)

In a survey of over 1,400 youth, Beauvais et al. (1985) found that over 82% of American Indian seventh-to-twelfth graders had used alcohol at least once, in contrast to 66% of non-Indian adolescents; 58% of American Indian adolescents, as compared to 27% of non-Indians, reported recent use of alcohol. The data of Oetting and Goldstein (1979) show that 12% of American Indian children drink beer, wine, or distilled spirits regularly by their ninth birthday and that 97% use alcohol by the time they reach the eleventh grade.

Substance abuse emerges as a serious problem in some Asian-American communities (Trimble, Padilla, & Bell, 1987) despite the frequent depiction of Asian-Americans as "model minorities."

Juveniles are known to be drug traffickers as well as users (Fulwood, 1987), leading to additional criminal and delinquent acts, which are widespread and range from stealing to assault and homicide. Such behavior, identified as commonplace among minority populations, is also evident in the dominant population group.

The negative physical, psychological, and social sequelae of drug abuse are widespread. The use of crack during pregnancy subjects the fetus to intrauterine addiction and withdrawal symptoms at birth and to the possibility of acquired immunodeficiency syndrome (AIDS) if the mother has been infected. An infant whose mother abused alcohol during pregnancy is likely to demonstrate fetal alcohol effects or to be born with full-blown fetal alcohol syndrome.

The psychological damage an individual substance abuser suffers covers a wide range of impairments. Particularly significant is the establishment of barriers that prevent adolescents from experiencing normal problem solving. The substances they abuse tend to impair their judgment, powers of discrimination, and ability to process information. Consequently, school failure becomes commonplace and relationships with family members become grossly impaired. As indicated previously, dysfunctional families and impaired family relationships serve as major contributors to the development of substance abuse by the children and adolescents in these families. The impact of substance abuse transcends the individual, a fact suggested by the following paragraph:

> Jerina Gervais heard her old boyfriend was out of jail, and the news made her nervous. He was a drug dealer, in and out of jail for as long as she'd known him, most recently for assaulting a police officer. But to Jerina, with neither father nor mother to care for her, he had been lover, protector and friend. What if he knocked on her door now, when she was trying to turn her life around? Would she fall for his flattery, accept his gifts and abandon her bright dreams for the future? (Gross, 1993, p. A1)

Kandel (1990) points to a link between parental drug use and control problems in children and identifies conduct disorders as an early precursor of drug use and delinquency in adolescents. The following vignette illustrates this

Clinical Vignette

Antonio's mother began to use cocaine before the school referred him to a child psychiatry clinic because of disturbed and disturbing behavior in his first-grade classroom. At that time, Antonio's diagnosis was attention-deficit hyperactivity disorder. Treatment was recommended, and Antonio's mother was referred to a drug treatment facility. As frequently happens in cases such as this, neither the mother nor clinic staff followed through on the recommendations. According to the clinic record, the case was closed 6 weeks after the diagnostic evaluation because of failed appointments and the inability of clinic staff to contact the mother.

At age 11, Antonio again was referred by his school because of assaultive behavior, alleged stealing, and possible drug use. Drug use was suspected because of a teacher's observation of a vacant expression in Antonio's eyes and frequent nodding. It was determined that Antonio had, in fact, begun to experiment with his mother's drugs.

Drug abuse compounds physical health problems, which are prevalent among inner-city minority populations. Addicts, whose health practices are poor, give scant attention to regular meals or the need for rest and sleep. Moreover, drugs suppress a range of physiological symptoms, thus masking the warning signs of illness, and drug abusers often tend to engage in other risk-taking behaviors that have a negative impact on health (Johnson, Williams, Dei, & Sanabria, 1990).

A study on the negative consequences of substance abuse among minority populations (Johnson et al., 1990) has found that alcoholism is a root cause of fatal automobile accidents and suicide in the American Indian population and is likely to account for a considerable percentage of spousal and child abuse. Fetal alcohol syndrome is another medical consequence of alcoholism in some American Indian groups. An increase in Latino victims of drug-related homicides and in Latino perpetrators of crime in New York City was reported in 1982 (U.S. Congress, 1989b). Deaths from drug overdoses and from combinations of drugs, particularly heroin and alcohol, are often reported for African-American substance abusers.

Other Mental Disorders

DSM-IV Draft Criteria (APA, 1993) provide guidance for other mental disorders that may afflict minority group populations, including eating disorders, gender identity disorders, elective mutism, mental retardation, and pervasive developmental disorder. These disorders do not emerge as particularly prevalent among minority populations. (Consequently, they are identified and elaborated upon here only briefly.) Nevertheless, the diagnostic process in cases of these disorders requires cultural sensitivity, that is, recognition of cultural factors and influences, in all stages—in history taking, testing, and the use of the DSM-IV multiaxial evaluation system.

Eating Disorders

The clinician who suspects an eating disorder in a child of a minority group first must determine the eating behaviors and dietary habits that are acceptable to the minority group. Information about the kinds of foods the family eats proves helpful in assessing the reasons for a child's obesity. One factor to consider is the high-calorie and starchy diet of poor families. In general, anorexia nervosa and bulimia continue to be rare or absent outside affluent Western cultures or Westernized cultures, such as Japan (Suematsu, Ishikawa, Kuboki, & Ito, 1985).

Pica, or the persistent eating of a nonnutritive substance, may be of particular concern in minority group populations. Infants suffering from this disorder typically eat paint, plaster, string, hair, or cloth; older children may eat animal droppings, sand, insects, leaves, or pebbles. The risk of lead poisoning, which may result from the ingestion of paint or paint-soaked plaster, is high for minority children who live under poor housing conditions.

However, once again, the clinician needs to be sensitive to the cultural background of the child and his or her family. The ingestion of soil and clay, for example, is widespread and acceptable behavior among many cultures; clay eating has flourished among the women in the Ewe of Southwestern Ghana (Vermeer, 1971) and among African-American women in the southern United States (Edwards et al., 1964). In contrast, reports from Senegal describe a folk illness called *pobough lang* (Beiser, 1974), which consists of compulsive dirt eating and symptoms of pallor, abdominal swelling, shortness of breath, edema, and weakness; depression, anxiety, hopelessness, and nightmares often accompany this syndrome.

Gender Identity Disorders

The most common feature of this disorder is a strong identification with and preference for the gender role characteristics of the opposite sex. Cultures with rigid and clearly demarcated gender role expectations often strongly prohibit any ambiguity or tendency toward opposite-sex behavior. For children, disapproval from playmates and from the adults in their family causes frequent and strong feelings of low self-esteem, a sense of not belonging, and, often, depression and social withdrawal. A case vignette illustrates.

Clinical Vignette

Paul, a 12-year-old boy from a Caribbean culture who had a homosexual orientation, dressed as a girl, indicated a wish to be a girl, and described his penis as disgusting. He presented with severe symptoms of depression, low self-esteem, and suicidal thinking. Scapegoated severely in his town of origin, Paul was never invited anywhere, was physically abused by his peers, and had become a disgrace to his family.

Paul's social development had been impaired by his cultural context. He could no longer tolerate being in his family and being the object of discriminatory slurs. To spite his family and peers, he increasingly and openly asserted his femininity and dressed accordingly.

During the intervention the clinician addressed the anger of the child and his family. The family came to accept Paul's homosexual orientation, and he was transferred to a more tolerant school. As Paul entered adolescence, he expressed happiness with his body, dressed appropriately, and felt better about himself.

Elective Mutism

Maternal overprotection and immigration from a non-English-speaking country are risk factors in elective mutism (Bradley & Skloman, 1975). Additional risk factors include hospitalization (Browne, Wilson, & Laybourne, 1963), frequent family separations (Kolvin & Fundudis, 1981), and physical trauma such as child abuse and rape (Hayden, 1980).

Clinical Vignette

Luisa, a 5-year-old girl who had been speaking Spanish at home, became electively mute upon entering preschool. She spoke English to some neighbors and to her older sibling at home, but she refused to speak at school.

Luisa's parents, who had migrated from a Latino country, experienced serious adjustment problems to both the culture and the language of the United States. This difficulty prevented them from obtaining good jobs. As the family experienced a loss in income and social status, the father became depressed.

The services of a Latino community group were recruited to help the parents adjust to their new culture. The father started English language classes, and Luisa, with the support of her teachers, gradually began to speak at school.

Reactive Attachment Disorders

This disorder is observed in children from inner-city and rural areas who have been exposed to severe neglect, understimulation, isolation, and deprivation. A case vignette illustrates.

Clinical Vignette

M.J., a 7-year-old African-American girl, was referred to a community health center because she fought on the school playground, had temper tantrums, acted overly sensitive to criticism, and was excessively clingy and needy of adult attention. At the time of the referral, M.J., the eldest of a sibship of four, lived with her maternal grandparents and her 2-year-old sister. Her 1-year-old brother lived in foster care. Her 6-month-old brother reportedly lived with the mother, but their whereabouts were unknown. The grandmother reported that M.J. had been physically abused at intervals during the first 4 years of her life with her mother. At age 4, subsequent to a report and investigation, a child protective agency placed her in foster care. For the past 2 years, M.J. and her sister had lived with their grandparents, who had been named their legal guardians.

M.J.'s behavior in the diagnostic session was characteristic of children who have been subjected to multiple placements; that is, she responded to the female examiner immediately and at the end of the interview kissed her and exclaimed, "I love you." She typically manifested indiscriminate sociability and was unable to exhibit appropiate selective attachments.

M.J. expressed a wish to live with her mother and admitted to feeling sad or mean at times. Her depressed mood and other reactions to loss were also apparent in her drawings and in the stories she developed.

Pervasive Developmental Disorders

Pervasive developmental disorders have been described as "a group of neuropsychiatric disorders characterized by specific delays and deviance in social and communicative skills, and a number of unusual behavioral features often subsumed under the rubric of insistence on sameness" (Volkmar, 1991, p. 499). Childhood psychosis is not included in this diagnostic category, which recognizes autistic disorder as a subtype, because of the difficulties in assessment and the absence of research confirming a correspondence between autistic disorders in childhood and adult psychosis. Although not included in *DSM-IV Draft Criteria* (APA, 1993), childhood schizophrenia nevertheless continues to be discussed in the literature (Volkmar, 1991).

Pervasive developmental disorders, more common among the male population and in siblings of the afflicted child than in the general population, occurs in children of families at all socioeconomic levels. There may be a period of normal development, ranging from a few months to a few years, before evidence of the disorder is observed.

Verbal and nonverbal communication defects usually are the dominant features of autistic disorder. If speech is present, it is not used for social interaction. The uncontrolled repetition of words is commonplace, as is pronoun reversal and abnormal intonation, pitch, and rhythm. Islands of unusual ability in certain areas may be observed, but the overall cognitive development is markedly impaired. Behavior is characterized by stereotyped body movements. The child becomes agitated with changes in routine, lacks interest in or awareness of others, and shows pronounced preoccupation with inanimate objects.

Clinical Vignette

An African-American couple sought help for their 2½-year-old son, Tony, who was demonstrating "bizarre behavior." The parents described normal behavior, in their perception, for the first 2 years of Tony's life. Tony had originally spoken a few words —"mama," "daddy," "bye-bye"—but had been mute for the past 6 months. Tony also seemed unaware of his parents.

Tony's mother first wondered if he was experiencing pain when he flapped his hands and then suspected he had a hearing problem when he did not respond to verbal commands to quiet down at times of hyperactivity. The pediatrician, however, ruled out any physical problem.

During the examination period Tony made no eye contact with the psychiatrist. He remained unresponsive to the examiner's verbal communication and warded off any efforts for physical contact. He exhibited no interest in any of the toys offered to him, but at one point he picked up a block and began to pound it on his head. Most of the time he ran aimlessly around the room.

The clinician's diagnosis of autistic disorder and his indication of a poor prognosis proved especially distressing to the father, who had entertained high hopes for his only son. Both parents had struggled with poverty throughout their lives and held middle-class aspirations. It was apparent that the father's investment in Tony represented, in part, the hope for realization through his son of some of his own unmet goals. The psychiatrist recommended a series of sessions with the parents as a first step in treatment planning.

Mental Retardation

Some of the causative factors in mental retardation are environmental in nature. Some cases are related to maternal alcohol consumption during pregnancy; others result from fetal malnutrition and lead poisoning. Mental retardation can also result from deprivation of social, linguistic, and affective stimulation. The lower socioeconomic classes seem overrepresented in cases of the milder types of mental retardation in which there is no specific biologic causation.

Some studies (Ramirez & Smith, 1978; Reschly & Jipson, 1976) suggest a high prevalence of mental retardation among American Indian children and youth. Piasecki et al. (1989) claims that the conclusions are invalid for the broad segment of the American Indian population because subjects in such studies were limited to those in boarding schools. An in-depth study by Joe (1980) determined that some developmental disabilities and neurosensory disorders are 4 to 13 times more prevalent among Native Americans, as compared to the population of the United States as a whole. These disabilities account, in part, for certain other findings, for example, that 5% of the 350 educable subjects were mentally handicapped and 34% were learning disabled (Joe, 1980).

Prematurity, which is coupled with low birth weight, is known to be one of the factors involved in developmental disorders. African-American adolescent mothers are at greatest risk for the delivery of low birth weight infants. These young mothers are least likely to receive adequate prenatal care, compounding the risk their children face (Carter, 1983).

The course of mental retardation, particularly the milder forms, is strongly associated with environmental influences: Positive influences improve the child's functioning; poor influences cause a deterioration. Early diagnosis and intervention provided by competent screening and service facilities can make a considerable difference. An awareness of the cultural meaning of mental retardation is crucial. Some cultures feel shame about the intellectual limitations of their children and may postpone or delay appropriate intervention.

In diagnosing developmental disorders the clinician must be sensitive to the parents, culture, and social class. Children arriving from agrarian and socioeconomically stressed societies with limited educational opportunities may have functioned appropriately within that system; consequently, their specific developmental disorder may not have been identified. Developmental problems may be observed when such children enter our highly industrialized society and a school system that requires particular skills. The child may be channeled toward a special class and may be given a diagnosis without adequate explanation to the family and without assessing if a stigma is associated with this new characterization. A case vignette illustrates the traumas experienced by a developmentally delayed child who was initially diagnosed as having a more severe form of mental retardation.

Clinical Vignette

Luis, a 4-year-old boy from a small Caribbean island, was a new arrival to New York City. His mother had recently died of terminal cancer, and Luis was sent to live with his aunt, his only surviving relative. Luis, who was not toilet trained, had no intelligible speech, could barely walk, had numerous repetitive mannerisms, lacked imaginative activity, and had few, if any, social skills. He did not respond to age-mates or adults.

Luis had been born to a poor single mother in a small agrarian village. His mother became ill with a slowly debilitating and terminal cancer soon after his birth. Unable to care for her child and with little social support, the mother had left Luis in a covered chicken hut, where he was fed but never talked to or stimulated.

After an extensive evaluation Luis was placed in a therapeutic all-day nursery. With the help of nursery staff and a devoted aunt, Luis began to respond. One year after treatment was implemented, Luis began to make gains in speech and motor development. His greatest advancement was in the social arena: he became an outgoing and smiling preschooler. On final assessment Luis was diagnosed with a mild mental retardation.

Specific Developmental Disorders

Developmental disorders are characterized by inadequate development of specific academic speech, language, and motor skills. Before making a diagnosis of a developmental disorder, the clinician needs to review the child's pediatric chart to rule out any vision or hearing problems. Additionally, the clinician must be aware of the quality of the child's present schooling. Some inner-city schools are unable to meet the needs of the increasing number of children in their classrooms. The schools are often understaffed and the teachers overworked. Many children may thus perform poorly on tests measuring academic functioning.

Children from families who speak non-Standard English or a language other than English must be evaluated carefully. They may demonstrate a limited vocabulary and speak in simple sentences or only in the present tense in Standard English but may be fully expressive in their language of origin. Some may be undergoing a transition to true bilingualism and may be struggling with limited skills in both languages.

Standardized measures to evaluate both intelligence and learning difficulties must be administered sensitively and, most of all, interpreted sensitively when utilized with inner-city children, who often attend inadequate schools and whose skills in an academically oriented world are difficult to measure. The clinician needs to consider the impact of high levels of chronic stress, of environments that lack stimulation for and encouragement of academic success, and of exposure to endless hours of television.

AXIS III OF DSM-IV: GENERAL MEDICAL CONDITIONS

The lives of all poor children but especially children of the minority poor, have always been marked by disadvantage, depression, danger, and death. Basic health care statistics provide a consistent picture of increased morbidity and mortality for this group of children (Mitchell & Heagarty, 1991). Axis III allows mental health clinicians to indicate any physical condition or disorder that is relevant to understanding or managing a patient. For the purpose of this diagnostic classification the medical condition must "cause clinically significant distress or impairment in social, occupational, or other important areas of functioning" (APA, 1993, p. B:7). Some clinical suggestions accompany the following review of the most prevalent physical problems associated with behavioral or cognitive difficulties in minority populations.

Infectious Diseases

The United States and South Africa are unique among industrialized nations in their failure to provide all children and families basic health protection against illness. The U.S. decline in immunization rates has been accompanied by a concomitant increase in the incidence of preventable childhood diseases. Nonwhite 1-year-old infants in the United States are less likely to be fully immunized against polio than

1-year-olds in 47 countries (*SOS America*, 1990). Despite advances in the development of antibiotic therapy, the rates of childhood contagious diseases, tuberculosis, and rheumatic fever continue to be significantly higher for minority children than for other groups (Mitchell & Heagarty, 1991). Thus, rates of hospitalization, missed school days due to medical illness, and disabilities are high and often interfere with the smooth psychosocial development of minority children.

Lead Poisoning

An estimated one in six children in the United States is at risk of lead poisoning. No group of children is free from lead exposure, but poor children in the inner cities face the greatest risks (*SOS America*, 1990). Clinicians who evaluate children who live in poverty-stricken areas must be aware of the possibility of lead poisoning and its potential consequences.

Children who reside in old and deteriorated housing and who are at the crawling stage or suffer from pica are exposed to high levels of lead. Minority children who reside in highly congested urban areas also may be exposed to lead in the soil and air from gasoline combustion. Some lead is present in areas with factories that produce lead-glazed ceramics. Folk remedies that use lead-containing substances are another source of exposure: For example, many low-income Mexican children may be treated for *empacho*, an illness manifested by gastrointestinal symptoms and diarrhea, with lead tetraoxide, or *azarcon*, with lead carbonate, or *albayalde*, or with lead monoxide, or *greta* (Balk, Garcia De Alba, Cueto, Ackerman, & Davison, 1989). The aggregate exposure to all these sources can produce an elevated toxicity risk (Mushak & Crocetti, 1989).

The U.S. Environmental Protection Agency (1986) warns that a blood level of "10 to 15 µg/dl and possibly lower" constitutes a level of concern for developmental neurotoxicity. High lead levels prove damaging and frequently are diagnosed and treated in pediatric clinics. Even though inconclusive, some well-controlled studies show a tendency for low to moderate blood lead levels in children to be related to higher scores on measures of aggressive/antisocial/hyperactive behaviors (Thomson et al., 1989) and to difficulties in visual motor integration (Winneke, Brockhaus, Ewers, Kramer, & Neuf, 1990) and visual spatial integration (Dietrich, Succop, Berger, Hammond, & Bornschein, 1991).

The mental health clinician must be aware of the need for supportive services for those children with high levels of lead but also sensitive to those minority children with moderate or lower lead levels who initially may be identified by their cognitive and behavioral difficulties, such as a learning disability or an attention deficit disorder with hyperactivity. Since many of these children are simultaneously exposed to a series of other insults in their environment, it comes as no surprise that they exhibit greater cognitive difficulties than do children with similar lead levels who come from families of higher socioeconomic status (Bellinger, Leviton, Needleman, Rabinowitz, & Waternaux, 1988). The clinician must try to identify potential risk factors during the initial history taking and should arrange for blood lead level testing if lead poisoning is suspected.

Fetal Alcohol Syndrome

Available data emphasize the need for the clinician to be alert to the possibility of fetal alcohol syndrome (FAS) and its sequelae in minority group children. Health units serving principally Navajo Pueblo tribes report an FAS prevalence similar to that of the overall U.S. population, whereas a much higher prevalence was reported for the Southwest Plains Indians (May, Hymbaugh, Aase, & Sumet, 1983). Factors such as cultural influences, patterns of alcohol consumption, nutrition, and metabolic differences have been postulated to play a role in this difference (Aase, Hymbaugh, May, & Sumet, 1983). African-Americans have a risk of FAS that is seven times as high as for whites, even after adjustment for the frequency of maternal alcohol intake, occurrence of chronic alcohol problems, and parity (number of children born) is made (Sokol et al., 1986).

FAS can cause prenatal and postnatal growth retardation, central nervous system involvement, and a characteristic face with short palpebral fissures, a thin upper lip, and an elongated flattened midface (Sokol & Clarren, 1989). Mental retardation and problems with learning, memory, and attention are common sequelae. Incoordination, hyperactivity, impulsiveness, and speech and hearing problems can be observed as well (Streissguth & La Due, 1985; Streissguth, Sampson, & Barr, 1989). Children often vary in the presentation of these symptoms; consequently, FAS may not always be easily identified. A thorough history of maternal alcohol abuse and a careful review of the prenatal chart is indicated.

Acquired Immunodeficiency Syndrome (AIDS)

The newborn child of a mother who has AIDS is at high risk of acquiring the disease. Unfortunately, numerous social stressors confront these mothers and contribute to their failure to identify their own HIV seropositivity during their pregnancy. In many cases these mothers also have a history of multiple substance abuse and have been exposed to multiple traumas themselves. Of those children infected during the prenatal period, 80% represent minority groups and the nation's poorest citizens (Centers for Disease Control, 1989). The figures also show that 23% of children (birth to age 12) with AIDS are Latinos (U.S. Congress, 1989b).

The developmental course for many of these children will be characterized by a gradual but progressive decline in language skills and in motor and adaptive functioning while others will experience an episodic course, with periods of deterioration alternating with periods of neurologic stability (Belman, Diamond, & Dickson, 1988). Infected children may lose previously acquired social skills, develop a change in gait, initiate toe walking, become apathetic, and decrease their gestures and vocalizations. Those in the final stages become mute, dull-eyed, and quadriparetic (having incomplete paralysis of the four limbs) (Belman et al., 1988; Belman, 1990). Loss of interest in school, psychomotor retardation, the development or worsening of attention deficit disorders, and an increase in emotional lability or social withdrawal may occur in older children (Belman, 1990). As the course of this illness may vary, the clinician must follow these cases carefully and watch for the development or worsening of cognitive functions and behavior. In view of the multiple secondary stressors in the family unit and in the school, it often proves difficult to determine the etiology of a new symptom.

Older male adolescents of ethnic minorities who reside in large urban areas predominate among adolescents with AIDS: African-Americans make up 12% of the male population aged 13 to 24 but represent 35% of the AIDS cases for this age group (U.S. Congress, 1989a). This higher proportion of cases reflects heterosexual contact and intravenous drug use among African-American and Latino adolescents and seems to explain in part the higher proportion of infected females in these groups (Gayle & D'Angelo, 1991). Adolescents who are runaways or crack users and who are involved with older male partners are at increased risk of AIDS infection as well (Stricof, Novick, Kennedy, & Welfuse, 1988; Fullilove & Fullilove, 1989; Remafedi, 1987).

Bouknight and Bouknight (1988) have addressed the effect of a culture's belief system on risk-taking behavior. For many minority communities, childbearing is highly valued, and male domination in matters of sexual behavior and contraceptive practices is common. Consequently, messages of condom use targeted to women may be ineffective. Lack of knowledge about prevention of HIV infection (DiClemente, Boyer, & Morales, 1988); homophobia in certain minority groups, leading to denial of bisexual or homosexual behavior (Mitchell & Heagarty, 1991); and health behavior patterns in which medical care is sought only during a medical crisis often combine with little education on health maintenance and a distrust of public agencies (Mitchell & Heagarty, 1991) to create additional risk factors.

Other Physical Problems

The clinician should inquire about allergies, asthma, tropical diseases, blood dyscrasias, parasitosis, or genetic illnesses to which certain cultural groups may be exposed or predisposed. It is particularly important to assess the prevalence of etiologic agents that may cause subtle or severe cognitive impairment in children. Infections, nutritional deficiency, and head injuries may vary across localities and cultural groups. Early signs of cognitive impairment may not be identified until a child is exposed to the high academic demands of a technical and industrialized society.

The presence of sickle cell anemia in this population needs to be considered. A case vignette illustrates the relevance of this information for a mental health clinician.

Clinical Vignette

Jamal, a 10-year-old African-American boy with sickle cell anemia, came to the mental health clinic with a complaint of headaches and frequent pains in his stomach. Jamal's mother had already taken him to a pediatrician because the symptoms were similar to those at the beginning of a sickle cell crisis, but there was no indication of any change in his blood morphology. The pediatrician referred her to a child psychiatrist who saw Jamal and decided to learn more about the disease. He worked closely with Jamal's primary doctor and identified current stressors in the child's life. The mother was involved in reducing the stressors and educated about the difference between somatic and real symptoms in her child.

An assessment of a child's dietary habits and nutritional status is crucial. School lunch may be the only balanced meal for inner-city children. Often, children arrive at school without having had breakfast and may be irritable, inattentive, and distracted as a consequence. Poor heating during the winter months at home and at school results in unresolved chronic upper respiratory infections, which affect a child's capacity and motivation to learn, as do injuries from the home-related accidents that are common in substandard housing.

AXIS IV OF DSM-IV: PSYCHOSOCIAL AND ENVIRONMENTAL PROBLEMS

The clinician's assessment of the severity of a particular psychosocial stressor on a particular patient needs to be based on his or her determination of the stress an "average" child in similar circumstances and with similar sociocultural values would experience from that particular stressor. Such an assessment also involves consideration of the amount of change the stressor causes in the patient's life, the degree to which the event is desired and under the control of the patient, and the number of other stressors the patient must cope with. Types of psychosocial stressors to be considered include problems with primary support groups, problems related to the social environment, and educational problems (APA, 1993, p. D:5).

Finally, the clinician must be certain that the evaluation of psychosocial stressors includes the impact of overt or covert discrimination by race, creed, or color; inadequate schools; and life in a community that is beset by crime and substance abuse and that offers few recreational opportunities. The following newspaper report describes some of the psychosocial stressors in the life of a inner-city adolescent:

> Marcus Tramble, an urban survivalist, follows [the] law [of the street] as closely as he can.
>
> For years his daily decisions have been governed by his fear of dying young, another victim of the violence that hovers over his world. There are places he will not go, clothes he will not wear, words he will not say and feelings he will not let out.
>
> Stay away from that street corner: it's a crack dealer's hangout. Don't wear a baseball cap; cocked the wrong way it can be a gang symbol and a magnet for violence. Never say anything, even in jest, that can be taken as an insult; retribution can be deadly.
>
> But some things Marcus cannot control: his skin color, his size, his youth. When he looks into the mirror he sees not a monster or a mugger but a slender brown-skinned teen-ager, 6 feet 3 inches tall, with hair cropped close on the sides and a smile that breaks out more easily than these mean streets would seem to warrant.
>
> When he goes out, though, Marcus feels accused of a crime he knows nothing about. (Terry, 1993, p. 1)

Clinicians must also consider a child's adaptive (or maladaptive) response style to a particular stressor and must be aware of culturally/ socially syntonic or dystonic responses. In the case of recent immigrants, clinicians must direct their attention to the psychosocial stressors related to cultural and economic shifts.

AXIS V OF DSM-IV: GLOBAL ASSESSMENT OF FUNCTIONING

Axis V allows clinicians to indicate their overall judgment of an individual's psychological, social, and occupational functioning on the Global Assessment of Functioning (GAF) Scale. DSM-III-R (APA, 1987, p. 20) specifies that two ratings on this scale need to be made: a rating of the level of functioning at the time of the evaluation and a rating of the highest level of functioning for at least a few months during the previous year. For children and adolescents this should cover at least a month during the school year. In view of the fact that symptoms are often a response to the frequent life stressors these children are exposed to, both assessments are crucial in making a prognosis.

The GAF Scale most likely provides the best assessment of the true functioning of the child. In a study in Puerto Rico, prevalence rates of all disorders based on DSM-III-R diagnoses yielded an estimate of 49.5% for children aged 4 to 16. When the presence of a DSM-III-R diagnosis was considered along with Children's Global Assessment Scale (CGAS) scores lower than 61, the prevalence decreased to 18.4% (Bird et al., 1990).

After making their own assessment, clinicians should compare their findings with those of other mental health professionals involved with the child as well as with the opinions of the child's parents and teachers.

CONCLUDING COMMENTS

The clinician's diagnostic tools undergo constant revision as researchers continue the ongoing struggle to resolve their many limitations. Hopefully, future developments will help clinicians organize behaviors more cogently, thus facilitating differentiation and diagnosis of true disorders, and will provide better information about appropriate approaches both for responding at the physiological and psychological levels of the patient and for intervening in the environment. Clinicians should be knowledgeable about the cultural idioms of dis-

tress and about culture-bound syndromes; elicit the parents' explana-
tory models of illness; contextualize the diagnosis; and be aware of
the potential cultural biases affecting the diagnosis and prognosis
(Kleinman, 1993). For now, clinicians need to be knowledgeable about
current diagnostic criteria in order to organize their understanding of
the presenting case, recommend treatment approaches, and deliver
services. The course of the psychiatric disorder or syndrome continues to be dependent not only upon the efforts of good clinicians but
upon the coping resources of the patient and family, family relationships (Jenkins & Karno, 1992), and successful involvement with the
welfare and medical systems.

When presenting diagnostic information to patients and their
families, the clinician should advise them of the limited state of the
art, take care not to blame the victim, present the information in a
clear and contextually sensitive manner, and allow ample time for
further discussion and exploration. All possible treatment alternatives
need to be explored thoroughly.

A comprehensive description of all current diagnostic categories
of mental disorder extends beyond the scope of this book. Consequently, the focus of this chapter has been on those diagnostic categories that are most frequently relevant to work with minority children. As many of the case vignettes in this book illustrate, success in
meeting the diagnostic challenge paves the way for selecting the most
appropriate treatment interventions, interventions that demonstrate
that the clinician as diagnostician and advocate can at times ameliorate or resolve the presenting problem.

THE TREATMENT
OF MINORITY CHILDREN

✦

An estimated 70% to 80% of approximately 7.5 to 9.5 million children with emotional problems are not getting the help they need (*SOS America*, 1990). Recent estimates for the population under 18 years of age needing treatment for mental illness at any one time ranges from 7 to 12 million or 10% of all children and adolescents in the country (Gould, Wunsch-Hitzig, & Dohrenwend, 1981).

Knowledge of child and adolescent psychiatric treatment lags significantly behind that of adult treatment. Treatment efficacy and specificity continue to be evasive and difficult subjects to approach both clinically and in research. Multiple approaches claim effectiveness for a host of psychiatric syndromes. Some approaches seem to work better than others for certain syndromes, but a flexible and integrated approach of several therapeutic interventions often is needed to maximize the impact of treatment. The added variables of rapid psychobiological developmental change in childhood, the exquisite reactiveness of children to their immediate environment, and the lack of consensus about what truly constitutes mental disorder in children compound the problem of providing effective treatment to minority group children.

CHAPTER 5

Culturally Sensitive
Therapeutic Interventions

✦

VARIABLES INFLUENCING TREATMENT
AND ITS EFFECTIVENESS

Service Utilization Patterns

The process of seeking mental health services emerges as a complex
phenomenon. Variables such as parental tolerance of deviant behavior, level of parental education and psychopathology, the extent of
externalizing or internalizing behavior on the part of the child, and
level of functional impairment often determine when and how the
parents seek help as well as whom they choose to approach. This process is more complex for the minority and culturally diverse populations.

A frequent claim is that some minority groups underutilize mental health services. For example, it has been reported that Mexican-
Americans do not seek counseling services either in community mental
health centers or in academic counseling centers (Keefe & Casas, 1980;
Sanchez & Atkinson, 1983; Wells, Hough, Golding, Burnam, &
Karno, 1987). This is explained in part by the fact that cultural groups
differ in their help-seeking behavior and in their treatment expectations (Giordano & Giordano, 1977; Tseng & McDermott, 1981).

African-Americans often mistrust help from traditional institutions other than their churches (McAdoo, 1977). They are likely to
tolerate problems and are not inclined to explain or understand them
because of a "strong and religious orientation" (Hines & Boyd-
Franklin, 1982, p. 10). To many, the "wages of sin" or failure to

"practice biblical principles" are acceptable explanations for their emotional problems.

For members of some cultures a certain amount of stigma accompanies mental illness. In addition, members of some cultures use somatic symptoms to express psychological distress; the psychological self is not separate from the physical self. Puerto Ricans (Garcia-Preto, 1982) and Chinese (Tseng & McDermott, 1981), for example, often express distress by somatizing and may seek services for physical, rather than psychological, distress. Furthermore, minority groups may perceive their problems as a consequence of their own actions or shortcomings or of the actions of others (Jones & Korchin, 1982; McGoldrick, 1982).

Other factors are equally important: Only 26% of the children receiving services in a Puerto Rican study saw mental health professionals in mental health facilities (Bird et al., 1991); the majority received services from guidance counselors in their public schools. This practice raises many policy and resource allocation questions: Are children with problems better identified and treated within the schools? Are the schools more accessible and sensitive to the particular communities they serve? Are children receiving help in the schools because of a paucity of better services in their communities?

Additionally, treatment facilities for those children from culturally diverse backgrounds must be accessible and provide comprehensive and culturally sensitive services. Rogler, Blumenthal, Malgady, and Costantino (1985) identified three ways in which mental health services can be rendered more culturally sensitive to ethnocultural minorities: increase accessibility to psychotherapy by locating mental health clinics in minority group neighborhoods close to public transportation; employ mental health workers who share the linguistic and cultural backgrounds of the patients; and create an ambience that reflects the cultural heritage of the client population. Friedson (1961) reported that low levels of professional health service utilization occur when there are differences between an ethnic group's and the professional community's understanding of an illness and its treatment and when a cohesive and extended indigenous lay referral structure exists.

In some cultures individuals seek relief and solutions outside the mental health system. To serve those who are unable to heal within these other networks, professionals must penetrate the lay referral structure by assimilating some members of the ethnic network into the professional structure. It has been suggested that a client's initial registration at a mental health facility be informal and immediate (Flores, 1978). Drop-in centers should be encouraged, and services should initially be crisis-oriented, with immediate social service assistance and/or medical care available. Any service delivery system or model that purports to be culturally sensitive must address the preferences and needs of the populations it seeks to serve.

Clinician Variables

Clinician variables, difficult but not impossible to assess, most likely exert a greater impact on the success or failure of treatment strategies with children than with adults. Clinician age, sex, and ethnicity, as well as empathic and perceptive skills, emerge as variables that need to balance well with theoretical orientation and an ability to interact and communicate with children. The clinician who works with children must be willing to be straightforward and honest, intellectually curious and flexible, and emotionally able to deal with the psychological challenges of the young patient.

Additionally, mental health workers who treat a member of any minority group must be aware that sociocultural factors from both the therapist's and the patient's culture enter the therapeutic relationship. By virtue of the training they receive, many therapists bring to the relationship the values and beliefs upon which Western psychology and psychiatry were founded; other therapists may come from countries and backgrounds immersed in Eastern philosophy and traditions. By contrast, the patient may hold an entirely different set of values and beliefs. No therapist can claim to be aware of all the nuances of a culture that differs from her or his own or to be free of cultural biases.

Many of these variables become compounded in work with inner-city children. Children often depend on adults to identify their symptoms and to refer and transport them to the appropriate services. As the impact of multiple environmental stressors interacts with family dynamics within a specific cultural framework, it becomes more difficult to differentiate sociocultural, familial, or child-related problems. Clinicians, who often need to implement a treatment strategy that embraces all three problem areas, are taxed to become environmental strategist, family therapist, and child expert. Commonly, clinicians need to juggle sociocultural principles with their neurodevelopmental knowledge to become eclectic, ecologically minded systems brokers without losing sight of the fine cultural, intrapsychic, and developmental dimensions of the assigned case.

Finally, to implement adequate approaches, clinicians must obtain the support of an effective interdisciplinary team, remain abreast of new knowledge evolving in the field, and garner the appropriate resources to implement comprehensive plans. Unfortunately, this represents the ideal, not the usual, situation. Clinicians often must limit their goals owing to "clinical overload" and consequently must limit the time they spend on interdisciplinary efforts and education. Their clinical skills become subservient to the priorities of the often underfunded agencies in which they work, and this results in the implementation of approaches that by their very nature are ineffective.

Many culturally sensitive treatment approaches have been developed despite these limitations. A review of these treatment approaches follows. The final portion of the chapter proposes a model that allows for the inclusion of culturally sensitive therapeutic interventions within a comprehensive theoretical framework appropriate for work with minority group children and their families.

CULTURALLY SENSITIVE TREATMENT APPROACHES: A REVIEW

Interpersonal Approaches

Katz (1981) suggests that individual treatment should address the cultural differences between the clinician and the patient as soon as possible and that prejudice and stereotyping can be bidirectional, that is, that stereotyping of both the dominant and the minority culture may occur. Clearly, patients should be evaluated on an individual basis, but therapists may erroneously attribute to their patients cultural traits that may not be present or may fail to recognize traits that are.

Pinderhughes (1989) observes that since the feelings aroused in clinicians who work with patients whose culture differs from their own "are more frequently than not negative and driven by anxiety, they can interfere with successful therapeutic outcome" (p. 21). Bradshaw (1978) calls attention to the fact that the cultural distance between therapist and client serves to trigger an unconscious use of distancing and defense mechanisms. Self-knowledge can control such maneuvers and enable the therapist to be more sensitive toward people of different cultures and races (Pinderhughes, 1989).

Cultural values about personal relationships affect the patient–therapist interaction. In the following excerpt Kunce and Vales (1984) discuss Mexican-American patients:

> When the counsellor becomes viewed as a personal friend, that counsellor may later be rejected for not living up to the client's expectations for overt assistance and concern. . . .

Another prevalent way of relating to persons in authority is to fore-stall responsibility or action by responding to requests in a genial, polite, and accommodating fashion that belies one's true intention of not con-forming. A closely allied strategy is the use of either flattery or saying what the official wants to hear to divert attention away from one's per-sonal problems. . . .

In the Mexican culture being late for appointments and social events is commonplace and under many circumstances expected. These types of behavior can create considerable frustration to the counsellor who needs to meet schedules. (pp. 104–105)

Minrath (1985) suggests that white therapists should examine their underlying prejudicial beliefs and attitudes. She delineates sev-eral unconscious reasons whites may want to work with minority populations, reasons that, if gone unexamined, could impede thera-peutic progress. These include a desire to resolve identity issues, to cure social ills, and to achieve a sense of superiority, as they actually view the minority patient as inferior. She also calls attention to the likelihood that clinicians, overwhelmed with "white guilt," often wonder about their own contribution to oppression and may become anxious and preoccupied when treating the urban poor. Therapists who become distant and detached are unable to listen sensitively to their patients. They become sympathetic instead of empathic and must consult a supervisor to resolve these issues.

A potential for conflict exists with culturally homogeneous patient–therapist dyads. Pinderhughes (1989) notes that clinicians can have a blind spot and may perceive patients from their own culture as being like themselves. This interferes with treatment, as these clini-cians fail to explore the meaning of events for their patient and assume the issues are similar to their own.

Many minority patients must be informed about the purpose of questions pertaining to clinical history, previous treatment informa-tion, family background, and psychosocial stressors (Tsui & Schultz, 1985). If during the initial assessment the need for a more psycho-dynamic approach is recommended, educating the patient about the therapeutic process becomes important. Patients, particularly immi-grant patients, may have had little exposure to mental health ap-proaches and may view such treatment as irrelevant to their illness and not return. For example, Yamamoto (1982) contends that to overcome the barrier to treatment on the part of Japanese-Americans, a good educational campaign is necessary.

Minority patients may perceive therapists to be knowledgeable experts who will guide the family's behavior in the proper course of action. Viewed as authority figures and respected as such, therapists need to convey an air of confidence and should not hesitate to make reference to their educational background and work experience (Lee, 1982). It may prove helpful for therapists to be well informed about the patient's history and to show the patient that they have considerable knowledge of his or her background. Thus, "How's your headache?" as the first question may be more sensitive than "How can I help you?" or "Can you tell me more about yourself?"

Therapists working with Asian-American patients must be sensitive to issues of shame and guilt when probing for personal information. To avoid leaving patients with the impression that they have "caused" their problems, therapists must help them understand that people often encounter difficult situations as the result of inevitable and unavoidable circumstances. In effect, the clinician uses the cultural belief in "fate to neutralize the client's excessive guilt and reponsibility" (Tsui & Schultz, 1985).

Many Asians express love through caring or tending to physical needs; consequently, "just listening" may be interpreted by them as "noncaring" (Hsu, 1983). An active demonstration of care, such as showing concern over a patient's physical condition or sleep pattern or prescribing some common remedies for the usual discomforts, is useful in establishing and maintaining good rapport (Hsu, 1983). Therapists should acknowledge and treat the patient's reported physical symptoms. A didactic component often facilitates the therapist's understanding that the patient's suffering is real. For those Asian-Americans who have not acculturated, comments such as "Your facial color looks better today" or "You ought to eat more vegetables" convey concern and care.

When rating the directive style of counseling, Korean subjects who were born in Korea and presently resided there provided higher ratings of counselor effectiveness, expertness, attractiveness, and trustworthiness than when therapy was nondirective (Foley & Fuqua, 1988). Of course these findings would only be relevant to first-generation Korean-Americans. The instruments used were the Counselor Rating Form and the Counselor Effectiveness Rating Scale.

Franklin (1982), who writes about individual therapy with urban African-American adolescents, identifies some ways traditional techniques can be modified to suit this population. Since many youths are referred by an outside authority figure, he suggests that it is important for the therapist not to be cast in the same role. To counteract this impression, a more active role is indicated in order for the therapist to be seen as empathic and caring. Additionally, therapists need to explain their own role as well as the extent of the adolescent's responsibility in the therapeutic process.

Paster (1985) makes a similar point and advocates the use of therapy contracts with poor, depressed, and acting-out African-American male adolescents. The therapist and youth agree upon a trial period of 6 to 8 weeks of therapy and discuss the adolescent's goals for therapy. At the end of the trial period the therapist and patient decide if a continuation of treatment is warranted or desired. Giving the adolescent an active part in the therapy "defuses dropout as a symbolic gesture of independence" (p. 413).

Franklin (1982) also delineates a series of "roles" that may be adapted by some adolescents to either test the therapist or stalemate the process of therapy:

> There are those who become mummified as a test of strength to endure the stress of silence; you will also encounter the seducer, who seeks validation from you as they do from their peers; the starer, who will rivet you with constant eye contact; and the abuser, who will verbally or physically try to intimidate you. The basic dynamic issue in the first sessions of therapy with the adolescent is one of control. The streetwise kid is very adept at maintaining control over the situation by adopting various roles. (p. 278)

The literature reports success in the use of psychoanalytically oriented individual psychotherapy of some inner-city African-American children (Meers, 1970; Spurlock & Cohen, 1969). The following vignette illustrates how combining the ego capacity, motivation, and energy levels of the patient with the motivation of the therapist allowed Carol, a 15-year-old African-American, to expand her ego and her life.

Clinical Vignette

Carol, the older of two daughters, was referred because of dizzy spells, mild palpitations, and anxiety attacks in school, where she was entering her junior high school year. She lived with her parents and sister in a housing project in the ghetto area. The family was supported by disability and blind assistance allotments because of the father's failing eyesight. Carol was seen for two periods of treatment by the same social worker: The first period ended when she completed high school, one-and-a-half years after referral. The second period was of two-and-a-half years' duration, from the time she was eighteen-and-a-half until she became twenty-one. Both parents were seen for the diagnostic evaluation. Neither parent was referred for treatment. Early in the treatment experience, a marked change in the family dynamics occurred: With a worsening of his visual problem, the father began to display paranoid and violent behavior. The mother responded by turning to Carol with the expectation that her "emergence into the labor market would provide an exit from life in the housing project ghetto." Carol, always a passive, compliant child with reaction formation defenses against anger, could not manage her rage over the obstruction of her long-standing wish to go to college, nor could she endure the guilt over separation wishes which defended her against sexual interest in boys. This is not to imply that Carol had no regressive wishes for the sadomasochistic and dependent gratification available from the mother. However, she effectively used her therapy to deal with the ambivalence, separation, and budding sexual interests so as to complete high school, to enter the local teacher's college, acquire part-time employment, and leave the therapist.

A bit over a year after termination of the first period of therapy, Carol called her therapist with complaints of panic and trembling on the job and in classroom recitations. She was taken back into treatment immediately, the foci of which were (1) to mitigate the intense rage and tie to the mother; (2) to support her against her regressive wishes; and (3) to help her achieve a sense of self-confidence in her reasonable dating patterns which were opposed by both parents.

The passive-aggressive defense against helplessness in the face of parental demands and social deprivation began to crumble as Carol experienced the therapist's confidence in her, which was supported by the larger culture. Carol's sense of autonomy expanded, and she became cognitively aware of the personal and social opportunity to make choices. Although she made much progress in achieving her goals, she could not move away from home when invited to do so by friends. (Spurlock & Cohen, 1969, pp. 28–29)

In the preceding vignette the therapist suggested that the patient apply for financial assistance as a means of relieving her guilt about choosing school rather than the full-time employment that would have allowed her to make a financial contribution to her family. Work with inner-city children, adolescents, and their families often calls for and involves collaborative efforts with another service agency to assist with handling pragmatic issues.

References have been made to the similarity of goals in individual psychotherapy with African-American children and those of the dominant group. There may be, however, a need to introduce parameters. As indicated previously, attention should be directed to specific culturally related transferences and countertransferences that may develop (Spurlock, 1985).

A segment of a resident's notes (minimally revised) provides a glimpse into psychotherapy with an 8-year-old African-American inner-city boy:

There was no need to introduce parameters in the individual treatment (which followed a period of work in a group). The child responded to confrontations with apparent interest and eagerness to examine a bit of behavior and readily supplied associations in the effort to "find other pieces to the puzzles of my life" (this was a reflection of his long-standing exposure to the television "soaps"). As in other therapeutic encounters, the therapist was supportive of the child's self-mastery and his movement in the direction of reinforcing those behaviors which decreased the sense of his inability to control his impulses. (Spurlock, 1985, p. 173)

In work with inner-city African-American children, Spurlock finds it helpful to see the patient and parents together for the initial session for the purpose of providing an explanation about the nature of the therapeutic process. This procedure is followed regardless of any previous contact with other staff. The rationale is twofold: to provide specific information about the process and ample time for questions and clarification and to grant the patient and the parent(s) an opportunity to size up the therapist and ask questions (such as "Have you ever worked with other families like us?"). This kind of orientation is particularly helpful with those families (regardless of race and ethnicity) who have experienced "investigative interviews" and are weary of revealing information that might disqualify them from the assistance they seek.

The telling of African folk tales is sometimes useful in work with African-American youngsters. Often, the content of the tale fosters or reinforces the self-esteem of youngsters who believe primarily negative things about the African-American culture. The playing of certain audiotapes (e.g., *African American Folktales* [Kaula, 1969], read by Brock Peters and Diana Sands) that incorporate a lesson in the narrative has been particularly useful in work with younger children as well as in training programs for mental health professionals who are unfamiliar with African-American culture.

Indigenous Healer–Therapist Interventions

The members of many cultures in the United States avail themselves of indigenous sources of help when they are under physical or emotional distress. Belief in these indigenous sources is so strong for some that this alone determines their health-seeking efforts. For others, the use of indigenous sources can be explained in part by several factors: a lack of awareness of the public or private health services in their area, the geographic and/or financial inaccessibility of services, the unavailability of culturally or linguistically sensitive services, and a previous failure on the part of public health services to reduce the distress.

Unfortunately, there is little in the literature (Bird & Canino, 1981) that describes the utilization pattern of indigenous healers for child- and adolescent-related problems. Clinicians who work in the public health sector must be aware of both the strengths and the limitations of indigenous assessment and treatment approaches and must be willing to respect and integrate these cultural beliefs into their theoretical framework, if necessary.

For example, clinicians need to devise ways to incorporate traditional American Indian therapies, such as sweat lodges, vision quests, and clan-based dances, into community-wide interventions (Beauvais et al., 1985). A combination of American Indian and Western techniques can be used with American Indians who believe in medicine men/women. The following vignette highlights such an approach:

Clinical Vignette

P.B., an 11-year-old Navajo girl, resided at a boarding school during the week and spent weekends with her family. P.B.'s 6-year-old brother had fallen into an irrigation ditch over the summer break and had suffered irreversible brain damage. During the second month of school, P.B.'s teachers and dormitory aides reported that she was extremely quiet and cried often. Additionally, P.B. was failing a majority of her subjects.

The school counselor made a referral to a local Indian mental health clinic. Both P.B. and her mother were seen. P.B. spoke of frequent dreams of deceased relatives since her brother's injury and admitted to hearing the voices of a deceased brother asking her to join him. She admitted to loss of appetite, difficulty in falling asleep, and fears of ghosts and spirits who were after her. The mother, school counselor, and one dormitory aide were educated about the expression of bereavement and depression in childhood, and all were encouraged to aid P.B. in talking about her feelings. The therapist, aware of the taboo against talking about the dead, encouraged P.B. to draw pictures, as a channel for ventilating her feelings. A traditional medicine man ceremony was held by the family, and P.B. was given antidepressant medication as she began ego-supportive therapy. Her symptoms gradually remitted over a period of 6 months.

Short-Term Therapy

Evelyn Lee (1988) observes that long-term talk therapy is too foreign for many Southeast Asian patients, many of whom are new immigrants. Such a claim has been made for Latino families as well. Thus,

short-term time-limited therapy that focuses on the presenting problems and on the present and immediate future has been recommended
for these groups. The therapy needs to be goal directed toward relieving symptoms or resolving a crisis. In the initial session the therapist
should identify a measurable goal, such as the regaining of the patient's
ability to eat, sleep, and work normally. The most effective approach
is that of crisis intervention, offering the patient immediate emotional
and environmental first-aid and the opportunity to express feelings
before plunging into history taking and finding solutions.

It often becomes necessary for the therapist to perform multiple
functions before engaging the patient in a therapeutic relationship,
functions such as serving as a social service worker by securing the
relevant and necessary social and medical assistance, serving as a health
educator who informs the client about the nature of Western medication and the role of psychotherapy in the treatment, and serving as a
family friend who demonstrates concern by concretely providing information, practical help, and sound and sensible advice to realistic problems. Therapists must convey expertise, temper clarity with cautiousness, and avoid establishing an egalitarian therapeutic relationship
(Tsui & Schultz, 1985). The relationship should be active, focused on
environmental manipulation, supportive, and free of extensive diagnostic evaluations (Hsu, 1983; Lee, 1988).

Often, brief and focused psychotherapy is indicated as an immediate follow-up to crisis intervention, as is illustrated by the following vignette (Spurlock, 1985):

Clinical Vignette

Eight-year-old Sarah was first seen in the emergency room where she had
been brought by her grandmother and several other relatives. The crisis
occurred because a young adult uncle, who had returned home "high
on some kind of dope," had abused Sarah. In a brief encounter with the
family, the psychiatry resident noted the grandmother to be a reservoir
of support. It was the grandmother who had been able to bring some
order to the chaotic situation that confronted her when she returned home
from her "day work" job and it was she who had arranged for the trip
to the hospital. She was able to provide some comfort to Sarah and per-
suade her to allow the nurse to examine her and talk to the doctor. Providing support to the grandmother and guidance for handling concrete
problems (the child's anxiety, immediate child care and protection, and
referral for help for the uncle) served as a focal point for the crisis intervention and the several subsequent sessions. The resident served as a
connecting link with a member of the child abuse team who was to follow the case. All involved agreed that ongoing assessment would be an
integral part of continued care. (p. 172)

Family Therapy

The experience and backgrounds of families within the same cultural group differ (Hsu, 1983; McGoldrick, Pearce, & Giordano, 1982). Within each cultural group, families also vary with respect to the reason for immigration, the level of acculturation or assimilation, language usage, and dynamics. Therefore, each family should be evaluated and treated with careful regard to its particular structure and the problem it presents. Furthermore, the therapist should function as a cultural interpreter and help the family recognize conflicts between the demands of the minority culture and those of the majority culture (Zuniga, 1988).

The often active involvement of minority family members in the welfare of their sick members can be effectively used to promote therapy within the family setting. This implies that health centers should offer mental health teams who can make home visits in order to provide early intervention and treatment rather than wait for patients to appear at their doorstep and thus risk the patient's suffering greater morbidity due to the delay (Wong, 1982; Jones & Korchin, 1982). To facilitate their provision of services, it is helpful for clinicians to recognize the tendency of many of these families to use informal networks (Jones & Korchin, 1982) and to respect the opinion of schoolteachers regarding their students' behavior.

Therapists should be aware of the extended kinship networks in, for example, African-American families and should search out "significant others who should be included in the family therapy process" (Hines & Boyd-Franklin, 1982, pp. 90–91). Often, patients and their families are unfamiliar with the setting and the process of therapy. Again, it is essential for therapists to inquire about their patients' feelings about the clinical setting and to instruct them about the therapeutic process.

Showing proper respect for the roles of family members is essential for developing and continuing a successful alliance. Many minority families believe the behavior of an individual family member to be a manifestation of the collective behavior pattern of the family. As deviant behavior often accompanies mental illness, the illness may bring shame and guilt to the parents (and especially to the father in Asian-American families), who may feel defeated by the act of turning to outsiders for help. In treating an Asian-American child, the reinforcement of the father's role within the family is extremely important at the initial stage of therapy. This may be accomplished by addressing initial inquiries, explanations, and requests to the father. The therapist's failure to do so may lead to the family's early termination of therapy (Hsu, 1983).

Some minority families attempt to personalize the therapeutic relationship. If the therapist refuses such an overture, the family may perceive the therapist as noncaring and thus untrustworthy. Chinese (Hsu, 1983) and Latino patients may bring the therapist food when they come for sessions. African-American patients may bring Christmas gifts. These behaviors may be interpreted as a breach of the professional relationship or as an attempt to manipulate or even bribe the therapist. However, from the patients' point of view, these are merely socially sanctioned ways to establish and maintain rapport, not attempts to gain favor.

To overcome the taboo that one should never discuss personal affairs with strangers, patients often attempt to incorporate the therapist into their family or clan network by inquiring about the therapist's personal background. The therapist should not react to such questions defensively or avoid responding to them altogether. Mostly, patients do not expect therapists to expose much of their background. They want only to bring the therapist closer to the family unit so that they can confide more freely and with greater security. For example, personal disclosure and an appropriate level of emotional expressiveness often prove the most effective ways to put Asian patients at ease (Tsui & Schultz, 1985).

Owing to the hierarchical structure of many minority families (McGoldrick et al., 1982), family members do not routinely sit together to share feelings. A parent's open expression of fear or sadness in front of the children might be interpreted as a loss of face in Asian-American families or as a sign of diminishing control in authoritative roles. For Asian-American and Latino families, verbal abuse by children in front of an outsider can provoke extreme embarrassment and anger. Therefore, family members should not be encouraged to express their feelings openly and to confront each other directly. This is especially true when conflicts exist between parents and children. An open challenge to authority is not tolerated well in these two groups. Thus, the therapist's primary task is not to encourage the younger generation to rebel openly or drastically against the older generation but to help them accomplish their goals without disturbing family harmony and violating parental authority.

Given the close-knit structure of these family systems, it often is impossible to engage the patient in treatment without soliciting the assistance of family members. Early involvement of family members in the treatment process forestalls the potential sabotaging of clinical work. Treatment efforts are doomed if they are viewed by family members as a threat to the integrity of the family and, consequently, to its survival (Tsui & Schultz, 1985). Japanese-American relatives, for example, frequently are available to participate as part of the treatment team; especially in outpatient care, clinicians must remember to involve them actively, advising them of ways to help the patient toward recovery (Yamamoto, 1982).

Finally, there is a family therapy model that describes these cultural and social systems. Termed the ESCAPE Model (Boynton, 1987), it underlines four steps the family therapist must make to adequately serve culturally different populations:

1. Engage the family within its context
2. Sensitize to the family's culture
3. Aware yourself of the culture's potential and positives
4. Know the environment where the culture clashes are played (p. 126)

Clinical Vignette

Manuel, a 13-year-old Cuban-American boy, was referred to the clinic for petty theft, lying, school truancy, and disrespectful behavior at home. On closer inspection the clinician discovered many difficulties in the family. The father, a strict but caring man, had recently lost his job. He had left Cuba as a child and had made it on his own despite great adversity. In his own words, "I skipped my own childhood. I started working at 13 to support my siblings. My father was very strict but that helped me to survive. I learned soon not to trust anybody." Manuel's mother had also suffered adversity. Wishing to compensate her children and protect them from similar experiences, she had showered them with affection but little discipline. She often unintentionally undermined her husband's strict discipline.

The father, now unemployed, could not understand his son's cavalier attitude toward his studies. His own frustrations and anger made him respond with exaggerated culturally determined role behavior. From a strict but effective father, he became an explosive and frustrated man who overdisciplined Manuel. His position as paterfamilias and breadwinner had been eroded, and his relationship to his wife had deteriorated as well. The stricter he became, the more protective of her children his wife became. Thus, parental discipline was inconsistent, sometimes too lenient and sometimes too strict, and it became the source of multiple marital disagreements.

The clinician, aware of the cultural patterns at work in this family, decided to see the parents initially. He respectfully addressed Mr. Perez first and, with the wife's tacit agreement, began the discussion by acknowledging the difficulties parents encounter in rearing children in a country where they are given great independence and are expected to be outspoken and by acknowledging that the children often sound disrespectful and too cocky to parents with other traditions. The clinician also described the value of old traditions, including the fine equilibrium between paternal strictness and authority and maternal warmth and lenience. Only then did he ask Manuel's parents for an account of what had occurred. In this way the clinician addressed issues of acculturation, showed respect for traditional roles, and provided support for the parents—but without joining them as allies and undermining his future relationship with Manuel.

As the parents discussed the present situation, the clinician was careful not to take sides. He attended silently to the insights on feelings that were revealed by the wife, and responded to the pragmatic, action-oriented approaches of the father. The clinician took care not to enter into issues about the couple prematurely, knowing that Mr. Perez would view this as intrusive and inappropriate. Aware of the need of Mr. Perez to save face and to salvage his pride during this time of high vulnerability, the clinician adeptly avoided themes that could open these issues and did not attempt to take over control of the family by suggesting solutions. Later, in a private session with Mr. Perez the clinician offered solutions after talking with social services and securing some possible job interviews for him.

The clinician provided support for the culturally sanctioned functions of women, that is, being attuned to feelings and wise about nurturance, and of men, being in charge of discipline and not spoiling children. As the first evaluation session ended, the clinician stated: "I certainly know how difficult it is to raise children these days. In the past, we had many other supports in the family and children were not so verbal and aware. There are many things we must adjust to constantly, and many answers we often do not have. So, let's meet again to discuss further the balance between discipline and nurturance." Thus, the clinician was able to personalize the relationship, join the family by offering some expertise without undermining their own capacities, and follow cultural norms in suggesting the need for some flexibility. The parents returned to the clinician, family therapy was instituted, and eventually Manuel became asymptomatic.

Group Approaches

Many clinicians feel that troubled inner-city children and adolescents whose relationships to adults (parents and teachers) is often impaired learn to depend more on their peer supports and communicate better within that context. Accordingly, they can benefit from group treatment approaches. For those whose cultures emphasize cooperation and value the group above the individual, group approaches may be especially suitable.

The Social Action Model (SAM) provides an alternative treatment strategy for poor people of color (Paster, 1986). SAM brings together oppressed people who may have internalized a sense of personal inadequacy because of devaluing experiences with the world and involves them in a socially relevant project. SAM is designed to reverse the "hopelessness and rage (that) lead to alienation, impotence, reckless endangerment, and worse" (Paster, 1986, p. 626) by giving participants a sense of personal and collective power.

Paster cites an example of a group of African-American and Latino youths who were recruited to participate in a project because of their involvement in petty criminal activity. Under the supervision of a paraprofessional, the boys were given a video camera and encouraged to make a film about inner-city living. They learned to coordinate and conduct interviews and to work cooperatively with each other and with authority figures. The film, subsequently shown on a cable television station, was successful. The participants felt empowered, and "this generated subsequent successful efforts that reinforced feelings of adequacy and self-worth" (Paster, 1986, p. 627).

"*Cuento*" therapy (storytelling therapy) uses traditional Puerto Rican folktales to support and transmit cultural values to Puerto Rican children. The theoretical premise of this therapy is that psychological problems experienced by bicultural Puerto Rican children are "partly due to a weakened cultural value system, a sense of distance from the surrounding society, lack of pride in ethnic roots, and the family's diminished role as a cultural agent of socialization" (Rogler & Procidano, 1986, p. 8). These folktales reinstate the child's culture as a source of pride and as a socializing agent. Some of the superficial details of the folktales are adapted to reflect an inner-city ecology, but the moral of the story remains unchanged. The use of folktales enhances the cultural congruence of the therapeutic modality.

> In addition to the intrinsic cultural values embodied in the original Puerto Rican stories, the adapted stories graft themes of adaptive functioning with the American culture into the plots. In this manner, based on the principles of modeling therapy, *cuento* therapy is intended to promote a new synthesis of bicultural symbols and thereby foster adaptive personality growth in children who are in conflict between two cultures. (Costantino, Malgady, & Rogler, 1988, pp. 22–23)

Costantino, Malgady, and Rogler (1988) adapted *cuento* therapy for preadolescents and early adolescents in the form of folk hero modeling therapy. In folk modeling therapy, Puerto Rican adolescents in a small group read the biography of a famous Puerto Rican. The therapist then analyzes the story, emphasizing the character traits of the hero or heroine that allow for survival and success in the face of such adversities as poverty and discrimination. After the story is read and analyzed, the participants are asked structured questions intended to draw parallels between the lives of the adolescents and that of the hero or heroine. The process reinforces adolescents' adaptive responses to adverse situations, identifies maladaptive responses as nonoptimal, and provides an opportunity to discuss the latter. At the conclusion of sessions either art projects or role-playing exercises allow the children an opportunity to demonstrate what they have learned and to put these lessons into practice. Interviews with participants after the therapy reveal that many enjoy the opportunity to learn about their cultural heritage. It instills in them a sense of identity and pride in being Puerto Rican.

Inclan and Herron (1989) use an "educational psychotherapy" group model in their work with inner-city Latino adolescents. Following an introduction, each of ten 90-minute sessions focuses on a particular theme: family and independence; sexuality; racism and discrimination; jobs and job interviewing; alcohol and drugs; and self-revelation, trust, and therapy. The sessions begin with a guided presentation, such as a film, that provides the context for the ensuing discussion of feelings. The educational presentation is a program in itself, but at its conclusion adolescents are given the opportunity to continue therapy in an ongoing group. Thus, the structured educational group may serve as an introduction to group psychotherapy. Inclan and Herron claim that the group approach is particularly successful at addressing the adolescent's concerns, fears, and guilt feelings associated with sexuality, an issue not usually raised in individual therapy sessions.

Kahn, Lewis, and Galvez (1974) reported that a group approach could be adapted to the treatment of delinquent American Indian youths. Initial group sessions offered formal presentations on topics likely to be relevant to adolescents, including dating, drugs, drinking, and family issues. Given the cultural norm against intimate disclosures to others, this approach allowed participants to discuss sensitive issues in abstract terms or in the third person. Despite this seemingly impersonal approach, group process developed, allowing several curative factors to emerge, such as modeling of appropriate behavior and ventilation of feelings. A marked decrease in recidivism rates for delinquency among participants provides quantitative support for the group approach.

Social Skills Learning Approaches

The bicultural competence and skills training model outlined by LaFromboise and Rowe (1983) suggests that social skills learned within one culture may not be appropriate within another cultural context. Rather than place emphasis on intrapsychic processes, this model espouses a situation-specific approach. The social skills training model "conceptualizes problematic behavior in terms of the specific discrepancies between the person's observed or self-reported behavior and behavior considered effective by an analysis of socially competent behavior within a culturally relevant setting" (LaFromboise & Rowe, 1983, p. 590).

Such a model draws heavily on social learning theory, as proposed by Bandura (1977), and may offer several advantages over other service delivery models. First, the program is less culturally biased than others since skills training can be tailored to varying cultural contexts. For example, an individual's responses and behaviors may differ according to the ethnic and cultural background of the other person in the social interaction. In assertiveness training, the degree to which one expresses one's wishes depends on the culture of the other person. Second, skills training may have proactive and preventive applications that break from the reactive nature of traditional mental health services. Third, the model can be applied to a wide range of problems presented to mental health workers.

However, the question of bicultural competence and training is not without its critics. Some question whether biculturalism is truly attainable. Others observe that one cultural lifestyle dominates or replaces the other by necessity and that personal preference leads to a stronger commitment to one lifestyle.

Another approach, skills enhancement, has been applied to substance abuse programs for American Indians. Didactic programs have been implemented using role-playing in groups to teach skills for preventing drug abuse. Bobo, Gilchrist, Cvetkovich, Trimble, and Schinke, (1988) describe a five-step problem-solving approach: Stop, Options, Decision, Action, and Self-Praise (SODAS). The program goal is to help American Indian youths make better decisions about drug use and resist peer pressure to drink or use drugs. Coupled with skills training, didactic materials may be used for lessons that focus on a historical review of drinking in American Indian communities, stereotypes about American Indians and alcohol, the religious use of hallucinogens, the social use of alcohol, and tribal and personal values. Such programs show some success in lowering rates of alcohol, marijuana, and inhalant use (Gilchrist, Schinke, Trimble, & Cvetkovich, 1987).

Skills training program participants demonstrate greater knowledge of substance abuse, increased interpersonal skills, improved attitudes about drug use, and greater success in resisting peer pressure to use drugs or alcohol (Schinke, 1988).

School Programs

James Comer, director of the Yale Child Study Center Schools Program, and his colleagues have created and implemented the School Development Program (SDP), which is based on the application of social and behavioral science principles to each individual aspect of a school program (Comer, 1980). The school governance and management team, the mental health team, and the parent participation program form the fundamental units of the SDP. These teams are interrelated and work together. Several committees and teams (e.g., steering committee and mental health team) are organized to function under the aegis of one of the units. The goals of the SDP, which is basically a preventive psychiatry approach, are to decrease behavioral problems and to increase coping skills of children. Such a school program model strives to make it feasible for children from lower socioeconomic and dysfunctional backgrounds to achieve high levels of education and to gain the opportunity to participate in the mainstream of society.

Two educators, McDaniel and Bielen (1990), developed Project Self-Esteem in California in 1978. A parent involvement program for improving self-esteem and preventing drug and alcohol abuse among children in kindergarten through sixth grade, Project Self-Esteem surveys children, teachers, and parents about the stressful happenings in the children's lives. Topics covered with teachers include multicultural issues, gender issues in education, parent involvement, positive discipline, and enhancing self-esteem in children. Recognition of one's uniqueness, distinctions between persons and their actions, communication skills, teasing and cheating, goal setting, accepting handicapped people, and alcohol and drug abuse—these are among the themes parents and children address. Project Self-Esteem, which is fully integrated into the regular school curriculum, involves a series of lessons, each with clear objectives, suggested readings, and age-appropriate materials.

Therapeutic Communities

Program development efforts require clinicians and researchers to recognize that children and adolescents internalize messages from the community about drug and alcohol use, delinquency, sex, education, and truancy. Therefore, programs must clearly reflect community reactions and feelings about these issues. The philosophy and treatment methods within a program must necessarily match the needs of the population the program purportedly serves (Shore & Von Fumetti, 1972). For example, Bobo et al. (1988) report that the American Indian board members of their program stipulated three criteria for cultural sensitivity: that intertribal cultural diversity be accounted for in the program, that emphasis be placed on the non-drug-abusing lifestyle of most American Indian people, and that emphasis be given to the perspective that abstinence is not the only appropriate behavior.

Another type of therapy that tries to counteract the negative effect of poor urban life on minority children is Unitas, a therapeutic community located in the South Bronx, New York. Unitas has created a multitude of symbolic families, each composed of up to 15 boys and girls. Two trained teenage residents act as the symbolic mother and father of the children, and Edward Eismann, the founder and director of the program, serves as the symbolic grandfather. The goal of the community is to prevent and remedy dysfunctional behavior by providing a milieu of order, discipline, and nurturance for the young children who often live in chaotic homes and environments. The community provides individual therapy, play therapy, classroom therapy, remedial reading, family therapy, and advocacy.

Eismann's theoretical position is that psychotherapy is "a systematic way of understanding and dealing with emotional hurts in an empathic re-educative manner" (Farber & Rogler, 1981, p. 31). He emphasizes the primacy of an empathic and caring healing relationship over insight in the process of psychological change. Unitas, sensitive to the culture and socioeconomic ecology of inner-city adolescents, adjusts traditional therapeutic interventions to meet the needs of urban youth.

Consultation Services

One should not underestimate the value of mental health services in the form of psychiatric consultation to schools and social agencies. Spurlock (1985) has addressed this issue in relation to African-American children, but consultation services can benefit a broad range of inner-city children and their families:

> Often, a consultant's initial task is to point out the need for the service providers to become familiar with the culture and the community from

which his or her charges come. Too frequently, the consultant's knowledge is limited. It is essential that the providers know that some of the modes of behaviors that they may identify as disorders may, indeed, be a non-pathological means of coping in a child's home environment. (p. 170)

For example, day care program staff may need a reminder to make use of culturally relevant readings rather than rely on fairy tales that are traditional in the dominant culture. The following African folktale, of Anase and his visitor, Turtle, is an example:

Anase, a cunning spider, tries to outwit his neighbors. He seldom succeeds. Turtle, tired and hungry, passes by the home of Anase. The aroma of freshly cooked fish and his own hunger pangs prompt Turtle to knock on Anase's door. Anase feels annoyed when he opens his door and sees the stranger, but he knows the unwritten law in his country that one never refuses hospitality to a passerby. He verbally welcomes Turtle and invites him to share the dinner that is about ready.

When Turtle extends one paw to help himself, Anase exclaims: "In my country, it is ill-mannered to come to the table without washing first." Turtle responds meekly to the criticism by struggling to the stream at the foot of the hill to wash his paws. But, his paws become dusty once again during his return to Anase's house.

Turtle finds Anase eating at a furious rate and sees that the platter is half-empty. Again, as Turtle reaches to help himself, Anase calls attention to his dusty paws and orders him to wash. Turtle responds as before. However, this time he takes great care to walk on the grass as he makes his return trip. To his dismay and regret, he finds that Anase has eaten all that remained of the meal. With a tone of sarcasm, Turtle thanks Anase for his warm hospitality and invites Anase to his home for a meal.

Some months later Anase visits Turtle, who warmly welcomes Anase and excuses himself to prepare the meal. Turtle is gone beneath the water for some time but finally surfaces to announce that dinner is ready. Anase dives head first into the water, sinks a few inches, and then resurfaces. He tries again and again but cannot reach the bed of the river. But, Anase is clever and determined that he can prevent a resurfacing by putting stones in his pockets. He does this and lands right at the dinner table. Anase finds before him the most delicious meal he ever has seen: oysters, clams, mussels, slices of eel, and a centerpiece of watercress and large pink shrimp. Turtle, already seated at the table, swallows a piece of eel and exclaims: "Oh, Anase, in my country it is ill-mannered to come to the table wearing a jacket; please take it off." Very, very slowly, Anase removes his jacket and leaves the table . . . and floats up . . . and out of sight.

Day care teachers can present this folktale as an enjoyable story or as a means of encouraging children to talk about what may happen when one tries to outsmart others for his or her own advantage.

Consultative experiences show that some providers, in their efforts to avoid cultural bias, tend to identify pathology in minority group members solely as the result of their experiences with racism and discrimination. Spurlock (1985) addresses this in relation to African-Americans:

> The diagnostician (or therapist) who views a black child only in terms of that child being a victim of racism and who dismisses any effort to evaluate intrapsychic factors mars the diagnostic process. Equally faulty is the clinician who is blinded to the differences of race or of class. (p. 168)

It is important to encourage providers to examine their countertransference reactions in their work with clients and to identify the particular significance of such reactions when working with people whose culture differs from their own (Spurlock, 1985).

Mental health professionals often are called upon to provide consultative services and/or crisis intervention within the schools. Frequently, such requests come in response to anxieties brought on by the violence that occurs within the school and the school environs. For example, a school nurse may ask for guidelines to quell a student's acute anxiety in response to witnessing a knifing in the school cafeteria or a principal may request assistance to help his staff and student body deal with the fears and anxieties that surface in his school on an almost daily basis.

It has proven useful to alert school personnel to the importance of anticipating certain kinds of problems in the school community and developing a plan to initiate a forum or meetings of small groups to facilitate the expression of feelings and offer suggestions for coping strategies and healings. Not all tragedies can be anticipated, of course; for those that cannot, crisis intervention must be initiated.

Inpatient and Partial Hospitalization Treatment

Vargas and Berlin (1991) call attention to the need for administrators and clinicians to be culturally responsive prior to a minority child's admission to an inpatient service.

> The typical children's hospital ostentatiously reflects the dominant culture in which it exists. The pictures on the walls, the style of the interior decorations and furniture, the layout of the rooms, offices, nursing station, and classrooms often represent the tastes and preferences of the

dominant culture rather than those of the ethnic minority patients it may serve. . . . To many young ethnic minority patients, the hospital's physical environment, intended to convey to them a genuine concern for their problems, speaks in a foreign tongue. (p. 15)

The Department of Psychiatry of San Francisco General Hospital (Zatzick & Lu, 1991) has developed a model to deal with these issues and to educate trainees about transcultural concerns. The clinical staff and the supervisory and clinical faculty of each of four focus units share a common linguistic and cultural background with a particular patient group. This decreases the dropout rate and improves the effectiveness of care (Lee, 1980, 1982; Wong, 1982). Each unit routinely celebrates ethnic holidays, and the occupational therapy groups orient their programs toward ethnic activities. Culturally sensitive evaluations and treatments, as well as the variations in symptom expression across cultures, are taught, thus helping the clinical staff learn to differentiate culturally sanctioned behaviors from psychopathology.

As in outpatient treatment, it is essential that clinicians be sensitive to the possibility that family members, including members of the extended family, may expect to be involved in the treatment process, a process with which they may be unfamiliar. Thus, it is essential to inquire about the patient's and family's feelings about the setting and to give information about the nature of the treatment process. In some instances the adult who is the decision maker for the family is not immediately available. To pressure the accompanying adult, even a biological parent, to make an immediate decision in the absence of the decision maker does not serve to develop trust and confidence. Vargas and Berlin (1991) provide a vivid illustration:

Fred, a 14-year-old, psychotic, Pueblo Indian boy had been referred for possible hospitalization with considerable urgency by the Pueblo social worker. Knowing Fred to come from a traditional Pueblo Indian family, the intake staff at the hospital recognized the evaluation for hospitalization could not take place until the maternal grandmother, who was essential to any decision making in the family, returned from a family visit in a neighboring state. On her return, the grandmother, along with the mother, father, patient, and patient's older brother, who acted as a translator, all attended the evaluation. (p. 17)

The case of Ines, a 16-year-old Latina brought to a hospital emergency room in response to a suicidal gesture, illustrates the need to involve an extended family member and avoid premature hospitalization:

Clinical Vignette

Ines came to the emergency room after an altercation with her mother precipitated a suicide attempt. The clinician on call did not want to release Ines to her mother, who had accompanied her, because the mother seemed equally distressed and angry. In response to questioning, the mother did not identify any other members of the household who could be contacted. Because there were no immediate resources in the community to refer the patient to, hospitalization on the pediatric ward was recommended. Both patient and mother were terrified of hospitalization, and mother refused to consider granting permission for the admission.

The attending psychiatrist, who was familiar with supportive networks, was consulted, and she suggested that contact be made with a member of the family's social network. A godmother was identified. She arrived at the hospital shortly after she was called, related well to Ines and her mother, and was able to calm them both. With the mother's permission, the patient was released to the temporary care of the godmother. An outpatient visit was scheduled for all three the following day. Subsequently, short-term family therapy was instituted.

Another case vignette illustrates the potential for a negative outcome if an inpatient facility fails to address the sociocultural issues fully:

Clinical Vignette

Jean Pierre, a husky 16-year-old boy from the West Indies, had been hospitalized in an inner-city hospital for over 6 months because of paranoid feelings, social withdrawal, and auditory hallucinations. A member of a large family, Jean Pierre had emigrated from the West Indies 1 year prior to hospitalization. His adjustment to the hospital routine continued to be difficult because he did not like the food and demonstrated "passive aggressive traits."

Jean Pierre's multiple nightmares persisted. He could not concentrate in school, and his academic skills continued to deteriorate. A multiplicity of antipsychotic medications proved ineffective despite dosages at maximum levels. Jean Pierre acted cautious and suspicious of the staff and was reluctant to become involved with his peers.

During a reevaluation interview with a culturally sensitive therapist, Jean Pierre confided his serious difficulties adjusting to the American way, his constant sense of being different from his African-American peers who were not West Indian, and his intense mourning for the family who had raised him back home. He had come to the United States expecting his previously absent mother to be warm and available, as his grandparents in the West Indies had been. Instead, he met an overwhelmed working mother who had three other children and a full-time job and who was often unable to visit him in the hospital.

On closer questioning, Jean Pierre confessed that he had been involved in some voodoo practices that had gone wrong when he had been asked to take a "potion." He did not want to elaborate further but indicated that subsequently he was no longer a man; "something" had happened. He had been told to follow some other steps to effect a "cure," but he was afraid to do so. Prior to his hospitalization Jean Pierre dreamed that he was in the ceremony again and was told that he would never be healed, that he would slowly deteriorate and die. After a careful mental status examination, the clinician concluded that the working diagnosis seemed to be a major depressive episode in an adolescent who had symptoms of mourning and loss and who was experiencing a sexual identity crisis secondary to an undisclosed sexual trauma.

A West Indian professional who was well versed in voodoo served as a consultant and reassured Jean Pierre that he would be well and that he apparently had fallen victim to people who abused the religion. Jean Pierre then was asked to prepare a paper on his culture and, with the help of the staff, to present it to his peers. Help was found for his overworked mother, who then could visit him more frequently. Jean Pierre's grandparents were contacted in the West Indies via telephone to talk with him. Antidepressant medication and a program to boost his male self-esteem and to help him understand his new culture were instituted. Many weeks later, Jean Pierre had improved significantly.

Pharmacology

Unfortunately, there have been a paucity of studies addressing the differential effect of psychopharmacology on ethnically or racially diverse groups of children. Certainly, it is important for clinicians to be aware of the family belief system with respect to mental illness. If family members regard it as a medical or physical illness, they will be more willing to comply with the medication. Some Indochinese groups believe that medication helps only in the acute phase and should be used for a short time. Long-term compliance in these groups may create a problem (Kroll et al., 1990). Many cultures utilize herbal drugs for the relief of symptoms. The clinician should ask the family to bring them, since some contain atropine-like substances that can produce or exacerbate anticholinergic effects (Chien, 1993). With Mexican-Americans living near the border, the clinician must be aware of the

fewer restrictions on drugs in Mexico and the consequent potential
for abuse of drugs such as amphetamines, barbiturates, and anxiolytics
(Martinez, 1993).

Substance Abuse Treatment

Semlitz and Gold (1986) call attention to the consensus of drug treatment professionals that successful treatment requires readjustment of
the addict's lifestyle in addition to therapy for physiologic drug dependence. Furthermore, many substance abusers need treatment for at
least two problems. Bailey (1989) suggests that no definitive treatment
for substance abuse exists but identifies four general categories of treatment philosophies and modalities: outpatient care, inpatient care,
aftercare, and residential therapeutic communities. These categories
have several features in common: all mandate abstinence from drugs,
group therapy with like patients, supplemental therapeutic intervention by self-help groups such as Narcotics Anonymous (NA) and
Alcoholics Anonymous (AA), and family therapy.

The drug-ridden environments of inner-city children and adolescents fail to support the goals of treatment, particularly cessation of
drug use. Drugs are big business in many of these communities, and
the seller needs customers. Further, the high rates of underemployment and unemployment, both of which stem in part from the limited availability of legal jobs in inner cities, serve to entice adolescents
to become involved in the drug business as a way out of their desper-
ate life situation.

Inpatient treatment can lend some protection, at least temporarily,
against negative influences from the external environment (e.g., by restricting the patient's access to drugs by limiting visitors and by isolat-
ing the patient from enabling family members and other individuals).
Detoxification is implemented as needed. Available psychotherapeutic
interventions include individual, group, and family treatment. Educational and vocational assessments and programming form an integral
component of many inpatient services. Day programs and regular group
therapy encounters are important features of aftercare. The high costs
of inpatient treatment, which varies from 6 to 24 months in therapeutic communities (Bailey, 1989), usually prove prohibitive for most inner-
city victims and those American Indians who live on reservations.

Kumpfer (1989), who provides a detailed and critical review of
risk factors and prevention strategies, notes the complexities involved
in the development and implementation of prevention programs. The
premise is that substance abuse does not develop in a vacuum but is

preceded by behavioral, cognitive, or emotional problems. Ideally, prevention efforts should focus on high-risk children. Pressures for such a focus resulted in passage of the Comprehensive Drug Rehabilitation and Treatment Act in 1986. The legislation mandates communities, prevention agencies, and schools to develop strategies for nine categories of youth who are believed to be at risk. Many minority group youngsters may belong to one or several of these categories, which are as follows: children of substance abusers, victims of physical/sexual/psychological abuse, school dropouts, pregnant teenagers, economically disadvantaged youth, delinquent youth, youth with mental health problems, suicidal youth, and disabled youth.

Most prevention programs have been implemented in schools. They offer films; didactic instruction; and presentations by physicians, law enforcement officers, recovering addicts, and nationally known celebrities. Grave concerns challenge the effectiveness of such programs. No hard data are available, but many in the field of addiction management believe that the parroting of slogans like "Just say no" and associated programs fail to make an appreciable impact on prevention.

Some community-based programs have been designed to be culturally specific. Soulbeat, one such program, uses churches and the public schools as vehicles in its focus on African-American families and youth (Maypole & Anderson, 1987). Soulbeat helps children to create and perform a skit with gospel music and dancing about an African-American family's problems with two teenagers who become involved with drugs. The performance ends with the cast engaging the church parishioners in a facts-and-misconceptions dialogue about drugs. The impact of these performances on youngsters has been particularly significant. "To be a 'Soulbeater' became a prestigious, ego-reinforcing experience. The 'Soulbeat' youngsters were observed to develop a group norm which discouraged drug use" (Maypole & Anderson, 1987, p. 138).

Individuals and groups in many communities take leadership roles in combating the problems generated by substance abuse. The clergy, assisted by parishioners, have achieved some success in inner-city communities across the United States ("Church and the Drug Crisis," 1989; "High Noon," 1989; Narine, 1989).

AN ETHNICALLY SENSITIVE STRESS PREVENTION AND INTERVENTION MODEL

All the aforementioned treatment approaches contribute to the clinical literature on the treatment of minority children and allow the clinician to be sensitive to the cultural context in which the child's symptoms evolve. With some exceptions, many of these approaches seem to relate to a variety of children with a wide spectrum of symptoms. Clearly, it is difficult to assess which treatment modality is most effective for a particular cultural group and at the same time most effective for a particular cluster of symptoms in a particular child within that group.

Some children appear socially distressed. Some experience low self-esteem. Some have endured various degrees of trauma. Some also suffer from diagnosable psychiatric disorders. Culture-specific issues may tend to blur in many multicultural inner-city areas where African-American, Latino, American Indian, and Asian-American children share neighborhoods, experiences, and stressors. Even within culturally homogeneous areas, children will be at different stages of acculturation. Some children may require an individual approach, others a family approach, and still others a psychopharmacological intervention. Some may require a combination of approaches. For example, a child with an attention deficit disorder who has been physically abused may require all of these approaches. Consequently, it often proves difficult to implement treatment interventions that are symptom or culture specific.

This reality, together with the fact that minority group children are exposed to an inordinate number of stressors, provides the basis for proposing a culturally sensitive therapeutic intervention model that integrates stress theory with prevention principles. The model permits the clinician to implement a comprehensive therapeutic intervention that recognizes the complexities of treating inner-city children who represent diverse cultures and suffer a variety of symptoms.

Components of the Model

Stress Theory

Cervantes and Castro (1985), who have reviewed stress theory and applied its principles to the Mexican-American population, divide the elements of stress theory into seven stages: potential stressors, appraisal of the stressor, internal and external mediators of stress, coping patterns, and short-term and long-term outcomes. Some of their principles prove relevant to other minority groups and are particularly applicable for the clinician who works with minority children and adolescents.

Potential Stressors

Potential stressors, the first stage, include different types of life circumstances that may be common but not inevitable and whose potential for stress may depend on preexisting conditions. For example, the process of migration may become a major stress for a family forced to migrate because of war and political persecution and, consequently, left with few resources to survive in the new country. Stress is mitigated considerably for the family who voluntarily migrates to a receptive and supportive host environment. Thus, the process of migration is potentially stressful, with the potential depending on the variables contributing to the person–environment interactions.

This stage is often described in terms of the concept of risk factors. In the case of children, parental dysfunction or illness, overcrowded living conditions, low social status, and prenatal and birth complications often emerge as risk factors. The cumulative occurrence of these factors, more than any single one, increases the likelihood of a negative outcome.

Appraisal of the Stressor

Appraisal of the stressor, the second stage, focuses on the ways different groups of individuals evaluate the stress associated with various events. For example, Hough, McGarney, Graham, and Timbers, (1982) suggest that any disruption of social support networks is associated with a greater expression of symptoms by those groups for whom such extended supports are of great importance. For children whose cultures highly value academic success a bad grade is experienced as highly distressful. For families from cultures that value social skills as crucial to the survival of the clan having a difficult, uncooperative, and oppositional child is a major tragedy.

Internal and External Mediators of Stress

Internal and external mediators form the third and fourth components. Internal mediators are traits associated with the individual, for example, locus of control, neurological intactness, social orientation, achievement motivation, and cognitive style. These traits influence the way the individual handles the stressor. Overly reactive and impulsive children experience stress differently than children who are essentially calm and pliable.

External mediators are social and familial factors that mitigate or exacerbate stress. For example, a stable family and a supportive school are external mediators that serve as protective factors for a child with a learning disability.

Coping Patterns

The fifth element is the coping pattern individuals use to reduce stress. Individuals may differ in their use of coping patterns despite the fact that they may have similar internal and external mediating variables. For example, some children withdraw from stress whereas others may approach it and attempt to diminish it by finding creative solutions. Children may approach stress with optimism and feelings of self-efficacy or may delegate others to find solutions for them.

Short-Term and Long-Term Outcomes

Both short-term and long-term outcomes, the final stages, provide feedback to individuals about the effectiveness of their coping strategies in reducing a stressor's impact and influence their appraisals of potential future stessors. Caplan (1964) observes that those subjects who cope effectively with a particular experience are more likely to come away from it with their coping abilities enhanced. Those who deal ineffectively are more likely to experience future pathological outcomes (Felner, 1984).

Principles of Primary, Secondary, and Tertiary Prevention

The principles of primary, secondary, and tertiary prevention emerge as particularly relevant in a discussion of minority group children. Primary prevention refers to attempts to reduce the incidence, or number of new cases within a given time period, of a disease or a disorder among a specified population. The approach uses two main strategies: health promotion and specific protection (Goldston, Yager, Heinicke, & Pynoos, 1990).

At some time a clinician should participate in primary prevention efforts with the support of professionals in public health, sociology, epidemiology, and education. Clinicians can offer consultation and mental health education and training to community organizations and become involved in the development of prevention policy. Clinicians can provide information to caretakers of children at risk, for example, children whose parents have been incarcerated, are mentally ill or substance abusers, or suffer a chronic medical disease. A clinician can educate the population at large about the risks of mental health problems in children with head injuries and epilepsy, the benefit of early referral for disruptive behaviors, the role of mental illness in adolescent suicide, and the associated mental health problems of adolescent substance abusers.

Secondary prevention consists of early diagnosis and treatment to reverse the progression of an existing disease or disorder. Its goal is to reduce prevalence by lessening duration (Bloom, 1969). Ideally, mental health services should be available in primary medical care settings, day care programs, and schools.

Finally, tertiary prevention efforts are directed toward maximizing the capacities of patients with irreversible conditions in order to reduce or limit the extent of their disability.

These three intervention strategies are approached within the sociocultural context of inner-city children who are at risk of emotional disabilities or who already manifest symptoms of psychiatric disorders. As it is our intent to focus on treatment strategies, the clinical application of our model addresses those issues most relevant to secondary and tertiary prevention strategies but fully acknowledges the crucial role of health promotion and specific protection.

Clinical Application of the Model

The proposed model requires the clinician first to make a good assessment of the psychosocial and environmental problems affecting the child and the family (see Table 1). Prior to implementing any culturally sensitive intervention, the clinician must assess the current frequency and intensity of each stressor, the strengths and vulnerabilities of the system, the stressor(s) impact on the family and the child, and the response each stressor has elicited. Other members of the multidisciplinary team should then be consulted for additional information. The clinician can then produce a list of priorities and develop a specific strategy designed to reduce stressors and increase strengths.

At this time the clinician identifies any need for additional expertise to implement the plan and discloses the intervention plan to the family. The clinician needs to be armed with a thorough and comprehensive history, a good preliminary diagnosis, and a system of priorities for intervention. The clinician now has the information necessary to implement a treatment that is sensitive to the belief system and expectations of the patient. These steps can be summarized as follows:

- Assessment of current frequency and intensity of each stressor and the response it elicits
- Assessment of strengths and vulnerabilities of the child, family, and environment
- Consultation with other professionals
- Determination of a realistic list of priorities

TABLE 1. Psychosocial and Environmental Problems

Problems with Primary Support Group (Childhood, Adult, Parent–Child). These include: death of family member; health problems in family; disruption of family by separation, divorce, or estrangement; removal from the home; remarriage of parent; sexual or physical abuse; parental overprotection; neglect of child; inadequate discipline; discord with siblings; birth of a sibling.

Problems Related to the Social Environment. These include: death or loss of friend; social isolation; living alone; difficulty with acculturation; discrimination; adjustment to life cycle transition (e.g., retirement).

Educational Problems. These include: illiteracy; academic problems; discord with teachers or classmates; inadequate school environment.

Occupational Problems. These include: unemployment; threat of job loss; stressful work schedule; difficult work condition; job dissatisfaction; job change; discord with boss or coworkers.

Housing Problems. These include: homelessness; inadequate housing; unsafe neighborhood; discord with neighbors or landlord.

Economic Problems. These include: extreme poverty; inadequate finances; insufficient welfare support.

Problems with Access to Health Care Services. These include: inadequate health care services; transportation to health care facilities unavailable; inadequate health insurance.

Problems Related to Interaction with the Legal System/Crime. These include: arrest; incarceration; litigation; victim of crime.

Other Psychosocial Problems. These include: exposure to disasters, war, other hostilities; discord with non-family caregivers (e.g., counselor, social worker, physician); unavailability of social service agencies.

Note. From American Psychiatric Association (1993, p. D:5). Copyright 1993 by the American Psychiatric Association. Reprinted by permission.

- Development of an intervention strategy
- Disclosure of intervention plan to the parents and the child and recruitment of family members (if available and indicated) as agents of change
- Implementation of an ethnically sensitive approach

Clinicians must be realistic about what they can change, humble about what they cannot modify, and prepared for unexpected challenges.

Presented in the following pages is an extensive case history that demonstrates the use of an ethnically sensitive stress prevention and intervention model and an approach that incorporates primary, secondary, and tertiary intervention.

Clinical Vignette

Aixa, a 13-year-old African-American girl, was referred to the clinic by her school for a recent episode in which she had threatened a girlfriend with a pair of scissors.

It was disclosed during the evaluation that at age 4, after a normal developmental history, Aixa had watched her drug-addicted mother kill her father, who had a history of criminal behavior, with a knife. Aixa was subsequently placed in a foster home. Between the ages of 6 and 8, she was sexually abused by one of her adolescent foster brothers. Aixa finally disclosed this information to a social worker and was sent to a new foster care home, which provided love and adequate supervision. She remained in the home and became an excellent and well-behaved student in a small and supportive school in the community. Despite frequent nightmares and worries about the murder and the sexual abuse, Aixa was adapting well. Her foster mother involved her in the neighborhood Baptist church and frequently spoke to her about the strengths of African-American women.

When Aixa reached her 12th birthday, her mother was cleared of all charges and asked the courts to return Aixa to her. The mother subsequently remarried and moved with Aixa to another community. Aixa's new inner-city neighborhood was located in an area well known for its high crime rate, ubiquitous drug dealers, and understaffed and underfunded schools. Aixa's previous symptoms worsened, and her nightmares became more intense. She was overly sensitive to the nonviolent but frequent arguments between her mother and her stepfather in their over-crowded apartment.

As Aixa entered adolescence, she was overstimulated by the uninhibited sexual comments of the boys in her school. She continued to manage academically and was considered to have good verbal skills and a sense of humor, but she was frequently explosive and short-tempered even upon slight provocation. She started to become sexually provocative toward the older boys, began to lie at home and in school, and adopted a demeanor of toughness in order to survive her new school setting. Aixa had been truant from school when family stability began to suffer. Aixa's mother began to experience increasing problems managing Aixa's behavior at home and felt overwhelmed and incompetent.

After a careful mental status examination diagnoses of conduct disorder, solitary aggressive type, and of delayed onset posttraumatic stress disorder were made. On Axis IV of DSM-IV she demonstrated problems with primary support group, educational problems, housing problems, and economic problems. Her rating on the Global Assessment of Functioning (Axis V) was moderate. Several environmental stressors were identified: overcrowding both in school and at home; low social status; exposure to crime, sex, and violence; foster care placement; poor student–teacher ratio; and frequent moves. Strengths included a good recreational facility in the community, which offered an ethnic pride program, and a nearby Baptist church. Among the family stressors to which Aixa was subjected were the following: death, criminality, psychopathology, substance abuse, inconsistent supervision and discipline, poor parental relationships, limited impulse control, instability, and inadequate models for identification. A background strength, which eroded quickly, was the influence of the stable and empowered foster parent with whom Aixa lived, a woman who had supervised her well and had offered her consistent and fair discipline.

Aixa was developing more impulsivity and lability in response to her multiple traumas and family history. Her endurance had eroded owing to the severity, prematurity, and cumulative effect of the multiple stressors, and her outlook on life was becoming increasingly negative. Although initially she had an inner locus of control, she increasingly (and justifiably) felt she would not be able to change things no matter what she did. Aixa's strengths included solid intelligence and verbal skills, good physical health, a sense of humor, a normal early neurodevelopmental history, and, until relatively recently, an autonomous and adaptable personality.

When primary prevention principles are applied in the present case, it is clear that we need to support public policies that provide better housing and schools, that ensure quality control of foster care placements, and that educate parents about the potential impact of violence, sexual abuse, drugs, crime, and family dysfunction on children.

Secondary prevention approaches in the case of Aixa were implemented immediately: The interdisciplinary team facilitated a referral of the family to the community recreational facility and also discussed with Axia's parents her previous involvement with the Baptist church. The team made themselves available to the child and family as a comprehensive health resource and made a commitment to help the family with any future medical needs and to serve, if necessary, as brokers with the educational system. Such an approach enabled the team to offer socioculturally sensitive resources and support networks both to enhance family members' self-esteem and sense of self-value and to protect the family from social isolation. In the process, the team also offered the concrete and immediate comprehensive services of the clinic—and did so prior to discussing the more abstract concepts of psychological dynamics and possible psychotherapy. During a school visit with the parents, the team identified a committed teacher as well as a part-time guidance counselor who promised to assist Aixa in finding positive activities for her unstructured time and, if indicated, to transfer her to a classroom with less provocative and more supportive peers. Psychological and educational tests confirmed Aixa's good intelligence and raised the possibility of an eventual transfer to a more structured and intellectually stimulating school. Aixa's mother, who permitted Aixa more frequent phone calls to the foster mother, responded to encouragement to establish a relationship with the foster mother for herself (it was learned that both families shared a migration from the same state in the south).

Once the members of the team had demonstrated their interest and reliability to the family and had discussed their findings fully, the parents were invited to join a parent-training group in the clinic, which included members of the same community. Until then the stepfather had delegated responsibility for all health care issues to the women in the family. A special appointment was made for him after working hours to emphasize the importance of his involvement. After several sessions it was evident that the stepfather had much to contribute and that he was willing to come periodically with his wife to discuss their marital problems. Meanwhile, Aixa was assigned to a female African-American therapist to help her resolve her traumatic experiences and better understand her present behavior. Applying the principle of tertiary prevention, the team identified a better drug rehabilitation program for the mother to help diminish the degree of disability caused by her long-standing problem.

Traditional norms of therapy frequently are modified to fit a cultural group, and certain therapies from those deemed appropriate for the specified group are selected over others. Therapies may be altered to address the consequences of living in an economically depressed environment as much as to accommodate indigenous cultural attributes, although this distinction is not necessarily made clear. In sum, the case of Aixa required multiple treatment approaches, all of which were incorporated within a culturally sensitive therapeutic intervention model that integrates stress theory with the principles of primary, secondary, and tertiary prevention.

CONCLUDING COMMENTS

Children who live in inner cities and on reservations are more likely to be subjected to chronic social stressors than are their counterparts in other communities. The psychiatric difficulties they experience—and there are many such difficulties—may be rooted in part in these untoward social stressors and may accentuate them. The range and intensity of stressful social factors in the community may contribute to a clinician's decision that a child is untreatable in his or her present environment or to the clinician's focusing on social factors at the expense of biological, neurophysiological, and psychiatric factors.

A clinician's focus on the disadvantage or deprivation associated with a child's cultural background may contribute to diagnostic errors or to a failure to complete the diagnostic and treatment process. In this context it is appropriate to remember the admonition of Chess (1969), who warned that the identification of cultural deprivation could "become a stereotype, which no matter how benevolently intended, ignores the rich diversity of individuals within the group" (p. 4).

CHAPTER **6**

The Clinician as Advocate

◆

RHINA'S WORLD

Rhina, like many minority children, is a victim of a broad range of social ills and unresponsive social policies. What is wrong with her world is perhaps best described by Rhina herself as the features that would never appear in her ideal world but are all too common in this world:

In My World

In my world there would be no war
In my world there would be no homeless
In my world there would be no hunger
In my world there would be no illegal drugs
In my world there would be no physical or sexual abuse towards children
In my world there would be no alcoholism
In my world there would be an abundance of love
In my world there would be communication between parents and children
In my world there would be understanding between countries
In my world there would be no hate for people from different races
In my world there would be three-day weekends
In this world there are wars
In this world there are homeless
In this world there are fatal illegal drugs
In this world there is mistreatment of innocent children
In this world there is no harmony between countries or races
Oh! How I wish I could have my world.

—*Rhina* (in Plantenga, 1991, p. 60)

EXPANDING THE ROLE OF THE CLINICIAN

Rhina's wish for a new world serves as the backdrop for a discussion on the need for expanding the role of clinicians to include that of advocate. To diagnose and treat children like Rhina without working to change a world that continues to impose multiple social stressors on them and to discriminate against them is at best both shortsighted and irresponsible.

The children's own words and their case vignettes document the need for clinicians to become advocates for their young clients. Accordingly, the comments on these final pages extend the earlier discussion of the principles of primary, secondary, and tertiary levels of prevention to include a proposal to add to the role of the clinician that of advocate for responsive social policy, advocate for the inclusion of a cultural perspective in training programs, and advocate for the child in the diagnostic and treatment process, respectively.

Advocate for Responsive Social Policy

Rhina's world, the world of many minority children, shouts to the clinician to take on the role of advocate for responsive social policy. To be truly effective in the provision of care to our child population requires primary prevention efforts outside the clinic and office doors. The children and families who seek the clinician's help need healthy, safe, and creative environments in which to live, work, and play. Clinicians can join forces with other professionals and advocacy groups in their social action efforts and can contribute their voice and their knowledge of child development, the potential deleterious effects of multiple social stressors, and necessary preventive measures to change the world of the children they diagnose and treat.

Advocate for the Component of Culture
in Clinician Training Programs

Clearly, deficiencies in professional training programs account for some of the problems related to the care of children and families in inner-city and reservation communities and reinforce the need for modifications to prevent such inadequacy. For some years, psychiatry colleagues have called for the formal introduction of a consideration of culture in psychiatric training programs and in the training of other mental health professionals, thus acknowledging that preju-

dicial attitudes and stereotypes about members of other cultures tend
to dull the diagnostic and treatment skills of clinicians:

> True understanding between patient and therapist of different cultures
> is made difficult not only by language barriers but also by the use of
> different body postures and expressions, the holding of different value
> systems, and the different modes used to communicate stress and affect.
> (Foulks, 1982, p. 244)

Elaine Pinderhughes (cited in Pinderhughes & Pinderhughes,
1982) developed a model training program in response to this problem:

> Members of one group in the presence of members of another group are
> likely to hide and deny any attitudes, thoughts, and feelings they deem
> offensive to the other group. The unspoken denied attitudes and thoughts
> may interfere with development of trust and may promote both conscious
> and unconscious behavior that interferes with development of alliances.
> This can cause major problems in intercultural, interracial, and inter-
> ethnic treatment interactions. (p. 254)

Pinderhughes bases her model on two reference points: the values of the trainee's own ethnic group and the relative power, or lack
of power, the trainee associates with his or her ethnic group. A modified form of the Pinderhughes model was found to be effective in a
child training program by one of us (JS) at the Children's Hospital
National Medical Center in Washington, DC. Incorporating the message of the Pinderhughes model into its trainee orientation week, the
child training program scheduled a series of sessions with incoming
trainees. At the sessions trainees shared their experiences of feeling
themselves to be in a powerless situation. The intent of this part of
the orientation program was to translate the recounting of these feelings into a discussion of the possible feelings of powerlessness and
vulnerability experienced by the patients the trainees would be seeing
in the months ahead. The use of a senior trainee in the role of facili-
tator proved helpful to these discussions. Orientation week for the
trainees also included an area tour with a community leader and the
opportunity to visit the affiliated hospital and meet staff. Such efforts
represent a start toward developing programs that train clinicians to
be knowledgeable about and sensitive to the cultures of the minority
populations they serve.

The clinician as advocate can encourage, support, organize, develop, and work to implement training programs that include in their
curriculum the study of the influence of the component of culture on

the diagnosis and treatment of mental disorders. Such advocacy, a secondary line of prevention, facilitates realization of the goal of training clinicians who are competent in providing culturally sensitive, responsive, and comprehensive evaluation and treatment to minority children and their families.

Child Advocate in the Diagnostic and Treatment Process

The clinician as advocate in the diagnostic and treatment process adds a tertiary line of prevention. Many of the case vignettes in this book illustrate the clinician in the role of child advocate in the diagnostic and treatment process. They demonstate the need for the culturally sensitive clinician to intervene in the child's home and school environment and the value of the clinician as advocate. As noted earlier, the clinician as diagnostician and advocate can at times ameliorate or resolve a child's presenting problem without a course of treatment beyond the initial evaluation and intervention. For other children, a successful diagnostic evaluation and subsequent early intervention and advocacy to eliminate or lessen the impact of social stressors pave the way for selecting the most appropriate course of ongoing therapeutic intervention. As advocate for minority children, the clinician expands his or her potential for effectiveness.

References

Aase, J. M., Hymbaugh, K. J., May, P. A., & Sumet, J. (1983). Epidemiology of fetal alcohol syndrome among American Indians of the Southeast. *Social Biology, 30,* 374–387.

Aboud, F. E. (1984). Social and cognitive bases of ethnic identity constancy. *Journal of Genetic Psychology, 145,* 227–229.

Aboud, F. E., & Mitchell, F. G. (1977). The effects of preference and self identification. *International Journal of Psychology, 12,* 1–17.

Aboud, F. E., & Skerry, S. A. (1983). Self and ethnic concepts in relation to ethnic constancy. *Canadian Journal of Behavioral Science, 15,* 14–26.

Achenbach, T. M. (1978). The Child Behavior Profile 1: Boys aged 6 through 11. *Journal of Consulting Clinical Psychology, 46,* 759–776.

Achenbach, T. M. (1979). The Child Behavior Profile: An empirically based system for assessing children's behavioral problems and competencies. *International Journal of Mental Health, 7,* 24–42.

Achenbach, T. M., & Edelbrock, C. S. (1981). Behavioral problems and competencies reported by parents of normal and disturbed children aged 4 through 16. *Monograph of the Society for Research in Child Development, 46*(188), 1–82.

Ackerson, L. M., Dick, R. W., Manson, S. M., & Baron, A. E. (1990). Properties of the Inventory to Diagnose Depression in American Indian adolescents. *Journal of the American Academy of Child and Adolescent Psychiatry, 29*(4), 601–607.

Adebimpe, V. R. (1981). Overview: White norms and psychiatric diagnosis of black patients. *American Journal of Psychiatry, 138*(3), 279–285.

Allodi, F. (1980). The psychiatric effects in children and families of victims of political persecution and torture. *Danish Medical Bulletin, 27,* 229–232.

Allport, G. (1954). *The nature of prejudice.* Cambridge, MA: Addison-Wesley.

American Psychiatric Association. (1987). *Diagnostic and statistical manual of mental disorders* (3rd ed., rev.). Washington, DC: Author.

American Psychiatric Association. (1993). *DSM-IV draft criteria*. Washington, DC: Author.

Anastasi, A. (1988). *Psychological testing* (6th ed.). New York: Macmillan.

Anthony, E. J. (1974). The syndrome of the psychologically invulnerable child. In E. J. Anthony & C. Koupernik (Eds.), *The child in his family: Children at psychiatric risk* (pp. 529–544). New York: Wiley.

Anthony, E. J. (1978). From birth to breakdown: A prospective study of vulnerability. In E. J. Anthony, C. Ceinland, & C. Koupernik (Eds.), *The child in his family: Vulnerable children* (Vol. 4, pp. 273–285). New York: Wiley.

Anthony, E. J. (1987). Risk, vulnerability, and resilience: An overview. In E. J. Anthony & B. J. Cohler (Eds.), *The invulnerable child* (pp 3–48). New York: Guilford Press.

Araneta, E. G. (1982). Filipino-Americans. In A. Gaw (Ed.), *Cross-cultural psychiatry* (pp. 55–68). Littleton, MA: John Wright.

Arce, A. A. (1982). Discussion: Cultural aspects of mental health care for hispanics. In A. Gaw (Ed.), *Cross-cultural psychiatry* (pp. 137–148). Littleton, MA: John Wright.

Arias, B. (1982). Educational television: Impact on the socialization of the Hispanic child. In G. L. Berry & C. Mitchell-Kernan (Eds.), *Television and the socialization of the minority group child* (pp. 203–211). New York: Academic Press.

Arroyo, W., & Eth, S. (1985). Children traumatized by Central American warfare. In S. Eth & R. S. Pynoos (Eds.), *Post-traumatic stress disorders in children* (pp. 103–120). Washington, DC: American Psychiatric Press.

Attneave, C. L. (1979). The American Indian child. In J. D. Noshpitz (Ed.), *Basic handbook of child psychiatry* (pp. 239–248). New York: Basic Books.

Ayalon, O. (1983). Coping with terrorism: The Israeli case. In D. Meichenbaum & M. Jaremko (Eds.), *Stress reduction and prevention* (pp. 293–339). New York: Plenum.

Bailey, G. W. (1989). Current perspectives on substance abuse in youth. *Journal of the American Academy of Child and Adolescent Psychiatry, 28*(2), 151–162.

Balk, R. D., Garcia De Alba, J., Cueto, L. M, Ackerman, A., & Davison, S. (1989). Lead-based remedies for empacho: Patterns and consequences. *Social Science Medicine, 29*(12), 1373–1379.

Bandura, A. (1977). *Social learning theory*. Englewood Cliffs, NJ: Prentice-Hall.

Barbarin, O. A. (1984). Racial themes in psychotherapy with blacks: Effects of training on the attitudes of black and white psychiatrists. *American Journal of Social Psychiatry, 4*(1), 13–20.

Barker, G. H., & Adams, W. T. (1963). Glue sniffers. *Sociology and Social Research, 47*(3), 298–310.

Barnes, E. J. (1969). Cultural retardation or shortcomings of assessment techniques. *Proceedings of the 47th Annual International Convention of the Council for Exceptional Children.* Washington, DC: Council for Exceptional Children.

Barth, F. (1969). *Ethnic groups and boundaries.* Boston: Little, Brown.

Bauermeister, J. J., Villamil-Forastieri, B., & Spielberger, C. D. (1976). Development and validation of the Spanish Form of the State–Trait Anxiety Inventory for Children (IDAREN). In C. D. Spilberger & R. Diaz-Guerrero (Eds.), *Cross-cultural anxiety* (Vol. 1, pp. 69–85). Washington, DC: Hemisphere.

Beauvais, F., Oetting, E. R., & Edwards, R. W. (1985). Trends in drug use of Indian adolescents living on reservations, 1975–1983. *American Journal of Drug and Alcohol Abuse, 11*(3, 4), 209–239.

Beiser, M. (1974). Indian mental health. *Psychiatric Annals, 4,* 6–8.

Bellinger, D., Leviton, A., Needleman, H., Rabinowitz, M., & Waternaux, C. (1988). Low-level lead exposure, social class, and infant development. *Neurotoxicology and Teratology, 10,* 497–503.

Belman, A. L. (1990). Aids and pediatric neurology. *Neurologic Clinics, 8*(3), 571–603.

Belman, A. L., Diamond, G., & Dickson, D. (1988). Pediatric acquired immune deficiency syndrome: Neurologic syndromes. *American Journal of Diseases of the Child, 149,* 29–35.

Bender, L. (1939). Behavior problems in Negro children. *Psychiatry, 2,* 213–228.

Berlin, I. N. (1986). Psychopathology and its antecedents among American Indian adolescents. In B. B. Lahey (Ed.), *Advances in clinical child psychology* (pp. 125–152). New York: Plenum.

Berlin, I. N. (1987). Suicide among American Indian adolescents. An overview. *Suicide and Life-Threatening Behavior, 17*(3), 218–232.

Bernard, V. W. (1953). Psychoanalysis and members of minority groups. *Journal of the American Psychoanalytic Association, 1,* 256–267.

Bird, H., & Canino, I. (1981). The sociopsychiatry of espiritismo: Findings of a study in a psychiatric population of Puerto Ricans and other Hispanic children. *Journal of the American Academy of Child Psychiatry, 20,* 725–740.

Bird, H. R., Canino, G., Gould, M. S., Ribera, J., Rubio-Stipec, M., Woodbury, M., Huertas-Goldman, S., & Sesman, M. (1987). Use of Child Behavior Checklist as a screening instrument for epidemiological research in child psychiatry: Results of a pilot study. *Journal of the American Academy of Child and Adolescent Psychiatry, 22*(2), 207–213.

Bird, H. R., Gould, M. S., Rubio-Stipec, M., Staghezza, B., & Canino, G. (1991). Screening for childhood psychopathology in the community using the Child Behavior Checklist. *Journal of the American Academy of Child and Adolescent Psychiatry, 30,* 116–123.

Bird, H. R., Yager, T. J., Staghezza, B., Gould, M. S., Canino, G., & Rubio-Stipec, M. (1990). Impairment in the epidemiological measurement of childhood psychopathology in the community. *Journal of the American Academy of Child and Adolescent Psychiatry, 29*(5), 796–803.

Black and minority health: Report of the Secretary's Task Force on Black & Minority Health. (1985). Washington, DC: U.S. Department of Health & Human Services.

Bloom, B. S. (1969). Letter to the editor. *Harvard Educational Review, 39,* 419–421.

Bobo, J., Gilchrist, L., Cvetkovich, G., Trimble, J., & Schinke, S. P. (1988). Cross-cultural service delivery to minority communities. *Journal of Community Psychology, 16,* 263–272.

Bonchard, T. J., & McGue, M. (1981). Familial studies of intelligence: A review. *Science, 212,* 1055–1059.

Boodman, S. G. (1990, April 17). Alcoholic mothers and their children. *Washington Post,* pp. 14–19.

Bouknight, L. G., & Bouknight, R. R. (1988). Acquired immunodeficiency syndrome in the black community: Focusing on education and the black male. *New York State Journal of Medicine, 88,* 232–235.

Boynton, G. (1987). Cross-cultural family therapy: The ESCAPE model. *American Journal of Family Therapy, 15*(2), 123–130.

Bradley, S., & Skloman, L. (1975). Elective mutism in immigrant families. *Journal of the American Academy of Child Psychiatry, 14,* 510–514.

Bradshaw, W. H. (1978). Training psychiatrists for working with blacks in basic residency programs. *American Journal of Psychiatry, 135*(12), 1520–1524.

Brander, T. (1943). Psychiatric observations among Finnish children during the Russo-Finnish War of 1939–1940. *Nervous Child, 2,* 313–314.

Brown, C. (1965). *Manchild in the promised land.* New York: Signet Books.

Browne, E., Wilson, V., & Laybourne, P. C. (1963). Diagnosis and treatment of elective mutism in children. *Journal of the American Academy of Child Psychiatry, 2,* 605–617.

Brozovosky, M., & Winkler, E. (1965). Glue sniffing in children and adolescents. *New York Journal of Medicine, 65*(5), 1984–1989.

Buchwald, D., Panwala, S., & Hooton, T. M. (1992). Use of traditional health practices by Southeast Asian refugees in a primary care clinic. *Western Journal of Medicine, 156,* 506–511.

Burlingham, D. T., & Freud, A. (1943). *War and children.* New York: Medieval War Books.

Burt, C. (1943). War neurosis in British children. *Nervous Child, 2,* 324–337.

Calnek, M. (1970). Racial factors in the countertransference: The black client. *American Journal of Orthopsychiatry, 40,* 39–46.

Canino, I. A. (1985). Taking a history. In D. Shaffer, A. Erhardt, & L. Greenhill (Eds.), *Diagnosis and treatment in pediatric psychiatry* (pp. 393–408). New York: Free Press.

Canino, I. A. (1988). The transcultural child. In C. Kestenbaum & D. Williams (Eds.), *Clinical assesments on children and adolescents* (pp. 1024–1042). New York: New York University Press.

Canino, I. A., & Canino, G. (1980). Impact of stress on the Puerto Rican family: Treatment considerations. *American Journal of Orthopsychiatry, 50*(3), 535–541.

Canino, I. A., Gould, M., Prupis, S., & Shaffer, D. (1986). A comparison of symptoms and diagnoses in Hispanic and black children in an outpatient mental health clinic. *Journal of the American Academy of Child Psychiatry, 25*(2), 254–259.

Cantwell, D. P. (1978). Hyperactivity and antisocial behavior. *Journal of the American Academy of Child Psychiatry, 17,* 252–262.

Caplan, G. (1964). *Principles of preventative psychiatry.* New York: Basic Books.

Carey-Trefzer, C. (1949). The results of a clinical study of war-damaged children who attended the Child Guidance Clinic, the Hospital for Sick Children, Great Ormond Street, London. *Journal of Mental Science, 95,* 535–559.

Carlin, J. E. (1979). The catastrophically uprooted child: Southeast Asian refugee children. In J. D. Noshpitz (Ed.), *Basic handbook of child psychiatry* (Vol. 1, pp. 290–300). New York: Basic Books.

Carlson, G., & Cantwell, D. P. (1980). A survey of depressive symptoms, syndromes and disorders in a child psychiatric population. *Journal of Child Psychology and Psychiatry, 21,* 19–25.

Carroll, J. K. (1981). Perspectives on marijuana use and abuse and recommendations for preventing abuse. *American Journal of Drug and Alcohol Abuse, 81,* 259–282.

Carter, J. H. (1983). Vision or sight: Health concerns for Afro-American children. In G. J. Powell (Ed.), *The psychosocial development of minority group children* (pp. 13–25). New York: Brunner/Mazel.

Cattell, R. B. (1959). *Handbook for the Culture Fair Intelligence Test: A measure of "G".* Champaign, IL: Institute for Personality and Ability Testing.

Cauce, A. M., Felner, R. D., & Primavera, J. (1982). Social support systems in high-risk adolescents: Structural components and adaptive impact. *American Journal of Community Psychology, 10,* 417–428.

Centers for Disease Control. (1989). Update: Acquired immunodeficiency syndrome, United States 1981–1988. *Morbidity and Mortality Weekly Report, 38,* 229–237.

Cervantes, R., & Castro, F. (1985). Stress, coping, and Mexican American mental health: A systematic review. *Hispanic Journal of Behavioral Science, 7,* 1–73.

Chess, S. (1969). Disadvantages of the "disadvantaged child." *American Journal of Orthopsychiatry, 39,* 4–6.

Chien, C. P. (1993). Ethnopsychopharmocology. In A. C. Gaw (Ed.), *Culture, ethnicity and mental illness* (pp. 413–430). Washington, DC: American Psychiatric Press.

Chu, C. R., Lubin, B., & Sue, S. (1984). Reliability and validity of the Chinese Depression Adjective Checklists. *Journal of Clinical Psychology, 40*(6), 1409–1413.

The church and the drug crisis. (1989, August). *Ebony,* pp. 160–164.

Clayton, R. R. (1986). Multiple drug use. *Recent Developments in Alcohol, 4,* 7–38.

Clevenger, J. (1982). Cultural aspects of mental health care for American Indians. In A. Gaw (Ed.), *Cross-cultural psychiatry* (pp. 149–158). Littleton, MA: John Wright.

Cohn, J., Holzer, K. I. M., Koch, L., & Severin, B. (1980). Children and torture: An investigation of Chilean immigrant children in Denmark. *Danish Medical Bulletin, 27*, 238–239.

Comer, J. P. (1980). *The school program: School power.* New York: Free Press.

Committee on cultural Psychiatry of the Group for the Advancement of Psychiatry. (1989). *Suicide and ethnicity in the United States.* New York: Brunner/Mazel.

Compas, B. E, Davis, G. E., Forsythe, C. J., & Wagner, B. M. (1985). *Assessment of daily life events during adolescence: The Adolescent Perceived Events Scale.* Unpublished manuscript, University of Vermont, Department of Psychology, Burlington.

Conrat, M., & Conrat, R. (1972). *Executive Order 9066: The internment of 110,000 Japanese-Americans.* Los Angeles: Anderson, Ritchie & Simon.

Coopersmith, S. (1967). *The antecedents of self-esteem.* San Francisco: Freeman.

Cormina, J. (1943). Repercussions of war on children as observed during the Spanish Civil War. *Nervous Child, 2*, 324–337.

Costantino, G., Malgady, R. G., & Rogler, L. H. (1988). *Cuento therapy: Folktales as a culturally sensitive psychotherapy for Puerto Rican children* (Monograph 12). New York: Fordham University, Hispanic Research Center.

Deykin, E. Y., Levy, J. C., & Wells, V. (1987). Adolescent depression and drug abuse. *American Journal of Public Health, 79*, 178–182.

DiClemente, R. J., Boyer, C. B., & Morales, E. S. (1988). Minorities and AIDS: Knowledge, attitudes, and misconceptions among black and Latino adolescents. *American Journal of Public Health, 78*, 55–57.

Dietrich, K. N., Succop, P. A., Berger, O. G., Hammond, P. B., & Bornschein, R. L. (1991). Lead exposure and the cognitive development of urban preschool children: The Cincinnati Lead Study cohort at age 4 years. *Neurotoxicology and Teratology, 13*, 203–211.

Dohrenwend, B. P., Dohrenwend, B. S., Gould, M. S., Link, B., Neugebauer, R., & Wunsch-Hitzig, R. (1980). *Mental illness in the United States: Epidemiological estimates.* New York: Praeger Press.

Dohrenwend, B. P., Levav, I., Shrout, P. E., Schwartz, S., Naveh, G., Link, B. G., Skodol, A. E., & Stueve, A. (1992). Socioeconomic status and psychiatric disorders: The causation-selection issue. *Science, 2*, 946–952.

Dorris, M. (1989). *The broken cord: A family's ongoing struggle with fetal alcohol syndrome.* New York: Harper & Row.

Dunsdon, M. I. (1941). A psychologist's contribution to air-raid problems. *Mental Health, 2*, 37–41.

Edwards, C. H., McDonald, S., Mitchell, J. R., Jones, L., Mason, L., & Trigg, L. (1964). Effect of clay and cornstarch intake on women and their infants. *Journal of the American Dietetic Association, 44*, 109–115.

Eggleston, P., & McFarland, S. (1975). Home–school interface patterns. *Viewpoints, 51,* 23–30.

Famularo, R., Stone, K., & Popper, C. (1985). Preadolescent alcohol abuse and dependence. *American Journal of Psychiatry, 140,* 1187–1189.

Farber, A., & Rogler, L. H. (1981). *Unitas: Hispanic and black children in a healing community* (Monograph 6). New York: Fordham University, Hispanic Research Center.

Farrington, D. P. (1986). The sociocultural context of childhood disorders. In H. C. Quay & J. S. Werry (Eds.), *Psychopathological disorders of childhood* (3rd ed., pp. 391–422). New York: Wiley.

Farrow, J. R., Rees, J. M., & Worthington-Robert, B. S. (1987). Health, developmental and nutritional status of adolescent alcohol and marijuana abusers. *Pediatrics, 79,* 218–223.

Felner, R. D. (1984). Vulnerability in childhood: A preventive framework for understanding childrens' efforts to cope with life stress and transitions. In M. C. Roberts & L. Peterson (Eds.), *Prevention of problems in childhood* (pp. 133–169). New York: Wiley.

Field, T. (Ed.). (1980). *High-risk infants and children.* New York: Academic Press.

Figueroa, R. A., & Sassenrath, J. M. (1989). A longitudinal study of the predictive validity of the System of Multicultural Pluralistic Assesment (SOMPA). *Psychology in the Schools, 26,* 5–19.

Fitzgerald, T. K. (1971). Education and identity: A reconsideration of some models of acculturation and identity. *New Zealand Council of Educational Studies,* pp. 45–57.

Flores, J. L. (1978). The utilization of a community mental health service by Mexican-Americans. *International Journal of Social Psychiatry, 24,* 271–275.

Foley, J. B., & Fuqua, D. R. (1988). The effects of status configuration and counseling style on Korean perspectives of counseling. *Journal of Cross-Cultural Psychology, 19*(4), 465– 480.

Fontana, A., & Dovidio, J. (1984). The relationship between stressful life events and school-related performances of Type A and Type B adolescents. *Journal of Human Stress 10*(1), 50–55.

Foulks, E. F. (1982). Discussion: Relevant generic issues. In A. Gaw (Ed.), *Cross-cultural psychiatry* (pp. 237–246). Littleton, MA: John Wright.

Franklin, A. J. (1982). Therapeutic interventions with urban black adolescents. In E. Jones & S. Korchin (Eds.), *Minority mental health* (pp. 267–295) New York: Praeger.

Friedson, E. (1961). *Patient's views of medical practice. A sample of subscribers to a prepaid medical plan in the Bronx.* New York: Russell Sage Foundation.

Fullilove, M. T., & Fullilove, R. E. (1989). Intersecting epidemics: Black teen crack use and sexually transmitted diseases. *Journal of the American Medical Women Association, 44,* 146–153.

Fulwood, I. (1987). Testimony at the joint hearing before the Select Committee on Narcotics Abuse and Control, House of Representatives and the Select Committee on Children, Youth and Families. In *The crack cocaine crisis* (pp. 59–61). Washington, DC: U.S. Government Printing Office.

Garbarino, J. (1975). A preliminary study of some ecological correlates of child abuse: The impact of socioeconomic stress on the mother. *Child Development, 47,* 178–185.

Garcia-Preto, N. (1982). Puerto Rican families. In M. McGoldrick, J. K. Pearce, & J. Giordano (Eds.), *Ethnicity and family therapy* (pp. 164–187) New York: Guilford Press.

Garmezy, N. (1981). Children under stress: Perspectives on antecedents and correlates of vulnerability and resistance to psychopathology. In A. I. Rabin, J. Aronoff, A. M. Barclay, & R. A. Zucker (Eds.), *Further explorations in personality* (pp. 196–270). New York: Wiley.

Garmezy, N. (1983). Stressors of childhood. In N. Garmezy & M. Rutter (Eds.), *Stress, coping and development in children* (pp. 43–84). New York: McGraw-Hill.

Garmezy, N., Masten, A. S., & Tellegen, A. (1984).The study of stress and competence in children: A building block for developmental psychopathology. *Child Development, 55*(1), 97–111

Gaw, A. (1982). Chinese Americans. In A. Gaw (Ed.), *Cross-cultural psychiatry* (pp. 1–29). Littleton, MA: John Wright.

Gayle, H. D., & D'Angelo, L. J. (1991). Epidemiology of AIDS and HIV infection in adolescents in pediatric AIDS. In P. A. Pizzo & C. M. Wilfert (Eds.), *The challenge of HIV infection in infants, children, and adolescents* (pp. 38–50). Baltimore, MD: Williams & Wilkins.

Gibbs, J. T. (1989). Black adolescents and youth: An update on an endangered species. In R. Jones (Ed.), *Black adolescents* (pp. 3–27). Berkeley, CA: Cobb & Henry.

Gilchrist, L., Schinke, S., Trimble, J., & Cvetkovich, G. (1987). Skills enhancement to prevent substance abuse among American Indian adolescents. *International Journal of the Addictions, 22*(9), 869–879.

Giordano, G. P., & Giordano, J. (1977). *The ethno-cultural factor in mental health: A literature review and bibliography.* New York: Institute on Pluralism and Group Identity.

Giordano, J. (1973). *Ethnicity and mental health.* New York: Institute of Pluralism and Group Identity.

Gittelman, R., Mannuzza, S., Shemker, R., & Bonagura, N. (1985). Hyperactive boys almost grown up. *Archives of General Psychiatry, 42,* 937–947.

Golden, S. M., & Duster, M. C. (1977). Hazards of misdiagnosis due to Vietnamese folk medicine. *Clinical Pediatrics, 16*(10), 949–950.

Goldston, S. E., Yager, J., Heinicke, C. M., & Pynoos, R. S. (Eds.). (1990). *Preventing mental health disturbances in childhood.* Washington, DC: American Psychiatric Press.

Gomez, A. G. (1982). Puerto Rican-Americans. In A. Gaw (Ed.), *Cross-cultural psychiatry* (pp. 109–136). Littleton, MA: John Wright.

Goodman, M. E. (1964). *Race awareness in young children* (rev. ed.). New York: Collier.

Gould, M. S., Wunsch Hitzig, R., & Dohrenwend, B. (1981). Estimating the prevalence of childhood psychopathology. *Journal of the American Academy of Child Psychiatry, 20,* 462–476.

Green, A. H. (1983). Child abuse: Dimensions of psychological trauma in abused children. *Journal of the American Academy of Child Psychiatry, 22,* 231–237.

Griffith, E. H., & Young, J. L. (1988). A cross-cultural introduction to the therapeutic aspects of christian religious ritual. In L. Coams & E. H. Griffith (Eds.), *Clinical guidelines in cross-cultural mental health* (pp. 69–89). New York: Wiley.

Gross, J. (1993, April 15). Boys and the street: Tempting Jerina, 18. *New York Times,* pp. A1, A16.

Guildford, J. S., Gupta, W., & Goldberg, L. (1972). *Relationship between teacher–pupil value disparities and the academic achievement, classroom behavior and school adjustment of elementary children* (ERIC Report No. ED 064667). Washington, DC: Office of Education.

Hakuta, K., & Garcia, E. (1989). Bilingualism and education. *American Psychologist, 44*(2), 374–379.

Harding, R. K., & Looney, J. G. (1977). Problems of Southeast Asian children in a refugee camp. *American Journal of Psychiatry, 134*(4), 407–411.

Hauser, S. T., Vieyra, M. A., & Jacobson, A. (1989). Family aspects of vulnerability and resilience in adolescence: A theoretical perspective. In R. Coles & T. Gugan (Eds.), *The change in our times: Studies in the development of resiliency* (pp. 109–133). New York: Brunner/Mazel.

Hayden, T. (1980). Classification of elective mutism. *Journal of the American Academy of Child Psychiatry, 19,* 118–133.

Heath, S. (1983). *Ways with words: Language, life, and work in communities and classrooms.* Cambridge, England: Cambridge University Press.

Heath, S. (1989). Oral and literate traditions among black Americans living in poverty. *American Psychologist, 44*(2), 367–373.

Helms, J. E. (1992). Why is there no study of cultural equivalence in standardized cognitive ability testing? *American Psychologist, 47,* 1083–1101.

Hess, R. D. (1969). Parental behavior and children's school achievement: Implications for Headstart. In E. Grotberg (Ed.), *Critical issues in research related to disadvantaged children.* Princeton, NJ: Educational Testing Services.

Hewlett, S. A. (1922). *When the bough breaks.* New York: Harper Perennial.

High noon at the housing project. (1989, August). *Ebony,* pp. 130–132.

Hilliard, A. G. (1983). Psychological factors associated with language in the education of the African-American child. *Journal of Negro Education, 52*(1), 24–34.

Hines, P. M., & Boyd-Franklin, N. (1982). Black families. In M. McGoldrick, J. K. Pearce, & J. Giordano (Eds.), *Ethnicity and family therapy,* (pp. 84–107). New York: Guilford Press.

Hollingshead, A. B., & Redlich, F. C. (1958). *Social class and mental illness.* New York: Wiley.

Holmes, T. H., & Masuda, M. (1974). Life change and illness susceptibility. In B. P. Dohrenwend & B. S. Dohrenwend (Eds.), *Stressful life events: Their nature and effects* (pp. 45–72). New York: Wiley.

Holmes, T. H., & Rahe, R. H. (1967). The Social Readjustment Rating Scale. *Journal of Psychosomatic Research, 11,* 213–218.

Homel, R., & Burns, A. (1989). Environmental quality and the well-being of children. *Social Indicators Research, 21,* 133–158.

Homeless families: Failed policies and young victims. (1991). Washington, DC: Children's Defense Fund.

Hough, R. I., McGarvey, W., Graham, J., & Timbers, D. (1982). *Cultural variations in the modeling of life change–illness relationships.* Unpublished manuscript.

Houston, S. A. (1971). A reexamination of some assumptions about the language of the disadvantaged child. In S. Chess & A. Thomas (Eds.), *Annual progress in child psychiatry and child development.* (pp. 233–250). New York: Brunner/Mazel.

Howard, A., & Scott, R. A. (1981). The study of minority groups in complex societies. In R. H. Munroe, R. L. Munroe, & B. B. Whiting (Eds.), *Handbook of cross-cultural human development* (pp. 113–152). New York: Garland.

Hsu, J. (1983). Asian family interaction patterns and their therapeutic implications. *International Journal of Family Psychiatry, 4*(4), 307–320.

Hughes, C. C. (1985). Glossary of "culture bound" or folk psychiatric syndromes. In R. C. Simmons & C. C. Hughes (Eds.), *The culture bound syndrome: Folk illnesses of psychiatric and anthroplogical interest* (pp. 469–505). Dordrecht, Netherlands: Reidel.

Husain, S. A., & Vandiver, T. (1984). *Suicide in children and adolescents.* New York: Spectrum.

Hwu, H., Yeh, E. K., Chang, L. Y., & Yeh, Y. L. (1986). Chinese Diagnostic Interview Schedule: II. A validity study on estimation of lifetime prevalence. *Acta Psychiatrica Scandinavica, 73*(4), 348–357.

Iiyama, P., & Kitano, H. H. L. (1982). Asian-Americans and the media. In G. L. Berry & C. Mitchell-Kernan (Eds.), *Television and the socialization of the minority child* (pp. 151–186). New York: Academic Press.

Inclan, J., & Herron, D. G. (1989). Puerto Rican adolescents. In J. T. Gibbs & L. N. Huang (Eds.), *Children of color* (pp. 251–277). San Francisco: Jossey-Bass.

Indian Health Service. (1984, June). *Indian Health Service Health Chart Book Series* (No. 421–166:4393). Washington, DC: U.S. Government Printing Office.

Jackson, A. M. (1984). Child neglect: An overview. In *Perspectives on child maltreatment in the mid '80's* (pp. 15–18). Washington, DC: Children's Bureau, National Center on Child Abuse and Neglect.

Jemmott, J. B., & Locke, S. E. (1984). Psychosocial factors, immunologic mediation, and human susceptibility to infectious diseases: How much do we know? *Psychological Bulletin, 95,* 78–108.

Jenkins, J. H., & Karno, M. (1992). The meaning of expressed emotion: Theoretical issues raised by cross-cultural research. *American Journal of Psychiatry, 149*(1), 9–21.

Joe, J. R. (1980). *Disabled children in Navajo society.* Ann Arbor, MI: Microfilms International.

Johnson, B. D., Williams, T., Dei, K. A., & Sanabria, H. (1990). Drug abuse in the inner city: Impact on hard-drug users and the community. In M. Tonry & J. R. Wilson (Eds.), *Drugs and crime* (pp. 9–67). Chicago: University of Chicago Press.

Johnson, J. H. (1986). *Developmental clinical psychology and psychiatry: Life events as stressors in childhood and adolescence* (Vol. 8). Beverly Hills, CA: Sage.

Johnston, L. D. (1985). The etiology and prevention of substance use: What can we learn fron recent historical changes? *National Institute of Drug Abuse Research Monograph Series, 56,* 155–177.

Jones, E. E., & Korchin, S. J. (1982). Minority mental health: Perspectives. In E. E. Jones & J. Korchin (Eds.), *Minority mental health* (pp. 3–36). New York: Praeger.

Jones, E. E., & Thorne, A. (1987). Rediscovery of the subject: Intercultural approaches to clinical assesment. *Journal of Consulting and Clinical Psychology, 55*(4), 488–495.

Kahn, M. W., Lewis, J., & Galvez, E. (1974). An evaluation study of a group therapy procedure with reservation adolescent Indians. *Psychotherapy: Theory, Research and Practice, 11*(3), 239–242.

Kandel, D. B. (1981). *Frequent marijuana use: Correlates, possible effects and reasons for using and quitting.* Paper presented at American Council on Marijuana Conference, "Treating the Marijuana Dependent Person," Bethesda, MD.

Kandel, D. B. (1990). Parenting styles, drug use and children's adjustment in families of young adults. *Journal of Marriage and the Family, 52,* 183–196.

Kashani, J. H., Keller, M. B., Solomon, N., Reid, J. C., & Mazzola, D. (1985). Double depression in adolescent abusers. *Journal of Affective Disorders, 8,* 153–157.

Kashani, J. H., Venzke, R., & Millar, E. A. (1981). Depression in children admitted to hospital for orthopoedic procedures. *British Journal of Psychiatry, 138,* 21–25.

Katz, P. (1976). The acquisition of racial attitudes in children. In P. A. Katz (Ed.), *Towards the elimination of racism* (pp. 125–154). New York: Pergamon Press.

Katz, P. (1981). Psychotherapy with native adolescents. *Canadian Journal of Psychiatry, 26,* 455–459.

Kauffman, C., Grunebaum, H., Cohler, B., & Garner, E. (1979). Superkids: Competent children of psychotic mothers. *American Journal of Psychiatry, 36,* 1398–1402.

Kaula, E. (Ed.). (1969). *Anase and his visitor, turtle* (Cassette Recording No. CDL 51309, Vol. 1). New York: Caedmon Records.

Keefe, S. E., & Casas, J. M. (1980). Mexican-Americans and mental health: A selected review and recommendation for mental health service delivery. *American Journal of Community Psychology, 8,* 303–323.

Kinzie, J. D., Manson, S., Do, T. V., Nguyen, T. T., Anh, B., & Than, N. P. (1982). Development and validation of a Vietnamese-language depression rating scale. *American Journal of Psychiatry, 139*(10), 1276–1281.

Kinzie, J. D., Sack, W., & Angell, R. N. (1986). The psychiatric effects of massive trauma on Cambodian children: The family, the home and the school. *Journal of the American Academy of Child Psychiatry, 25,* 377–383.

Kleinfeld, J., & Bloom, J. (1977). Boarding schools: Effects on the mental health of Eskimo adolescents. *American Journal of Psychiatry, 134*(4), 411–417.

Kleinman, A. (1977). Depression, somatization and the new cross-cultural psychiatry. *Social Science and Medicine, 11*(1), 3–10.

Kleinman, A. (1993). How culture is important to DSM-IV. In J. E. Mezzich, A. Kleinman, H. Fabrega, B. Good, G. Johnson-Powell, K. M. Lin, S. Manson, & D. Parron (Eds.), *Cultural proposals and supporting papers for DSM-IV* (pp. 13–33). Washington, DC: DSM-IV Task Force, American Psychiatric Association.

Kolvin, J., & Fundudis, T.(1981). Elective mute children: Psychological development and background factors. *Journal of Child Psychology, 22,* 219–232.

Kozol, J. (1991). *Savage inequalities.* New York: Crown.

Kroll, J., Linde, P., Habenicht, M., Chan, S., Yang, M., Vang, T., Souvannasoth, L., Nguyen, T., Ly, M., Nguyen, H., & Vang, Y. (1990). Medication compliance, antidepressant blood levels, and side effects in Southeast Asian patients. *Journal of Clinical Psychopharmacology, 10*(4), 279–283.

Kumpfer, K. L. (1989). Prevention of alcohol and drug abuse: A critical review of risk factors and prevention strategies. In N. B. Enzer, I. Philips, & D. Shaffer (Eds.), *Prevention of mental disorders, alcohol, and other drug use in children and adolescents* (Office for Substance Abuse Prevention Monograph No. 2, pp. 310–371). Rockville, MD: U.S. Department of Health and Human Services.

Kunce, J. T., & Vales, L. F. (1984). The Mexican American: Implications for cross-cultural rehabilitation counseling. *Rehabilitation Counselling Bulletin, 28,* 97–108.

LaFromboise, T. D., & BigFoot, D. S. (1988). Cultural and cognitive considerations in the prevention of American Indian adolescent suicide. *Journal of Adolescence, 11,* 139–153.

LaFromboise, T. D., & Rowe, W. (1983). Skills training for bicultural competence: Rationale and application. *Journal of Counseling Psychology, 30,* 589–595.

Lambert, N. M. (1979). Contributions of school classification, sex, and ethnic status to adaptive behavior assessment. *Journal of School Psychology, 17*(1), 3–16.

La Vietes, R. (1979). The Puerto Rican child. In J. D. Noshpitz (Ed.), *Basic handbook of child psychiatry* (Vol. 1, pp. 264–271). New York: Basic Books.

Lawrence, D. B., & Russ, S. W. (1985). *Mediating variables between life stress and symptoms among young adolescents.* Paper presented at the Annual Meeting of the American Psychological Association, Los Angeles.

Le, D. D. (1983). Mental health and Vietnamese children. In G. J. Powell (Ed.), *The psychosocial development of minority children* (pp. 373–384). New York: Brunner/Mazel.

Leacock, E. B. (1969). *Teaching and learning in city schools.* New York: Basic Books.

Lee, E. (1980). Mental health services for the Asian-Americans: Problems and alternatives. In U.S. Commission of Civil Rights (Ed.), *Civil rights issues of Asian and Pacific Americans: Myths and realities* (pp. 734–756). Washington, DC: U.S. Government Printing Office.

Lee, E. (1982). A social systems approach to assessment and treatment for Chinese American families. In M. McGoldrick, J. K. Pearce, & J. Giordano (Eds.), *Ethnicity and family therapy* (pp. 527–551) New York: Guilford Press.

Lee, E. (1988). Cultural factors in working with Southeast Asian refugee adolescents. *Journal of Adolescents, 11,* 167–179.

Lee, F. R. (1993, April 6). With no parents, Ladetta, 18, presses on. *New York Times,* pp. A1, B6.

Leighton, A. H. (1982). Relevant generic issues. In A. Gaw (Ed.), *Cross-cultural psychiatry* (pp. 199–236). Littleton, MA: John Wright.

Leong, F. T. L. (1986). Counseling and psychotherapy with Asian-Americans: Review of the literature. *Journal of Counseling Psychology, 33*(2), 196–206.

Lin, K. M., Kleinman, A., & Lin, T. (1981). Overview of mental disorders in Chinese cultures: Review of epidemiological and clinical studies. In A. Kleinman, K. M. Lin (Eds.), *Normal and abnormal behavior in Chinese culture* (pp. 237–271). Dordrecht, Netherlands: D. Reidel.

Looff, D. (1979). Sociocultural factors in etiology. In J. D. Noshpitz (Ed.), *Basic handbook of child psychiatry* (Vol. 2, pp. 87–99). New York: Basic Books.

Looney, J. G. (1979). Consulting to children in crisis. *Child Psychiatry and Human Development, 10*(1), 5–14.

Lopez, S., & Nunez, J. A. (1987). Cultural factors considered in selected diagnostic criteria and interview schedules. *Journal of Abnormal Psychology, 96*(3), 270–272.

MacVicar, K. (1979). Psychotherapy of sexually abused girls. *Journal of the American Academy of Child Psychiatry, 18,* 340–353.

Malgady, R. C., Costantino, G., & Rogler, L. H. (1984). Development of a Thematic Apperception Test (TEMAS) for urban Hispanic children. *Journal of Consulting and Clinical Psychology, 52*(6), 989–996.

Malone, C. (1979). Child psychiatry and family theory: An overview. *Journal of the American Academy of Child Psychiatry, 18,* 4–21.

Manson, S. M., Ackerson, L. M., Dick, R. W., Baron, A. E., & Fleming, C. M.

(1990). Depressive symptoms among American Indian adolescents: Psychometric characteristics of the Center for Epidemiological Studies Depression Scale (CES-D). *Psychological Assessment, 2*(3), 231–237.

Marcos, L. (1979). Effects of interpreters on the evaluation of psychopathology in non-English-speaking patients. *American Journal of Psychiatry, 136*(2), 171–174.

Marsella, A. J., Sanborn, K. O., Kameoka, V., Shizuru, L. & Brennan, J. (1975). Cross-validation of self-report measures of depression among normal populations of Japanese, Chinese and Caucasian ancestry. *Journal of Clinical Psychology, 31*(2), 281–287.

Martinez, C. (1993). Psychiatric care of Mexican-Americans. In A. C. Gaw (Ed.), *Culture, ethnicity and mental illness* (pp. 431– 466). Washington, DC: American Psychiatric Press.

Matluck, J. H. (1978). *Cultural norms and classroom discourse: Communication problems in the multi-ethnic school setting.* Paper presented at a meeting of the American Educational Research Association, Toronto.

May, P. A., Hymbaugh, K. J., Aase, J. M., & Sumet, J. (1983). Epidemiology of fetal alcohol syndrome among American Indians of the southwest. *Social Biology, 30,* 374–387.

Maypole, D. E., & Anderson, R. B. (1987). Culture-specific substance abuse prevention for blacks. *Community Mental Health Journal, 23*(2), 135–139.

McAdoo, H. (1977). Family therapy in the black community. *American Journal of Orthopsychiatry, 47,* 75–79.

McCandless, B. (1967). *Children: Behavior and development* (2nd ed.). New York: Holt, Rinehart & Winston.

McDaniel, S., & Bielin, I. N. (1990). *Project self-esteem.* (Available from Enhancing Education, P.O. Box 16001, Newport Beach, CA, 92659)

McFee, M. (1968). The 150% man: A product of Blackfeet acculturation. *American Anthropologist, 70,* 1096–1103.

McGoldrick, M. (1982). Ethnicity and family therapy: An overview. In M. McGoldrick, J. K. Pearce, & J. Giordano (Eds.), *Ethnicity and family therapy* (pp. 3–30). New York: Guilford Press.

McGoldrick, M., Pearce, J. K., & Giordano, J. (Eds.). (1982). *Ethnicity and family therapy.* New York: Guilford Press.

Meers, D. R. (1970). Contributions of a ghetto culture to symptom formation. *Psychoanalytic Study of the Child, 25,* 209–230.

Mercer, J. R. (1979). *System of Multicultural Pluralistic Assessment Technical Manual.* New York: Psychological Corporation.

Mercier, M. H. (1943). The suffering of French children. *Nervous Child, 2,* 308–312.

Miller, J. D., Cisin, I., Gardner-Keaton, H., Harrell, A. V., Wirtz, P. W., Abelson, H. I., & Fishburne, P. M. (1983). *National survey on drug abuse: Main findings 1982* (DHHS Publication No. ADM 83–1263). Rockville, MD: National Institute on Drug Abuse.

Miller-Jones, D. (1989). Culture and testing. *American Psychologist, 44*(2), 360–366.

Minrath, M. (1985). Breaking the race barrier: The white therapist in interracial psychotherapy. *Journal of Psychosocial Nursing, 23*(8), 19–24.

Minturn, L., & Lambert, W. (1964). *Mothers of six cultures: Antecedents of child rearing.* New York: Wiley.

Miramontes, O. (1987). Oral reading miscues of Hispanic students: Implications for assessment of learning disabilities. *Journal of Learning Disabilites, 20*(10), 627–632.

Mitchell, J. L., & Heagarty, M. (1991). Special consideration for minorites in pediatric AIDS. In P. A. Pizzo & C. M. Wilfert (Eds.), *The challenge of HIV infection in infants, children, and adolescents* (pp. 704–713) Baltimore, MD: Williams & Wilkins.

Morrison, M. A. (1991). Overview: Kids and drugs. *Psychiatric Annals, 21*(2), 72–73.

Murphy, L. B., & Moriarty, A. E. (1976). *Vulnerability, coping, and growth from infancy to adolescence.* New Haven, CT: Yale University Press.

Mushak, P., & Crocetti, A. F. (1989). Review: Determination of numbers of lead-exposed American children as a function of lead source: Integrated summary of a report to the U.S. Congress on childhood lead poisoning. *Environmental Residence, 50*(2), 210–229.

Myers, H. F., & King, L. M.(1983). Mental health issues in the development of the black American child. In G. J. Powell (Ed.), *The psychosocial development of minority group children* (pp. 275–306). New York: Brunner/Mazel.

Narine, D. (1989, August). The billionaire and the students. *Ebony,* pp. 146–150.

National Black child Development Institute. (1989). *Who will care when parents can't?* (Report). Washington, DC: Author.

Norris, D. M., & Spurlock, J. (1992). Racial and cultural issues impacting on countertransference. In J. R. Brandell (Ed.), *Countertransference in psychotherapy with children and adolescents* (pp. 91–123). Northvale, NJ: Aronson.

Norton, D. G. (1983). Black family life patterns: The development of self and cognitive development of black children. In G. J. Powell (Ed.), *The psychosocial development of minority group children* (pp. 187–193). New York: Brunner/Mazel.

Oberndorf, C. P. (1954). Selectivity and options for psychiatry. *American Journal of Psychiatry, 110,* 754–758.

Oetting, E. R., & Goldstein, G. S. (1979). Drug use among Native American adolescents. In G. Beschner & A. Friedman (Eds.), *Youth drug abuse* (pp. 409–441). Lexington, MA: Lexington.

Ogbu, J. U. (1978). *Minority education and caste: The American system in cross-cultural perspective.* New York: Academic Press.

Ogbu, J. U. (1981). Origins of human competence: A cultural ecological perspective. *Child Development, 52,* 413–429.

Ogbu, J. U. (1986). The consequences of the American caste system. In U. Neisser (Ed.), *The school achievement of minority children* (pp. 19–56). Hillsdale, NJ: Erlbaum.

Opler, M. K., & Singer, J. L. (1956). Ethnic differences in behavior and psychopathology: Italian and Irish. *International Journal of Social Psychiatry, 1,* 11–17.

Ortiz, A., & Maldonado-Colon, E. (1986). Recognizing learning disabilities in bilingual children: How to lessen inappropiate referrals of language minority students to special education. *Journal of Reading, Writing, and Learning Disabilities International, 2*(1), 43–56.

Ortiz, A., & Yates, J. R. (1983). Linguistically and culturally diverse handicapped students: Implications for manpower planning. *Journal of the National Association of Bilingual Education, 7*(3), 41–53.

Padilla, A., & Garza, B. M. (1975). IQ tests: A case of cultural myopia. *National Elementary Principal, 54* (March/April), 53–58.

Padilla, E. R. & Wyatt, G. E. (1983). The effects of intelligence and achievement testing on minority children. In G. J. Powell (Ed.), *The psychosocial development of minority group children* (pp. 417–437) New York: Brunner/Mazel.

Palacios, M., & Franco, J. N. (1986). Counselling Mexican-American women. *Journal of Multicultural Counselling and Development, 14*(3), 124–131.

Papajohn, J., & Spiegel, J. (1975). *Transition in families.* San Francisco: Jossey-Bass.

Papanek, E. (1942). My experiences with fugitive children in Europe. *The Nervous Child, 2,* 301–307.

Paster, V. (1985). Adapting psychotherapy for the depressed, unacculturated, acting out, black male adolescent. *Psychotherapy, 22*(2), 408–417.

Paster, V. (1986). A social action model of intervention for difficult to reach populations. *American Journal of Orthopsychiatry, 56*(4), 625–629.

Philipus, M. J. (1971). Successful and unsuccessful approaches to mental health services for an urban Hispano-American population. *American Journal of Public Health, 61,* 820–830.

Piasecki, J. M., Manson, S. M., & Biernoff, M. P. (1989). Abuse and neglect of American Indian children: Findings from a survey of federal providers. *American Indian and Alaskan Native Mental Health Research, 22,* 43–62.

Pierce, C. M. (1988). Stress in the workplace. In A. F. Coner-Edwards & J. Spurlock (Eds.), *Black families in crisis: The middle class* (pp. 27–34). New York: Brunner/Mazel.

Pinderhughes, E. (1989). *Understanding race, ethnicity and power: The key to efficacy in clinical practice.* New York: Free Press.

Pinderhughes, C. A., & Pinderhughes, E. B. (1982). Perspectives of the training directors. In A. Gaw (Ed.), *Cross-cultural psychiatry* (pp. 247–284). Littleton, MA: J. Wright.

Plantenga, B. (Ed.). (1991). *Like open bright windows.* New York: Poets in Public Service.

Plomin, R. (1983). Childhood temperament. In B. B. Lahey & A. Kazdin (Eds.), *Advances in clinical child psychology* (Vol. 6, pp. 45–92). New York: Plenum.

Porter, J. D. W. (1971). *Black child, white child: The development of racial attitudes.* Cambridge, MA: Harvard University Press.

Powell, G. J. (1982). The impact of television on the self-concept development of minority group children. In G. L. Berry & C. Mitchell-Kernan (Eds.), *Television and the socialization of the minority child* (pp. 105–149). New York: Academic Press.

Powell, G. J. (Ed.). (1983). *The psychosocial development of minority children*. New York: Brunner/Mazel.

Price, C. S., & Cuellar, I. (1981). The effects of language and related variables on the expression of psychopathology in Mexican American psychiatric patients. *Hispanic Journal of Behavioral Sciences, 3,* 145–160.

Prince, R. (1989). [Review of *Social phobia among Japanese: Clinical, family and cultural exploration*]. *Transcultural Psychiatric Research Review, 26,* 137–147.

Public Health Service, U.S. Department of Health and Human Services. (1990). *Healthy people 2000: National health promotion and prevention objectives*. (DHHS Publication No. PHS 91–50212). Washington, DC: U.S. Government Printing Office.

Ramirez, B., & Smith, B. J. (1978). Federal mandates for the handicapped: Implications for American Indian children. *Exceptional Children, 44*(7), 521–528.

Ramirez, M. (1983). *Psychology of the Americas: Mestizo perspectives on personality and mental health*. New York: Academic Press.

Ramirez, M., & Castaneda, A. (1974): *Cultural democracy, bicognitive development, and education*. New York: Academic Press.

Ramsey, P. G. (1986). Young children's thinking about ethnic differences. In J. S. Phinney & M. J. Rotheram (Eds.), *Children's ethnic socialization: Pluralism and development* (pp. 55–72). Newbury Park, CA: Sage.

Red Horse, J. (1983). Family structure and value orientation in American Indians. *Social Casework, 61*(8), 462–467.

Reinhart, M. A., & Rhus, H. (1984). Moxibustion: Another traumatic folk remedy. *Clinical Pediatrics, 24*(1), 58–59.

Remafedi, G. (1987). Adolescent homosexuality: Psychosocial and medical implications. *Pediatrics, 79,* 331–337.

Rendon, M. (1974). Transcultural aspects of Puerto Rican mental illness in New York. *International Journal of Social Psychiatry, 20,* 18–24.

Report of the Secretary's Task Force on Black and Minority Health. (1985, August). In T. E. Malone (Chairperson), *U.S. Department of Health and Human Services: Vol. 1. Executive summary, National Institutes of Health*. Washington, DC: National Academy Press.

Reschly, D. J., & Jipson, F. J. (1976). Ethnicity, geographic locale, age, sex, and urban–rural residence as variables in the prevalence of mild retardation. *American Journal of Mental Deficiency, 81*(2), 154–161.

Robins, L. N. (1978). Sturdy childhood predictors of adults' antisocial behavior. *Psychological Medicine, 8,* 611–622.

Rogler, L. H., Blumenthal, R., Malgady, R., & Costantino, G. (1985). *Hispanics and culturally sensitive mental health services* (Research Bulletin, 8[3–4]). New York: Fordham University, Hispanic Research Center.

Rogler, L. H., & Procidano, M. (1986). The effect of social networks on marital roles: A test of the Bott hypothesis in an international context. *Journal of Marriage and the Family, 48,* 693–701.

Rosen, D., & Frank, J. D. (1962). Negroes in psychotherapy. *American Journal of Psychiatry, 119,* 456–460.

Rosenberg, M., & Simmons, R. G. (1972). *Black and white self-esteem: The urban school child.* Washington, DC: American Sociological Association.

Rosenthal, D. A. (1986). Ethnic identity development in adolescents. In J. S. Phinney & M. J. Rotheram (Eds.), *Children's ethnic socialization: Pluralism and development* (pp. 156–179). Newbury Park, CA: Sage.

Rotheram, M. J., & Phinney, J. S. (1986). Introduction: Definitions and perspectives in the study of children's ethnic socialization. In J. S. Phinney & M. J. Rotheram (Eds.), *Children's ethnic socialization: Pluralism and development* (pp. 10–28). Newbury Park, CA: Sage.

Ruiz, E. J. (1975). Influence of bilingualism on communication in groups. *International Journal of Group Psychotherapy, 25*(4), 391–395.

Rutter, M. (1979). Protective factors in children's response to stress and disadvantage. In M. W. Kent & J. E. Rolf (Eds.), *Primary prevention of psychopathology: Vol. 3. Social competence in children* (pp. 49–74). Hanover, NH: University Press of New England.

Rutter, M. (1981). The city and the child. *Journal of Orthopsychiatry, 51,* 610–625.

Rutter, M. (1982). The city and the child. In S. Chess & A. Thomas (Eds.), *Annual progress in child psychiatry and child development* (pp. 353–370). New York: Brunner/Mazel.

Rutter, M. (1987). Psychosocial resilience and protective mechanisms. *American Journal of Orthopsychiatry, 57*(3), 316–331.

Rutter, M., Maughan, B., Mortimore, P., Ouston, J., & Smith, A. (1979). *Fifteen thousand hours: Secondary schools and their effects on children.* Cambridge, MA: Harvard University Press.

Rutter, M., Yule, B., & Quentin, D. (1975). Attainment and adjustment in two geographical areas: Some factors accounting for area differences. *British Journal of Psychiatry, 126,* 520–533.

Sack, W., Angell, R. N., Kinzie, J. D., & Rath, B. (1986). The psychiatric effects of massive trauma in Cambodian children: The family, the home and the school. *Journal of the American Academy of Child Psychiatry, 25,* 377–383.

Sanchez, A. R., & Atkinson, D. R. (1983). Mexican-American cultural commitment, preference for counselor ethnicity and willingness to use counseling. *Journal of Counseling Psychology, 30,* 215–220.

Sandler, I. N., & Block, N. (1979). Life stress and maladaptation of children. *American Journal of Community Psychology, 7*(4), 425–440.

Sansonnet-Hayden, H., Haley, G., Marriage, K., & Fine, S. (1987). Sexual abuse and psychopathology in hospitalized adolescents. *Journal of the American Academy of Child and Adolescent Psychiatry, 26,* 753–757.

Schinke, S. P. (1988). Preventing substance abuse among American Indian adolescents: A bicultural competence skill approach. *Journal of Counseling Psychology, 35*(1), 87–90.

Semlitz, L., & Gold, M. S. (1986). Adolescent drug use: Diagnosis, treatment and prevention. *Psychiatric Clinics of North America, 9*(3), 455–473.

Senour, M. (1977). Psychology of the Chicana. In J. L. Martinez (Ed.), *Chicano psychology* (pp. 329–340). New York: Academic Press.

Shaffer, D., Gould, M., Brasic, J., Ambrosini, P., Fisher, P., Bird, H., & Aluwahlia, S. (1983). A Children's Global Assessment Scale (CGAS). *Archives of General Psychiatry, 40,* 1228–1231.

Shore, J. H., & Von Fumetti, B. (1972). Three alcohol programs for American Indians. *American Journal of Psychiatry, 128*(11), 1450–1454.

Shore, J. N., & Manson, S. (1981). Cross-cultural studies of depression among American Indians and Alaska Natives. *White Cloud Journal, 2*(2), 5–12.

Smith, D. E., Ehrlich, M. A., & Seymour, R. B. (1991). Current trends in adolescent drug use. *Psychiatric Annals, 21*(2), 74–79.

Smith, J. W. (1988). Black middle-class education in the 1980's. In A. C. Edwards & J. Spurlock (Eds.), *Black families in crisis: The middle class.* (pp. 129–138). New York: Brunner/Mazel.

Smith L. (1944). *Killers of the dream.* New York: Norton.

Sokol, R. J., Ager, J., Martier, S., Debanner, S., Ernhart, C., Kuzma, J., & Miller, S. I. (1986). Significant determinants of susceptibility of alcohol teratogenicity. *Annals of the New York Academy of Sciences, 447,* 87–102.

Sokol, R. J., & Clarren, S. K. (1989). Guidelines for use of terminology describing the impact of prenatal alcohol on the offspring. *Alcoholism: Clinical and Experimental Research, 13*(4), 597–598.

SOS America: A Children's defense budget. (1990). Washington, DC: Children's Defense Fund.

Spencer, M. B. (1982). Pre-school children's social cognition and cultural cognition: A cognitive developmental interpretation of race dissonance findings. *Journal of Psychology, 112,* 275–296.

Spiegel, J. P. (1976). Cultural aspects of transference and countertransference revisited. *Journal of the American Academy of Psychoanalysis, 4,* 447–468.

Spielberger, C. D., Gonzalez, F., Martinez, A., Natalicio, L. F., & Natalicio, D. S. (1971). Development of the Spanish edition of the State-Trait Anxiety Inventory. *Interamerican Journal of Psychology, 5,* 145–185.

Spurlock, J. (1985). Assessment and therapeutic intervention of black children. *Journal of the American Academy of Child Psychiatry, 24,* 168–174.

Spurlock, J. (1986). Development of self concept in Afro-American children. *Hospital and Community Psychiatry, 37*(1), 66–70.

Spurlock, J., & Cohen, R. S. (1969). Should the poor get none? *Journal of the American Academy of Child Psychiatry, 8,* 16–35.

The State of America's Children. (1991). Washington, DC: Children's Defense Fund.

Streissguth, A. P., & La Due, R. A. (1985). Psychological and behavioral effects in children prenatally exposed to alcohol. *Alcohol Health and Research World, 10*(1), 6–12.

Streissguth, A. P., Sampson, P. D., & Barr, H. M. (1989). Neurobehavioral dose-response effects on prenatal alcohol exposure in humans from infancy to adulthood. *Annals of the New York Academy of Sciences, 562,* 145–158.

Stricof, R., Novick, L. F., Kennedy, J., & Welfuse, I. (1988). *Sero prevalence of adolescents at a homeless facility.* Paper presented at the American Public Health Association Conference, Boston.

Sue, S., & Chin, R. (1983). The mental health of Chinese-American children: Stressors and resources. In G. J. Powell (Ed.), *The psychosocial development of minority group children* (pp. 385–397). New York: Brunner/Mazel.

Sue, S., & Sue, D. W. (1974). MMPI comparisons between Asian-American and non-Asian-American students utilizing a student health psychiatric clinic. *Journal of Counselling Psychology, 21*(5), 423–427.

Suematsu, H., Ishikawa, H., Kuboki, T., & Ito,, T. (1985). Statistical studies in anorexia nervosa in Japan: Detailed clinical data on 1,011 patients. *Psychotherapy and Psychosomatics, 43*(2), 96–103.

Szapocznik, J., Scopetta, M., & Tillman, W. (1978). What changes, what stays the same, and what affects acculturative change in Cuban immigrant families? In J. Szapocznik & J. Herrera (Eds.), *Cuban-Americans: Acculturation, adjustment and the family.* Miami: Florida University Press.

Taylor, O. L., & Payne, K. T. (1983). Culturally valid testing: A proactive approach. *Topics in Language Disorders, 3*(3), 8–20.

Taylor, R. (1976). Psychosocial development among black children and youth: A reexamination. *American Journal of Orthopsychiatry, 46*(1), 4–19.

Terry, D. (1993, April 11). Fear and ghosts: The world of Marcus, 19. *New York Times*, pp. A1, A16.

Thomas, A. (1962). Pseudotransference reactions due to cultural stereotyping. *American Journal of Orthopsychiatry, 32*, 894–900.

Thompson, J. W., & Walker, R. D. (1988). Adolescent suicide among American Indians and Alaskan Natives. *Psychiatric Annals, 20*(3), 128–133.

Thomson, G. O. B., Raab, G. M., Hepburn, W. S., Hunter, R., Fulton, M., & Laxen, D. P. H. (1989). Blood lead levels and children's behavior results from the Edingburgh Lead Study. *Journal of Child Psychology and Psychiatry, 30*(4), 515–528.

Topper, M. D. (1987). The traditional Navajo Mexican man: Therapist, counselor, and community leader. *Journal of Psychoanalytic Anthropology, 10*(3), 217–249.

Trimble, J. E., Padilla, A. M., & Bell, C. S. (1987). *Drug use among ethnic minorities* (DHHS Publication No. ADM 87–1474). Washington, DC: U.S. Government Printing Office.

Trueba, H. T. (1986). Beyond language: Social and cultural factors in schooling language minority students. *Anthropology and Education Quarterly, 17*, 255–259.

Tseng, N. S., & McDermott, J. F. (1981). *Cultural mind and therapy: An introduction to cultural psychiatry.* New York: Brunner/Mazel.

Tsui, P., & Schultz, G. L. (1985). Failure of rapport: Why psychotherapeutic engagement fails in the treatment of Asian clients. *American Journal of Orthopsychiatry, 55*(4), 561–569.

Tsushima, W. T., & Onorato, V. A. (1982). Comparison of MMPI scores of white and Japanese-American medical patients. *Journal of Consulting and Clinical Psychology, 50*(1), 150–151.

U.S. children and their families: Current conditions and recent trends: A report of the Select Committee on Children, Youth and Families (U.S. House of Representatives, 101st Congress Union Calendar No. 219, Report 101– 356). (1989, November). Wasington, DC: Government Printing Office.

U.S. Congress, House, Select Committee on Children, Youth and Families, 101st Cong. (1989a, July). *Barriers and opportunities for America's young black men.* Washington, DC: U.S. Government Printing Office.

U.S. Congress, House, Select Committee on Children, Youth and Families, 101st Cong. (1989b, September). *Hispanic children and their families: A key to our nation's future.* Washington, DC: U.S. Government Printing Office.

U.S. Environmental Protection Agency. (1986). *Air quality criteria for lead* (EPA Report No. EPA-600/8–83/028af-df, 4V). Research Triangle Park, NC: Environmental Criteria and Assessment Office. (NTIS No. PB 87–142378)

Van Oss, B., Marin, G., & Padilla, A. (1983). *Utilization of traditional and montraditional sources of care among Hispanics.* Paper presented at the American Psychological Association Annual Meeting, Montreal.

Vargas, L. A., & Berlin, I. N. (1991). Culturally responsive inpatient care of children and adolescents. In I. N. Berlin & R. L. Hendren (Eds.), *Psychiatric inpatient care of children and adolescents: A multicultural approach* (pp. 14–34). New York: Wiley.

Vega, W. A., Hough, R., & Romero, A. (1983). Family life patterns of Mexican-Americans. In G. J. Powell (Ed.), *The psychosocial development of minority group children* (pp. 194–215). New York: Brunner/Mazel.

Vermeer, D. (1971). Geophagy among the Ewe of Ghana. *Ethnology, 10,* 56–72.

Volkmar, F. R. (1991). Autism and the pervasive developmental disorders. In M. Lewis (Ed.), *Child and adolescent psychiatry: A comprehensive textbook* (pp. 499–508). Baltimore: Williams & Wilkins.

Vygotsky, L. (1978). *Mind and society: The development of higher psychological process.* Cambridge, MA: Harvard University Press.

Weisz, J. R., Suwanlert, S., Chaiyasit, W., Weiss, B., Achenbach, T. M., & Walter, B. R. (1987). Epidemiology of behavioral and emotional problems among Thai and American children: Parent reports for ages 6 to 11. *Journal of the American Academy of Child and Adolescent Psychiatry, 26*(6), 890–897.

Wells, K. B., Hough, R. L., Golding, J. M., Burnam, M. A., & Karno, M. (1987). Which Mexican-Americans underutilize health services? *American Journal of Psychiatry, 144*(7), 918–922.

Werner, E. E. (1961). *Personality characteristics of men and women who successfully assimilated stress during their formative years.* Paper presented at the Bi-Annual Meeting of the Society for Research in Child Development, State College, PA.

Werner, E. E., & Smith, R. S. (1982). *Vulnerable but invincible: A study of resilient children.* New York: McGraw-Hill.

Westermeyer, J. (1974). The "drunken Indian": Myths and realities. *Psychiatric Annals, 4*(11), 29–36.

Westermeyer, J. (1979). The Apple syndrome in Minnesota: A complication of racial ethnic discontinuity. *Journal of Operational Psychiatry, 10*(2), 134–139.

Westermeyer, J. (1987). Clinical considerations in cross-cultural diagnosis. *Hospital and Community Psychiatry, 38*(2), 160–165.

Westermeyer, J., Vang, T. F., & Neider, J. (1983). Migration and mental health among Hmong refugees: Association of pre- and postmigration with self-rating scales. *Journal of Nervous and Mental Disease, 171*(2), 92–96.

Whiting, B. B., & Whiting, J. W. (1975). *Children of six cultures: A psychocultural analysis.* Cambridge, MA: Harvard University Press.

Williams, C. L. (1987). Issues surrounding psychological testing of minority patients. *Hospital and Community Psychiatry, 38*(2), 184–189.

Williams, C. L., & Westermeyer, J. (1983). Psychiatric problems among adolescent Southeast Asian refugees: A descriptive study. *Journal of Nervous Mental Diseases, 171,* 79–85.

Williams, J. S. R., & Moreland, J. K. (1976). *Race, color, and the young child.* Chapel Hill: University of North Carolina Press.

Williams, R. L. (1970). Danger: Testing and dehumanizing black children. *Clinical Child Psychology Newsletter, 9*(1), 5–6.

Williams, R. L., Binkin, N. J., & Clingman, E. (in press). Pregnancy outcomes among Hispanic women in California. *American Journal of Public Health.*

Wilson, W. J. (1978). *The truly disadvantaged.* Chicago: University of Chicago Press.

Winneke, G., Brockhaus, A., Ewers, V., Kramer, V., & Neuf, M. (1990). Results from the European multi center study on lead neurotoxicity in children: Implications for risk assesment. *Neurotoxicology and Teratology, 12,* 553–559.

Wolkind, S., & Rutter, M. (1985). *Sociocultural factors in child and adolescent psychiatry.* Boston: Blackwell Scientific.

Wong, H. Z. (1982). Asian and Pacific Americans. In L. R. Snowden (Ed.), *Reaching the underserved: Mental health needs of neglected populations* (pp. 185–204). Beverly Hills, CA: Sage.

World Health Organization. (1992). *The ICD-10 classification of mental and behavioral disorders.* Geneva, Switzerland: Author.

Yamamoto, J. (1978). Therapy for Asian-Americans. *Journal of the National Medical Association, 70*(4), 267–270.

Yamamoto, J. (1982). Japanese-Americans. In A. Gaw (Ed.), *Cross-cultural psychiatry* (pp. 31–53). Boston: John Wright.

Yamamoto, J., & Iga, M. (1983). Emotional growth of Japanese-American children. In G. J. Powell, A. Morales, A. Romero, & J. Yamamoto (Eds.), *The psychosocial development of minority children* (pp. 167–178). New York: Brunner/Mazel.

Yamamoto, J., James, E., & Polley, N. (1968). Cultural problems in psychiatric therapy. *Archives of General Psychiatry, 19,* 45–49.

Yamamoto, J., Lam, J., Choi, W. I., Reece, S., Lo, S., Hahn, D. S., & Fairbanks, L. (1982). The psychiatric status schedule for Asian-Americans. *American Journal of Psychiatry, 139*(9), 1181–1184.

Yates, A. (1987). Current status and future directions of research on the American Indian child. *American Journal of Psychiatry, 144*(9), 1135–1142.

Yeatman, G. W., & Dang, V. V. (1980). Cao Gio (coin rubbing): Vietnamese attitudes toward health care. *Journal of the American Medical Association, 244*(24), 2748–2749.

Yu, P. (1979). *Parental attributions as predictors of child competence in families with a parent with a history of psychiatric disturbance.* Unpublished doctoral dissertation, University of Rochester, Rochester, NY.

Zatzick, D. F., & Lu, F. G. (1991). The ethnic minority focus unit as a training site in transcultural psychiatry. *Academic Psychiatry, 15,* 218–225.

Zuniga, M. (1988). Assessment issues of north Chicanos: Practice implications. *Psychotherapy, 25*(2), 288–293.

Index